The Visitor's Guide
to
HAMPSHIRE & ISLE OF WIGHT

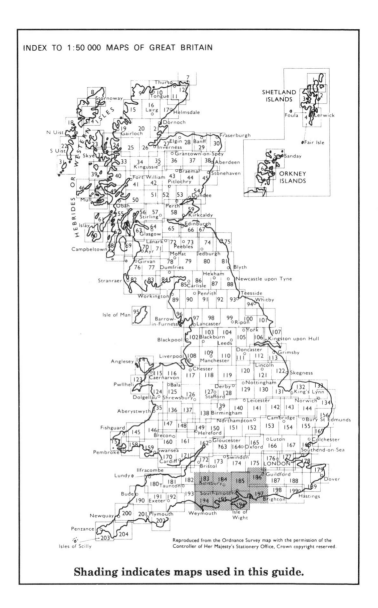

INDEX TO 1:50 000 MAPS OF GREAT BRITAIN

Shading indicates maps used in this guide.

THE
VISITOR'S GUIDE TO
HAMPSHIRE
& ISLE OF WIGHT

JOHN BARTON

MPC

HUNTER
PUBLISHING INC

Published by:
Moorland Publishing Co Ltd,
Moor Farm Road,
Airfield Estate,
Ashbourne,
Derbyshire DE6 1HD
England

British Library Cataloguing in
Publication Data:
Barton, John
   The visitor's guide to Hampshire
   & Isle of Wight. - 2nd ed.
   1. Hampshire - Visitor's guides
   2. Isle of Wight - Visitor's guides
   I. Title
   914.22'704858

ISBN 0 86190 353 6 (paperback)
ISBN 0 86190 352 8 (hardback)

Published in the USA by:
Hunter Publishing Inc,
300 Raritan Center Parkway,
CN 94, Edison, NJ 08818
ISBN 1 55650 239 7 (USA)

Colour and black & white
origination by:
Scantrans, Singapore

Printed in the UK by:
Richard Clay Ltd, Bungay, Suffolk

Cover photograph: *HMS Warrior,
Portsmouth* (MPC Picture Collection)

Illustrations have been supplied as
follows: MPC Picture Collection: pp
170 (both), 178 (top), 179 (bottom
& inset), 183, 198 (both), 210, 211
(both), 218 (top), 222 (bottom).

All other illustrations are from the
author.

CONTENTS

Key to Symbols Used in Text Margin and on Maps

Recommended walk

Parkland

Archaeological site

Nature reserve/Animal interest

Birdlife

Garden

Tourist Information Office

Church/Ecclesiastical site

Building of interest

Castle/Fortification

Museum/Art gallery

Beautiful view/Scenery, Natural phenomenon

Other place of interest

Water sports

Interesting railway

Industrial archaeology

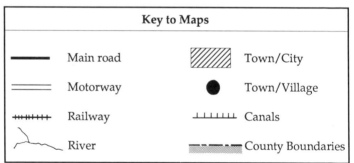

Key to Maps

Main road

Motorway

Railway

River

Town/City

Town/Village

Canals

County Boundaries

Note on the Maps

The maps drawn for each chapter, while comprehensive, are not designed to be used as route maps, but rather to locate the main towns, villages and places of interest. For exploration, visitors are recommended to use the 1:50,000 (approximately $1^1/_4$ in to the mile) Ordnance Survey 'Landranger' maps. The sheets covering the areas included in this book are shown on the frontispiece.

INTRODUCTION

Hampshire has more to offer the visitor than most other counties of England. Unspoilt scenery, rivers and coast, beautiful country houses, attractive villages and interesting market towns, ancient monuments and churches are all part of the natural and man-made scene, the ancient blending with the medieval and modern to make a fascinating landscape.

No area in England of comparable size has as many varied attractions as the Isle of Wight. A coast of cliffs and sandy beaches, splendid viewpoints, towns and villages, manor houses, country parks, museums, leisure centres, nature trails and footpaths — all within an island only 23 miles by 13 miles.

The visitor to Hampshire who expects to find a closely built-up area will be surprised by the many miles of undulating downland mainly given over to farming. In fact, away from the Southampton-Portsmouth coastal belt, the county is largely unspoilt, with small towns and villages separated by farmland, heath and forest. There is a great deal of woodland, much of it open to the public. Hampshire is the third most densely wooded county in England — 16 per cent of its area is woodland and over a half of this wooded area is 'ancient' woodland, ie pre-1700.

Chalk underlies most of north and central Hampshire and gives rise to the characteristic landscape of open downland. Sand and gravel heaths occur in the north-east and also in the south-west, some partly within the New Forest. The commonest stone is flint, which has often been used for building, usually in combination with brick or stone. The main rivers are the Test, Itchen and Avon, which rise in the chalklands and are famous for their salmon and trout-

7

fishing. The wildlife and vegetation of Hampshire and the Isle of Wight are probably unsurpassed in Great Britain in their diversity and richness. Woodland, grassland, heath and marsh provide habitats for an astonishing range of plants, animals and insects, some of them among the rarest in the country. Much of this natural history can be studied at the many nature reserves open to visitors.

Hampshire's position in the centre of southern England, close to the English Channel, and the importance of Winchester as the former capital of England have ensured a vital historic role for the county. Southampton, a port since Roman times, and Portsmouth, a dockyard for nearly 800 years, have both played a leading part in English history. These three cities, with such long and fascinating histories and with so much of their heritage surviving, are a major part of Hampshire's attraction.

The county's name was first recorded in 757, as *Hamtunscir*, ie 'the shire of Hamtun'; the official name of the county until 1959 was 'The County of Southampton'. It was one of the first four recognised English counties.

There are over 450 scheduled ancient monuments in the county. The earliest of these are the earthen long barrows of the neolithic people, the first farmers; about forty of these barrows survive. There are also hundreds of Bronze Age round barrows in the county. From the seventh century BC onwards the Iron Age tribes constructed the immense hill-forts that are such prominent features of the landscape. Several of them, such as those at Danebury Hill and Old Winchester Hill, can be visited.

Not much is known of the Roman invasion of Hampshire but evidently it met with little resistance. The county was not primarily a military zone; both before and after the invasion it was a thriving agricultural area. There were two main towns, Winchester and Silchester, the former being one of the five largest towns in Roman Britain. Three of the many Roman villas can be visited — at Newport and Brading in the Isle of Wight, and at Rockbourne. A long period of peace ended in the late third century AD when marauders necessitated the construction of the 'Saxon shore' forts, one of which, at Portchester, is the most impressive Roman fort in Britain.

After centuries of trouble and uncertainty, Saxon Hampshire became part of Alfred's kingdom of Wessex with Winchester as its capital. The period before and after the Norman invasion was a prosperous time for Hampshire and trade with Europe flourished.

The greatest cultural contribution the county made at this time was the output of illuminated manuscripts from the Winchester monasteries. Winchester was pre-eminent in the twelfth century but was overshadowed later by Southampton, which became a leading port.

Much of the medieval landscape survives to this day. Field boundaries, roads, street patterns, houses, churches, deer parks (of which there were about thirty in the sixteenth century), cultivation terraces (lynchets) and remains of deserted villages are all part of the medieval heritage.

The Civil War brought to Hampshire its share of conflicts, notably at Cheriton and Basing House. The countryside suffered greatly from the marauding armies and churches were often desecrated by the troops. The eighteenth and early nineteenth centuries were prosperous for Hampshire and the Isle of Wight, at least for the wealthy, as evidenced by the fine country houses, great and small, many of which can be visited. But they were also times of great change, in transport, agriculture and industry; turnpike roads, canals and railways came in turn. The first completed railway line in the county was from London to Southampton in 1840. The rural landscape was greatly changed too by the enclosure of the old open fields.

Some disused railway lines are now used as public footpaths and other relics of the industrial age can be seen in the county's museums and at other places. The eighteenth century also saw the birth of the seaside resort; Southampton's temporary revival then was partly due to the popularity of sea-bathing.

The present century has seen rapid and extensive urban growth in Hampshire, but little in the Isle of Wight. Southampton and Portsmouth have grown to become large industrial and commercial cities, and the largest oil refinery in Britain is at Fawley on Southampton Water. However, there are now many more facilities for leisure activities, more parks and sports centres, and more access to historic buildings and the countryside.

There are not as many country houses in Hampshire as in some other counties, though those that are open to the public are of outstanding interest. The county makes up for this with its castles and fortifications, many situated on the coast such as Portchester Castle, Hurst Castle and others. The two great periods of church building in Hampshire were the Norman-Early English transitional (about 1180-1220) and the Victorian. Those visitors interested in parish churches will find many fine examples of these periods, such

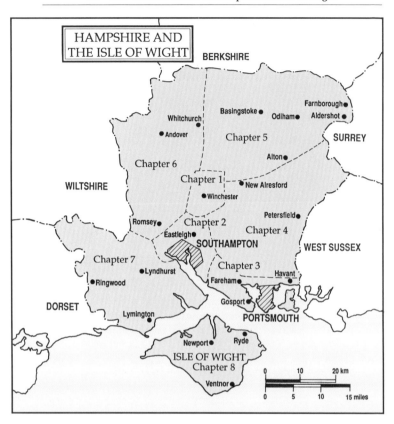

HAMPSHIRE AND THE ISLE OF WIGHT

BERKSHIRE

SURREY

WEST SUSSEX

WILTSHIRE

DORSET

Whitchurch
● Andover
Basingstoke ●
Odiham ●
Farnborough ●
Aldershot ●
Chapter 5
Alton ●
Chapter 6
Chapter 1
● New Alresford
● Winchester
Romsey ●
Chapter 2
Petersfield ●
Eastleigh ●
SOUTHAMPTON
Chapter 4
Chapter 7
● Lyndhurst
Chapter 3
Havant
● Ringwood
Fareham ●
Gosport ●
PORTSMOUTH
Lymington
Newport ●
Ryde
ISLE OF WIGHT
Chapter 8
Ventnor ●

0   10   20 km

0   5   10   15 miles

as St Cross (Winchester) and Lyndhurst respectively. The churches of Hampshire and the Isle of Wight are not so grand as those of Suffolk or the Cotswolds but they contain a wealth of monuments, furniture and interesting details.

The richness of Hampshire's heritage of buildings and ancient monuments is only one of the attractions of the county, though possibly the chief one to many visitors. The countryside can offer nature trails, walks, country parks, nature reserves and the incomparable New Forest; there are abundant opportunities to study plants and trees, wildlife, and shore and marine life. The county caters for all tastes in the way of sports — golf, sailing and gliding to name just three. There are many theatres and cinemas and countless excellent hotels and restaurants.

The Victorians opened up the Isle of Wight to tourists, following the lead set by Queen Victoria, and many of the towns have more than a flavour of that period. The Isle of Wight should be visited not only for its great variety of attractions but also because it has an atmosphere all its own. It is a walker's paradise — over 500 miles of footpaths, including a magnificent coastal path. The island has everything the visitor could want, yet remains largely unspoilt.

The climate is never extreme, the sea having a moderating influence. Snow does not last long and the Isle of Wight in particular can be visited all the year round. So welcome to Hampshire and the Isle of Wight!

1

IN AND AROUND WINCHESTER

The site of Winchester was a natural place for a settlement, at the point where a river cut through the chalk downs. The earliest known settlement was on St Catherine's Hill, where the Iron Age hill-fort was preceded by an unenclosed camp. The hill-fort was abandoned about 100BC. There was another enclosed settlement on the west side of the city at what is now known as Oram's Arbour, the defences of which were probably constructed after the abandonment of St Catherine's Hill.

The Romans established their town on the west side of the River Itchen and later surrounded it with a defensive wall; they named it *Venta Belgarum*, 'the town of the Belgae'. It became an important market centre with several roads radiating from it.

Much of the archaeological evidence for Roman Winchester is difficult to reach, because of subsequent medieval building all over the city. However, it is evident that in the later first century AD Roman Winchester became fully urbanized, with a grid pattern of streets, town houses and defences. Through the next three centuries it acquired all the status symbols of an important Roman centre — public buildings, large houses and an encircling stone wall.

In the seventh century the Saxons founded Old Minster, the first cathedral in Winchester. The site of this first great church, near the present cathedral, has been revealed by excavations. In AD662 the bishop's throne was moved to Winchester from Dorchester on the Thames and this marked the beginning of Winchester's long ecclesiastical supremacy in Wessex. The most famous of the Saxon bishops was St Swithun, though he held that post for only 10 years. Alfred, arguably the greatest of all English kings, successfully opposed the Danes; he made Winchester his capital and lived there in his palace. Winchester under Alfred became a great centre of religion, learning and the arts through its monastic institutions. He founded the nuns' minster (Nunnaminster) and New Minster (built after his death).

In the late ninth century a new town was founded, its extent being determined by the existing Roman defences. The street plan, which survives today, was laid out, and the Roman wall was rebuilt.

From the time of Alfred to that of Henry II, Winchester was one of the most important cities in Europe, the capital of Wessex and then of England. Saxon Winchester was the greatest ecclesiastical centre in England — its three minsters occupied one-quarter of the area of the town. Edward the Confessor was crowned here in 1043.

William the Conqueror made Winchester his capital after the Norman Conquest. He rebuilt the royal palace, which was in the vicinity of the present church of St Lawrence, and constructed a castle on the hill on the west side of the city. The first Norman Bishop of Winchester, Walkelin, was not appointed until 1070 however, and the cathedral was not begun until 1079. It was in Winchester that the famous *Domesday Book* was compiled and written, though Winchester itself was not included in the survey until much later.

Winchester reached the peak of its prosperity in about 1150; it was then probably the second largest town in England, highly developed and densely built-up. The narrow streets of the city were full of traders, especially those dealing in wool and cloth, which as in so many English towns formed the staple industry. Winchester attracted merchants from all over Britain and Europe. The population was about 8,000, a figure not reached again until after 1820. The Winchester Domesday, compiled in 1110 and 1148, gives the most detailed description of any European city of the early Middle Ages. There were fifty-seven churches within its walls in the late thirteenth century; today only one of them survives.

Much of our knowledge of Roman, Saxon and medieval Winchester comes from the many excavations that have been conducted in various parts of the city since 1961, as and when opportunities have arisen. By the thoroughness of these excavations and the recording of their finds it can be said that no city in Europe surpasses Winchester in the knowledge of its past history.

St Giles's Fair, held annually throughout the Middle Ages on the

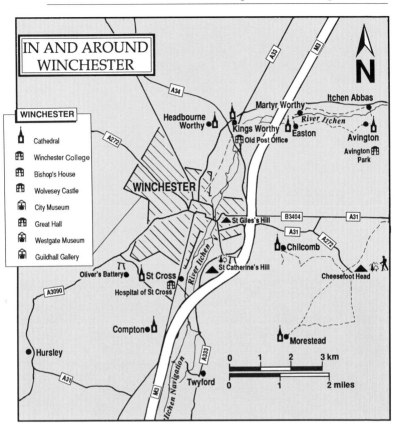

hill outside the town, was one of the largest in Europe. It started to decline at the end of the thirteenth century but its prosperity outlived that of Winchester itself.

After about 1150 Winchester's importance declined; much of its wealth moved to London and it ceased to be the capital. The city was ravaged by the Black Death in 1348-9. At the end of the fourteenth century the clothing industry brought about a revival, but it was short-lived. Winchester's decline started in the western half of the city and by the end of the Middle Ages much of the area within the city walls was covered by fields and orchards, and remained so until the nineteenth century.

In the latter part of the fourteenth century the College of St Mary, the first of England's public schools, was built on its present site, and the nave of the cathedral was rebuilt by Bishops Edington and Wykeham. At the Reformation the Benedictine monastery was dissolved. Fortunately the cathedral survived, with a dean and chapter instead of a prior and monks, but Hyde abbey and St Mary's abbey (the nunnery) were destroyed.

In the Civil War the city, a Royalist centre, suffered many attacks; it was eventually captured by Cromwell and the castle, except the Great Hall, was destroyed.

There was considerable destruction in the city during the Commonwealth period; Wolvesey Castle, the bishops' palace, was also damaged. Most of the damage inflicted on the cathedral during its long history was perpetrated at this time — choir-stalls, statues and the west window were destroyed. Indeed it was even suggested that the cathedral itself should be demolished, but it survived for the second time in its history, as did the college.

After the Middle Ages Winchester's pre-eminent wealth and prestige had gone for ever, but after the Restoration its decline was arrested and the city settled into its role as the county town and a market and social centre.

King Charles II decided to build a palace at Winchester, on the site of the old castle; it was to have had an avenue of trees leading down to the west front of the cathedral. One wing was completed (by Wren) before the King's death and then the plans were shelved. The gentry built many seventeenth- and eighteenth-century houses in the city, of which several survive in the Close, High Street and elsewhere.

In the eighteenth century Winchester was a quiet country town and continued so until the railway in 1840 brought increased trade and prosperity, and the population increased to its level of the twelfth century. There was very little industry in nineteenth-century Winchester; it was also by then an important military centre.

Winchester is one of the richest cities in England in its architecture and historical associations. There is so much to see within a small area that it is best to explore the city on foot. The cathedral, college and St Cross Hospital should on no account be missed so they will be described first.

Winchester cathedral was founded in 1079 and consecrated in 1093; it was the church of the Benedictine monastery of St Swithun.

It is one of the great churches of the world, in terms of both beauty and size. The view of the nave from the west end is awe-inspiring; this is William of Wykeham's masterpiece of Perpendicular Gothic architecture and a marvel of building craftsmanship. From here one can appreciate the great length of the cathedral — it is the longest medieval church in Europe (556ft). The Norman nave was even longer, but in the fourteenth century it was shortened at the west end by about 40ft. An inscription in the close wall marks the extent of the former west end of the nave.

The transepts present a stark contrast to the lofty nave. These, with the tower and the crypt, are the only surviving parts of the original Norman building. The first tower fell down in 1107, to spite William Rufus according to legend. In the transepts, with their massive walls and small windows, it is possible to visualise what the cathedral looked like in the twelfth century and to appreciate the incredible achievement of the Norman masons under Bishop Walkelin who completed it in just over 40 years with very limited means.

The Perpendicular nave was begun at the west end by Bishop Edington and continued by Bishop William of Wykeham and his master mason William de Wynford. They retained the pillars of the Norman nave and disguised them with clustered shafts, and these pillars are thus much more solid than is normal with Perpendicular arcades. The nave is the most satisfying part of the cathedral, its twelve bays exhibiting little change of detail. The west front was the work of Edington; Nikolaus Pevsner describes it as 'disappointing'.

There is little evidence now of the Norman nave and the Norman chancel. The cathedral was extended eastwards in 1202 by Bishops de Lucy and des Roches to form the retrochoir and the Lady Chapel, though the latter was remodelled in the late fifteenth century. The interior of the retrochoir is very beautiful, though to appreciate it properly one must try to ignore the chapels and furnishings that have been placed in it. The retrochoir was built primarily to accommodate the pilgrims who came to the shrine of St Swithun.

So chronologically, there are the Norman transepts, tower and crypt, the retrochoir, the nave, the remodelling of the Lady Chapel and finally the remodelling of the chancel in the early sixteenth century by Bishop Fox, who retained its fourteenth-century arcades. Having fixed the dates of the various parts of the cathedral in one's mind it is time to look at the furnishings and memorials, in which Winchester is as rich as any cathedral in England.

Perhaps the most-visited memorial in the cathedral is that of Jane Austen in the north aisle of the nave. Her gravestone in the floor makes no mention of her literary achievements, but the memorial on the wall and the stained-glass window above it (1900 by Kempe) make amends.

Near her grave stands the font made of black marble from Tournai in Belgium; there are only seven such fonts in England, four of them in Hampshire. It is elaborately carved in fine Romanesque style; on two sides are scenes of legends attributed to the life of St Nicholas, on the other two sides doves and a beast.

The two **chantry chapels** in the nave commemorate the two bishops responsible for the rebuilding of the nave, Edington and Wykeham. They also illustrate the change in architectural style between the death of Edington in 1366 and Wykeham in 1404. Edington's chapel still has Decorated motifs, as seen on his Purbeck marble tomb-chest, but Wykeham's is almost wholly Perpendicular in style. The contrast shows the change from simplicity to soaring grandeur.

Under the crossing facing the north transept is the **Chapel of the Holy Sepulchre** (about 1200). It has a series of twelfth- and early thirteenth-century wall-paintings, which are among the best of that period in the country. They include *Deposition and Entombment of Christ*, *Doubting Thomas* and *Entry into Jerusalem*.

In the **Silkstede chapel** in the south transept is the grave of Izaak Walton, the author of *The Compleat Angler*, the classic work on angling. Above is his memorial window with the legend 'Study to be quiet', one of his favourite texts. He was living with his daughter in the Close when he died in 1683 at the age of 90.

The two wooden benches of about 1200 in the transept are thought to be the oldest pieces of oak furniture in the country. The **Pilgrim Gates**, perhaps the oldest wrought-iron gates in England, are probably thirteenth century as the design details are similar to those on Queen Eleanor's tomb in Westminster Abbey.

The choir-stalls are thought to be the oldest surviving set in England (about 1308). The misericords on their undersides, which supported the monks during the interminable services, may not be closely examined, but they display a wealth of carving, much of it humorous. There are monsters, a mermaid, a monkey and a family of musical pigs.

The large tomb in the chancel is supposedly that of William II, the

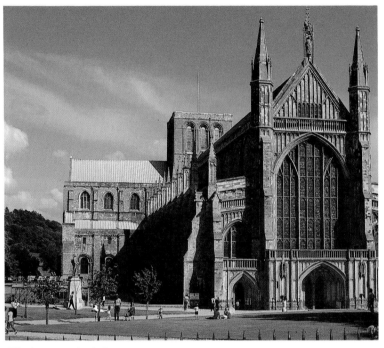

Winchester cathedral

little-lamented king who was mysteriously killed in the New Forest in 1100, and whose body was unceremoniously brought to the cathedral on a cart the day after his death.

The great stone **reredos** dates from the fifteenth century. The original statues were destroyed at the time of the Reformation and the present ones are of the late nineteenth century. The choir screen (by Sir George Gilbert Scott) is a fine piece of woodwork, but imagine the vista from the west end of the nave if the screen was not there!

The chests on top of the side screens are said to contain the bones of several Saxon kings; the bones were scattered by Cromwell's troops and whether they were subsequently pieced together correctly is doubtful. Behind the reredos are the chantries of Bishops Fox and Gardiner. Fox died in 1528 and was responsible for the east window and the chancel screens. Gardiner died in 1555, and his

Places of Interest in Winchester

Winchester Cathedral and the Close
Founded 1079. The longest medieval church in Europe and one of the most beautiful. Many graves, including those of Jane Austen and Izaak Walton.
Cathedral library in the oldest book-room in Europe, with the famous Winchester Bible, one of the most beautiful manuscript books in the world.
The Pilgrims' Hall in the Close has the earliest hammer-beam roof in England.
Triforium Gallery has decorative stonework and sculptures from the cathedral.
Cathedral treasury with Hampshire silver church plate exhibition.

Winchester College
The first public school in England, founded 1382. Many original buildings survive, including the first schoolroom. College chapel, cloister, Fromond chantry chapel, and war cloister.

Wolvesey Castle
(English Heritage)
Ruins of the palace of the Bishops of Winchester.

Royal Green Jackets Museum
Peninsula Barracks

Royal Hussars Regimental Museum
Peninsula Barracks

Gurkha Museum
Peninsula Barracks

Light Infantry Museum
Peninsula Barracks

Four museums with interesting military relics.

Great Hall of Winchester Castle
Finest medieval castle hall in England after Westminster Hall. Famous Round Table, supposedly of King Arthur.

Royal Hampshire Regiment Museum
Southgate Street
Displays and mementoes of the regiment's history.

City Museum, The Square
Westgate Museum, High Street
Exhibits relating to the history of Winchester.

Guildhall Gallery
The Broadway
Exhibitions of paintings and crafts, mainly by Hampshire artists and craftsmen, changing every month or two.

City Mill
(National Trust)
Old corn-mill on the River Itchen.

St Giles's Hill
Site of St Giles's Fair, one of the great annual fairs of the Middle Ages. Splendid view over Winchester.

Historic Resources Centre
Hyde Street
Information and displays relating to the history of Winchester.

Winchester Heritage Centre
Upper Brook Street
Exhibition and audio-visual display recounting the development of Winchester through the ages.

The Crusades Experience
St John's House, The Broadway
Audio-visual re-creation of the medieval crusades.

chapel is part Gothic and part early Renaissance in design.

The shrine of St Swithun in the retrochoir dates only from 1962, 1100 years after his death; in 1538 his shrine had been destroyed by Henry VIII's commissioners. The site of his grave is marked by a stone outside the cathedral. He was buried outside Old Minster so that the rain would fall on his grave. On 15 July 971 his body was moved inside and so the legend arose that rain on that day would be followed by 40 days of rain.

On the floor of the retrochoir is the largest and oldest area of medieval tiles in England. The bronze figure of William Walker recalls his heroic work as a diver in the years 1906-12 when single-handed he underpinned with concrete the whole east end of the cathedral and saved it from collapse. He is certainly Winchester's greatest unsung hero.

The two **chantry chapels** in the retrochoir are those of Bishops Beaufort (died 1447) and Waynflete (died 1486). The effigy of Beaufort is a seventeenth-century copy. The Waynflete chapel has a complex but magnificent vault.

The **Lady Chapel** was extended in 1486 to mark the christening of Henry VII's son Arthur. The original wall-paintings of about 1500 are very faint so they are covered with protective panels painted with facsimile impressions. The originals would have been in far more brilliant colours, and may have been inspired by those in Eton College Chapel. There are some much earlier wall-paintings in the vault of the **Guardian Angels' Chapel**. The monument of Lord Portland (1634) is one of the best of that date in England, ahead of its time with its classical surround.

The **crypt**, entered from the north transept, is open only in summer because of flooding. The Norman crypt is a remarkably complete example, the work of Bishop Walkelin. The eastern crypt dates from 1189-1204, the same period as the early Lady Chapel. The architecture is very simple — flat vaulting and rough stonework, though the crypt under the Lady Chapel has a rib vault.

The **cathedral library**, with its thousands of volumes of rare books, is housed in the oldest book-room in Europe, dating from about 1150. Here is displayed the famous Winchester Bible, one of the most beautiful illuminated manuscript books in the world. It was begun soon after 1160 by the Winchester School of artists and by good fortune survived the Reformation and the Civil War. Though the text is complete, work on the coloured illustrations ceased after

25-30 years. It was not intended for ordinary use and was originally bound in two volumes (it is now in four). Also on display are two Dutch globes by the cartographer Blaeu, a celestial globe of 1640 and a terrestrial globe.

In the **Triforium Gallery** there is a display of Romanesque decorative stonework (mainly capitals from the cloisters), sculptures from the great reredos that were torn down at the Reformation, Queen Mary's supposed wedding chair, and fragments that may be from St Swithun's shrine.

The **cathedral treasury** contains a constantly changing exhibition of silver plate from the cathedral, Wolvesey Castle and Hampshire churches.

The foundations of **Old Minster** can be seen outside the cathedral on the north side; it was founded about AD648 and became a cathedral about AD662. It was enlarged several times and finally in AD974-994 was rebuilt on a greater scale than ever, when it became probably the greatest church in England, at the centre of a populous city. This quarter of the city was a royal and ecclesiastical precinct without parallel in northern Europe.

Old Minster was a place of pilgrimage to the shrine of St Swithun, and the scene of coronations (eg Edward the Confessor) and burials of kings (eg Alfred and Canute). Its diocese extended from London to the Isle of Wight. Old Minster was demolished in 1093, immediately after the consecration of the new cathedral.

New Minster, founded in 901-3, stood very close to Old Minster and was intended for use as the town church. It was moved to Hyde in 1100. **Nunnaminster**, founded in the late ninth century, was also part of the great complex of monastic buildings that occupied about one-quarter of the area of the early medieval town, a concentration unique in England.

The **cloister** was on the south side of the cathedral, surrounded by the buildings of St Swithun's Priory. The cloister has been destroyed, but the medieval **Prior's Hall** survives near the Deanery. Adjoining the Pilgrims' School is the **Pilgrims' Hall** (open to visitors); it has the earliest wooden hammer-beam roof so far known in England. Opposite the school is the timber-framed range of old stables, now used as classrooms. The exploration of the Close is a pleasant experience.

Just beyond St Swithun's Gate is **King's Gate**, one of the two surviving gateways of the medieval city. Above it is the church of St

Kingsgate Street, Winchester

Swithun, one of the few in England in this curious position; it was founded to serve the people who worked at St Swithun's Priory. To the left is College Street; Jane Austen died at No 8. She came here from her home at Chawton in order to be near her doctor. Picturesque Kingsgate Street has several fine Georgian houses, some with their original bow-windows. At **St Michael's church** look for the Saxon sundial on the south wall.

Winchester College, founded in 1382 as the College of St Mary, is the oldest English public school. It was built 1387-93 (at a cost of just over £1,000!) and many of the original buildings survive. There were originally seventy 'poor and needy' scholars, whose tuition was almost entirely devoted to classics and grammar. There are now in addition about 580 'Commoners', who do not live in the college. Chamber Court has been the centre of college life for 600 years; around it are the rooms of the scholars, and on the south side is the hall, immediately above the very earliest schoolroom. There are guided tours of the college in summer. The chapel and the cloister are part of the original buildings.

The chapel, extensively restored in the nineteenth century, is dignified and beautiful. The original wooden ceiling and lierne vault survive; they were constructed by the craftsmen who also built the roof of Westminster Hall. The bench-ends and the misericords under the benches are original; the latter depict dragons, a crippled man, a pelican and a shepherd among others.

In the Middle Ages Fellows of the college were buried in the cloister and lessons were held here in summer. Earl Wavell, the famous soldier of World War II, is buried here. In the centre of the cloister is the Fromond chantry chapel, completed in 1446. The upper floor is once again in use as a library, its original purpose. The red-brick building beyond is known as 'School' and was built in 1683-7 as an additional schoolroom. The war cloister commemorates in panels the former scholars who fell in the two world wars.

At the far end of College Street on the left is the **Bishop's House**, the surviving part of the house built in 1684 by Thomas Fitch (not by Christopher Wren as is sometimes supposed) for Bishop Morley at

Bishop's House, Winchester

the time when Charles II often visited Winchester. Beyond it are the ruins of the twelfth-century **Wolvesey Castle**. The palace, or castle, of Wolvesey was the work of two bishops, Giffard and de Blois, who was the grandson of the Conqueror. Giffard's West Hall has been described as the largest known non-monastic building of its date in England, other than Westminster Hall; very little of it survives. Much more remains of de Blois's East Hall of the early twelfth century; it was a fortified building with nearly forty rooms surrounding a central courtyard. De Blois also built a wall between the two halls and a moat, which came in useful in the war between King Stephen and his sister Matilda.

Wolvesey Castle was used for several hundred years for the visits of royalty and nobility until it was demolished in 1786. Probably its last great event was the wedding reception for Queen Mary and Philip II of Spain in 1554.

The best way to approach **St Cross** is by a footpath from College Walk across the water-meadows by the River Itchen (about a mile). Away to the left is St Catherine's Hill with its distinctive clump of beech trees. One can also reach St Cross by car or bus via St Cross Road. The Hospital of St Cross was founded by Bishop Henry de Blois in 1136 and is the oldest almshouse in England, having been used for this purpose ever since that time. The original provision was for the housing of thirteen old men and free dinners every day for 100 other poor men. In 1446 Bishop Beaufort extended the hospital to include thirty-five members of his Order of Noble Poverty, 'distressed gentlefolk' of the time. Today the brothers of the original foundation wear black cloaks and those of the Beaufort foundation wear red cloaks. The traditional 'Wayfarer's Dole' of bread and ale can be claimed by visitors at the porter's lodge.

Nearly all the buildings date from the 1446 rebuilding, with the notable exception of the church. Grouped round the square, they present a scene of great beauty and tranquillity; it is almost as if time has stood still for 500 years. On the west side are the lodgings of the brothers; each of them has three rooms. Adjoining the impressive gatehouse is the hall; the dining-room and the old kitchen with its original fireplace are open to visitors. Lovers of Trollope may like to know that Hiram's Hospital in *The Warden* was based on St Cross.

The church is one of the best examples in England of the transitional period of architecture between Norman and Early English. It was built during the period 1170-1230, a time in which ecclesiastical building reached its peak in Hampshire. The earliest work is at the east end and in the transepts.

The Romanesque and Gothic details of the church adjoin each other or overlap, so there is no order to the transition in styles. The chancel exterior is clearly wholly Norman; the north transept has some pointed windows, but the south transept has not. The nave aisles on the east are Norman but become wholly Early English to the west. The tower is said to have been rebuilt in 1384. The interior is more complicated, made more so by Butterfield's restoration in the nineteenth century. Nevertheless the result is a church of great dignity, powerful rather than beautiful. Features of special interest are the Norman font, the lectern of 1509, a brass to John de Campeden (1410), thirteenth-century wall-paintings and a triptych of 1512 by the Flemish artist van Mabuse.

Many other places of interest in Winchester can be seen by walking, with diversions, from West Gate along High Street to St Giles's Hill. **West Gate**, one of the two surviving medieval gateways of the old city, stands on the line of the city wall. It was once used as a prison and is now a museum. On the inside walls are inscriptions cut by prisoners; other exhibits include armour, a city coffer and the medieval weights and measures of the city. The ceiling, from Winchester College, was made for Queen Mary's wedding in 1554. There is a good view of High Street from the roof.

A short distance beyond West Gate is the former **Peninsula Barracks**, which stands on the site of the medieval castle, destroyed after the Civil War. The site was purchased from the City Corporation for five shillings by Charles II, who then commissioned Christopher Wren to build a palace there. It was never completed, and was burnt down in 1894.

The **Royal Green Jackets Museum** is open to visitors and has a large collection of war relics, with special emphasis on the North American campaign and the Peninsula War. Fifty-six Victoria Crosses were won by the three regiments that formed the Royal Green Jackets and thirty-two of these are on display. There are three other regimental museums here, those of the **Royal Hussars**, the **Gurkhas** and the **Light Infantry**.

Near West Gate is the **Plague Monument**, erected in 1759 to mark the spot, just outside the city wall, to which the markets were removed at the time of the plague in 1666. South of West Gate is the **Great Hall**, all that survives of the medieval castle. It is considered to be the best medieval hall in the country, after Westminster Hall. It dates from the early thirteenth century; the fine arcade piers are of Purbeck marble. It was built in the form of a double cube (110ft by 55ft by 55ft) with five bays. It once had dormer windows instead of the present straight eaves.

The famous Round Table, traditionally associated with King Arthur, hangs on the west wall; it has been dated to the mid-thirteenth century, and was perhaps commissioned by Edward I. It was painted in the early sixteenth century with a figure of King Arthur (probably a likeness of the young Henry VIII), the Tudor rose in the centre and the names of twenty-four knights around the circumference. The painting may have been done in preparation for a state visit by the Holy Roman Emperor Charles V.

Henry III was born in the castle in 1207, and Henry V was there before going to Agincourt. The Great Hall itself has witnessed many historic events — several meetings of the English Parliament (the first in 1246, the last in 1449), the trial of Walter Raleigh in 1603, and the trials presided over by the infamous Judge Jeffreys. The bronze statue of Queen Victoria finally ended up here after standing in various spots in the city; it commemorates the Queen's Golden Jubilee.

Near the entrance to the Great Hall are remains of the **old castle**, including a round tower (about 1222) and part of the curtain-wall. Behind the Great Hall is **Queen Eleanor's Garden**, a re-creation of a thirteenth-century garden.

In High Street notice the variety of Georgian and Victorian buildings, some with original shop-fronts and doorways. To the left is Jewry Street, a name that recalls the part of the city inhabited in early medieval times by Jewish traders and money-lenders. They lived amicably with the other citizens until the general expulsion of Jews from England in the late thirteenth century. The most prominent building in Jewry Street is the public library, formerly the Corn Exchange. To the right in Southgate Street, in Serle's House, is the **Royal Hampshire Regiment Museum**. This contains many relics from the regiment's campaigns, with a special display of the Gallipoli landings in 1915. The regiment was formed in 1881 and two companies from the 1st Battalion were the first into France on D-Day.

High Street can be regained by following Symond's Street, parallel to and east of Southgate Street. Here is **Christ's Hospital**, a row of almshouses built in 1607 at the expense of Peter Symonds, a Winchester man who became a London merchant.

Further along High Street is the old **Guildhall**, now a bank, with its remarkable bracket clock made by a local craftsman. Every evening at 8 o'clock a curfew bell is rung from here, a tradition maintained since Norman times. Opposite is **God Begot House**, on the site of the manor house that belonged to Emma, wife of Canute. A stop for refreshment can be made at **The Royal Oak**, which claims

Places of Interest Around Winchester

The Itchen Valley
Walks along the River Itchen through unspoilt water-meadows between Martyr Worthy, Itchen Abbas, Avington and Easton. Trout-fishing at Avington.

Headbourne Worthy
Saxon church with remains of a remarkable rood.

Avington Park and Church
Seventeenth-century mansion and park. The state rooms are open in summer. The best Georgian church in Hampshire, with original furniture. Picnic park west of the village.

Cheesefoot Head
3 miles east of Winchester on the A272
Good viewpoint and starting-point for walks over the downs.

St Cross Hospital and Church
The oldest almshouse in England. Visitors can request the 'Wayfarer's Dole'. The church is a fine example of the transitional Norman style.

Itchen Navigation
Canal from Winchester to Southampton, in use 1710-1869. Its 10-mile length can be followed by public footpath.

St Catherine's Hill
Superb view over Winchester. Crowned by an impressive Iron Age hill-fort. The Mizmaze is an old turf-cut maze. The hill is a nature reserve, the whole of it open to visitors.

Twyford Waterworks
Hazeley Road, Twyford
Small water-pumping station of Edwardian date.

to have the oldest bar in England.

In High Street stands the medieval **High Cross**, known as the Butter Cross because here there was once a market; here also the town-crier used to shout his news and in fact still does, because the city employs an official town-crier. The entrance to **St Lawrence**, the only surviving medieval church within the old city, is in the passage behind the cross. The church stands on the site of the former Norman royal palace, perhaps even on the site of the royal chapel, and is unusual in being almost completely surrounded by shops and offices. In St Lawrence each new bishop is presented to the mayor and citizens before his enthronement. The **Eclipse Inn**, round the corner, was once its rectory. Also about here stood William the Conqueror's palace; fragments of it survive in nearby buildings.

The **City Museum** in the Square has many interesting exhibits.

There are several Roman mosaic floors, including an almost complete one from a villa at Sparsholt. Many finds from the Lankhills Roman cemetery and from the recent excavations at the Brooks in Winchester are on display. An important exhibit is the Winchester Reliquary, a purse-shaped container for relics, made of bronze and gilt in the ninth century AD and a unique object from Anglo-Saxon England. Two Victorian shops have been reconstructed in the museum, a tobacconist's and a chemist's exactly as they stood in High Street. Market Lane leads back to High Street via the tower of St Maurice's church, all that survives; high up on the wall a Saxon sundial faces the cathedral.

Where High Street widens to become the Broadway stands the ornate Victorian **Guildhall**; here is the Tourist Information Centre and the Guildhall Gallery. In the centre of the Broadway is an imposing statue of King Alfred, erected in 1901 to commemorate the 1,000th anniversary of his death, but in fact 2 years too late because he died in AD899! **St John's Hospital** opposite consists of twenty-one almshouses and a medieval hall and chapel.

City Bridge over the Itchen once marked the eastern boundary of the city; East Gate stood here. That part of the city beyond the river was called the Soke. **City Mill** by the bridge was rebuilt in 1744 and is now a youth hostel owned by the National Trust (open in summer). **St Peter's church** in Chesil Street has a Norman tower, and is now used as a theatre by the local dramatic society; its medieval rectory stands on the corner opposite.

In St John's Street is the **church of St John the Baptist**, the most interesting and oldest surviving parish church in Winchester. It was neglected for a long period and perhaps for that reason was not thought worthy of restoration. There was a church here in 1142, when it was acquired by St Denys Priory in Southampton. The nave arcades with their round pillars and slightly pointed arches date from about 1200. There are traces of late thirteenth-century wall-paintings. A rare feature is the external rood stair-turret and door.

Further on is **The Old Blue Boar**, once an inn, now the oldest house in Winchester (about 1340). From here it is not far to the top of **St Giles's Hill**, which offers a fine view over the city. The fair held here in the Middle Ages was one of the largest in Europe, attended by traders from all over England. The bishop took as much as £150 annually from the fair, a large sum in those days.

A path from the west side of the recreation centre leads to the abbey gatehouse, all that survives of Hyde Abbey, which was founded here in 1110 when the monks of New Minster moved from the city centre. The gatehouse is later however — fifteenth century. When a new gaol was built on the site of the abbey church in 1787 some coffins were destroyed, one of them almost certainly being that of King Alfred who had been reburied here — a sad ending for England's greatest king. The present church of St Bartholomew has a Norman south doorway. The Historic Resources Centre at Hyde is open to visitors and displays information relating to the city's history.

An interesting and pleasant walk can be taken from the recreation centre to **Kings Worthy** (about $1^1/_2$ miles); by road take the A3090 via Hyde Street. From the end of Saxon Road the path to Kings Worthy, which follows closely the line of the Roman road to Silchester, is known as Nuns Walk and was the beginning of the medieval Pilgrims' Way from Winchester to Canterbury via the Itchen valley. The old part of Kings Worthy lies around the church, which has a medieval tower. The Old Post Office, a timber-framed house near the church, was one of the earliest post offices in England. The Cart and Horses has the authentic air of an old coaching inn.

The church at **Headbourne Worthy**, on the road to Winchester, has a rare and remarkable relic — a Saxon rood or cross with the life-size figures, severely mutilated, of Christ, the Virgin and St John. It is inside the church on what was once perhaps the exterior west wall of the nave. The church is Saxon — see the west doorway. There is a brass of 1434 to John Kent, a scholar of Winchester College. **Avington** is reached via the A31 to Alton and a left turn one mile beyond its junction with the A272. A delightful 4-mile round walk can be taken along both sides of the Itchen valley from the picnic park west of the village. One mile west lies **Easton**, a large village with many pretty thatched cottages (but no shop!), picturesquely situated above the river. The church is late Norman with a peculiar steeple. In the chancel is a monument to Agatha Barlow, whose five daughters each married a bishop!

The road north crosses the river and a footpath along the north bank leads to **Martyr Worthy**, an attractive one-street village also with a Norman church, which has two fine original doorways. The name of the village derives from Henri la Martre, who held the manor in 1201. Opposite the church the path crosses fields to Chilland and Itchen Abbas. The River Itchen has a constant flow of clear

Avington Park

water and is famous for its trout; this stretch of the river is particularly beautiful and peaceful. Plant-lovers will discover many species that enjoy water habitats. Charles Kingsley used to stay at **Itchen Abbas**, and it is said that he wrote *The Water-Babies* at the Plough Inn that preceded the present one. The church was rebuilt in the Norman style in the nineteenth century. In the churchyard is the grave of the gypsy John Hughes, said to have been the last man in England to be hanged for horse-stealing (in 1825), as an example to others. The road south leads to Avington.

Nearer Alresford is **Itchen Stoke**, with its unusual Victorian church based on the design of the church of Sainte Chapelle in Paris. The tiles in the floor of the apse are in the form of a maze similar to the one in Chartres cathedral.

Avington Park was rebuilt in the late seventeenth century and has been refaced and added to since. The wood-and-plaster portico on the west front is a very early example. Charles II stayed here, and later it was bought by John Shelley, brother of the poet. The state rooms, including the library, ballroom and drawing-room, are open in summer. The church is completely unspoilt Georgian, built 1768-

71, and undoubtedly the best of this period in Hampshire. All the furniture is original, of mahogany supposedly from a Spanish Armada ship; even the hat-pegs remain on the walls. There is a barrel-organ, which plays thirty-one hymns, and a 'Vinegar' Bible of 1717. Fishing is available at the Avington lakes.

Cheesefoot Head on the Petersfield Road is reached via the A31 and a left turn. Here one can park and take walks across the downs. One path across Fawley Down leads to **Morestead** (2 miles). It is hard to realise that this track was once the main road from London via Alton to Southampton and used throughout the Middle Ages; in fact it was the first Winchester bypass! At Morestead is a small undedicated Norman church. This area was in the past celebrated for rabbits — sadly this is not so today.

The village of **Chilcomb** is reached by a turning off the A31 a mile east of Winchester. St Andrew's church is a small and unspoilt Norman building beneath the downs at the end of a lane, incredibly remote and peaceful though only 2 miles from Winchester. The manor of Chilcomb, given to Old Minster by King Cynegils in AD635, covered a very large area around Winchester at the time of Domesday.

St Catherine's Hill is best approached on foot by the tow-path of

The Itchen Navigation at Shawford

the **Itchen Navigation** from its terminus at Wharf Hill. An Act of 1665 authorised the construction of the Itchen Navigation 'by improving the river and making new cuts'; it was completed in 1710 from Winchester to Woodmill, Southampton, and had fifteen locks. It was last used as a canal in 1869. A public footpath follows the whole of its $10^1/_2$ miles and makes an interesting day's walk.

St Catherine's Hill is a stiff climb but the view of Winchester from the top is well worth the effort. The hill is crowned by the massive rampart and ditch of an Iron Age hill-fort that was the site of the first important settlement in the area. In the beech tree plantation is the site of a twelfth-century chapel, and to the east of it is the Mizmaze, a turf-cut maze, probably seventeenth century in date, which has given pleasure to generations of children (and adults!). The hill is a nature reserve in the care of the Hampshire and Isle of Wight Naturalists' Trust. It has a good range of chalk plants and insects, and is one of the places where the bee orchid and the frog orchid can be found.

Twyford, the first village south of Winchester on the A333, has interesting literary associations. At Twyford House, on the main road above the church, Benjamin Franklin, famous American statesman and writer, wrote some of his autobiography. At the lower end of Queen Street was a school where Alexander Pope, as a pupil in 1697, was expelled for making fun of his tutor. At the present school on the main road Thomas Hughes, the author of *Tom Brown's Schooldays*, was a pupil; he described it unflatteringly in his book.

There were six mills at Twyford when *Domesday Book* was compiled, when the Bishop of Winchester was lord of the manor. Twyford church was rebuilt by Waterhouse in 1876-7. Inside there is a copy of the Elizabethan seating arrangement, when the parishioners were allocated seats according to their status. The yew tree in the churchyard is said to be the oldest clipped yew in the country.

The B3386 crosses the river to **Compton**, 'the village in a valley'. The church here is most unusual for it has two naves and two chancels. The church was extended in 1905; the Norman chancel is now a chapel and there is a superbly carved Norman doorway.

From Compton the A31 leads in 3 miles to **Hursley**, famous for two widely differing men. The first, Richard Cromwell, son of Oliver, married the daughter of the squire of Hursley. He was living at the Lodge when he became Lord Protector of England after the death of his father in 1658. At the Restoration he fled to the Continent for 20 years and never saw his wife again. His grave is said to be under the chancel. The second, John Keble, was leader of the Oxford Movement and author of *The Christian Year*. He was vicar from 1836 to 1866, and the church was rebuilt in 1848 with the royalties from his books. He lies in the churchyard with his wife, who outlived him by only 6 weeks. The great house in the park is now occupied by the firm of IBM.

The union workhouse at Hursley was the smallest in England; it covered only four parishes, later extended to six before moving to Chandler's Ford. The workhouse was converted from a row of cottages and has now reverted to houses again (The Square in Collins Lane). Parts of the bank of the medieval deer park can be seen in Ampfield Wood; a public footpath crosses it in places. Note the wide ditch on the inside of the bank; it was once deep enough to prevent the deer from escaping.

At **Oliver's Battery**, between Hursley and Winchester, is a Romano-British enclosure, now an ancient monument. The name derives from its possible use in the Civil War by the Roundheads as a base from which to attack Winchester.

2

IN AND AROUND SOUTHAMPTON

S outhampton, one of the most historic cities in Britain, has taken full advantage of its position between two rivers giving easy access inland, on a deep-water natural harbour, with the benefit of double high tides. The history of Southampton goes back almost 2,000 years, to the Roman port of *Clausentum* on a small peninsula on the east bank of the Itchen at Bitterne. The bank and ditch that protected the settlement were visible until the area was built over in the nineteenth century. *Clausentum* originated in the first century AD and by the fourth century it had been reduced in area and surrounded by a defensive stone wall. Excavations in 1951-4 revealed the remains of stone buildings, including a bath-house.

The next known settlement, the Saxon port of *Hamwic*, was on the opposite bank, in the present St Mary's area. Excavations have shown that it was one of the largest towns in Europe at that time, and probably the earliest planned Saxon town in England. It is now thought that the town of *Hamtun*, which was important enough to give its name to the county, was the same place as *Hamwic* and not as previously supposed two separate towns. So the county was named *Hamtunscir*, and the *Domesday Book* version *Hantescire* gives us the modern abbreviation Hants.

St Mary's church originated as the minster church of Saxon *Hamwic*. Many finds were made in the St Mary's area when it was built over in the mid-nineteenth century but most of them have been lost. Further excavations since the last war culminated in 1978-83 in the uncovering of a large area of the Saxon town in the Seven Dials

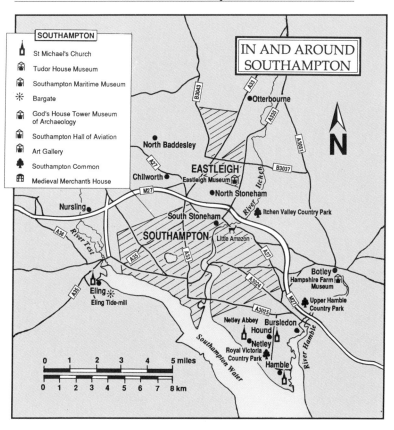

SOUTHAMPTON

- St Michael's Church
- Tudor House Museum
- Southampton Maritime Museum
- Bargate
- God's House Tower Museum of Archaeology
- Southampton Hall of Aviation
- Art Gallery
- Southampton Common
- Medieval Merchant's House

IN AND AROUND SOUTHAMPTON

district; this seemed to confirm that *Hamwic* was the first post-Roman planned town in north-west Europe. The population has been estimated at 4,000-8,000, which if correct means that *Hamwic* was the largest town in England in the eighth century.

That *Hamwic* traded with many parts of Europe is clear from the different coins and fragments of glass and pottery that have been found. It is also clear that many diverse crafts and industries were carried on in the town. The decline of *Hamwic* began at the time of Winchester's revival under King Alfred, and the loss of its international trade finally led to its demise in the late ninth century.

A new settlement emerged before the Conquest on the site of the later Anglo-Norman town; its main axis was on the line of what is now High Street and it was surrounded by fields and marshes. By 1086 it had a population of nearly 1,000.

After the Norman Conquest two separate communities grew up, an English one centred on English Street (the present High Street) and a French one centred on French Street. In the late twelfth century and throughout the thirteenth century many timber houses were rebuilt of stone, evidence of the town's prosperity because stone was expensive. Remains of several houses of this period can be seen, including the so-called 'King John's House' and 'Canute's Palace'. After about 1300 timber became the chief building material once again, and that is why more buildings survive from the thirteenth century than from the later medieval period. The medieval street layout survived until recent times.

For 500 years Southampton was one of England's leading ports; its chief trade was the import of wine and the export of wool. For much of this time the merchants of Southampton had been reluctant to finance the fortification of the town. Even after the French raid of 1338, when much of the town was laid waste and many people were slaughtered, they were still reluctant to do so. The Black Death caused a further postponement, but by 1385 the stone walls and towers of the town's defences were almost complete, the castle had been rebuilt and Southampton had become one of the strongest fortified towns in England. Its walls had twenty-nine towers, and seven gateways of which four survive; the remains of its town walls are among the best in England.

In 1445 Southampton was incorporated as a borough and in 1447 it became a county of a town (not to be confused with the 'County of Southampton' ie Hampshire). Southampton experienced an economic recovery in the fifteenth century, largely through the export of wool; a warehouse of this time survives (the Wool House). The port was a hive of activity; it was the chief port of call in England for Italian ships, and many Italian merchants lived in the vicinity of Bugle Street and Westgate Street. But this second great period of prosperity came to an end in the mid-sixteenth century, when the trade with Italy ceased and London came to the fore as a port.

The construction of castles along the Solent shore in the 1540s made the town defences of Southampton superfluous and from then on they were not properly maintained. In spite of the fluctuations in its trade and prosperity, Southampton's population continued to grow until in 1600 it numbered about 4,000. Several visitations of the plague reduced the numbers and it did not reach that figure again for some time. Southampton had been a pleasant place in which to live; a visitor in the sixteenth century would have seen a town with gardens, orchards, many fine buildings and a High Street as handsome as any in England, but by 1600 an air of decay hung over the town.

Later, the town again suffered a decline, but in the eighteenth century the discovery of a mineral spring and the increasing popularity of sea-bathing were exploited to the full to bring a temporary revival of prosperity. Southampton became one of the country's leading spas, a resort of royalty and the aristocracy. The spring, of chalybeate water, was north-west of Bargate, near the western shore; for good measure the site was laid out as a pleasure garden. By the 1760s bathing-houses had been built near the quays; they were filled with sea-water at each tide. One of these, the Long Rooms at West Quay, had an assembly room that became the centre of social activities. The streets were lit in 1782-3 (by gas in 1820) but the lamps served only to accentuate the cleanliness of High Street and the filth of the side streets. The spa period was finished by 1820 but even greater days were to come.

The opening of the Outer Dock in 1842 and the Inner Dock in 1851 brought an enormous increase in trade, helped by the opening of the railway to London in 1840. It soon became clear that steamships and the passengers they carried would be vital to the prosperity of the port. In 1843 Southampton replaced Falmouth as the principal mail packet port. After the purchase of the docks by the London and South Western Railway Company in 1892 Southampton never looked back; between 1892 and 1914 the volume of shipping using the port rose threefold. It was the only port that could be entered at any time by the largest vessels, and it became Britain's leading passenger port.

Its importance in wartime was seen in the Crimean War, Boer War, World War I and World War II, when the bulk of the British expeditionary forces passed through the port (over 8,000,000 in 1914-18). Other notable events in the history of the docks were the coming of the White Star Line in 1907, the Cunard Line in 1919, the installation of a floating dock in 1924 and the opening of the Ocean Terminal in 1950.

In the nineteenth century the population rose rapidly and most of the country estates on the outskirts of the town were built over.

Including the suburbs, the population reached 100,000 in 1901 (it is now over 200,000). It was therefore as well that the old common fields were designated public parks in 1844, as was Southampton Common.

Horse-drawn trams were introduced in 1879, and these were electrified in 1900. The 1920s and 1930s saw much expansion in the town, and the prosperity resulted in the growth of civic amenities such as the new Civic Centre.

Southampton has made a remarkable recovery from the devastation of the last war, when over 3,500 buildings were destroyed, including many in the historic High Street. As a final honour in 1964 it became a city.

Southampton's important buildings therefore reflect its three great periods of prosperity. First, those of medieval date in the old town, south of Bargate; these include the town walls and gateways, the Wool House, St Michael's church and St Julian's chapel. Second, those of the spa period of 1750-1820, notably the terraced houses in Carlton Crescent, Bedford Place and Rockstone Place. Third, those of the late nineteenth century to the present day, notably the Civic Centre.

Today Southampton has a larger proportion of its area devoted to parks and commons than most cities, and is particularly fortunate to have its Common and a fine sports centre.

Bargate, one of the best medieval gatehouses in Britain, has been the most famous landmark in Southampton for 800 years now, so it is an appropriate place to start a perambulation of the town walls. It was built to guard the main road into the town. It has been used as a toll-gate, prison, guildhall and museum. The original Norman archway dates from about 1175, and the two flanking towers were added a hundred years later. The upper floor was the medieval guild-hall. Trams had to be specially modified to go under the archway when all traffic went through Bargate. In 1914 the Corporation recommended its removal, but better counsels prevailed.

The wall on the south side of Bargate Street leads to **Arundel Tower**, at the north-west corner of the town walls. This tower was nicknamed 'Windwhistle', and the next one 'Catchcold', because until the nineteenth century the sea lapped the whole length of the western wall, which felt the full force of westerly winds. This stretch of the walls is the best surviving part; the arcades have apertures at the top through which missiles could be dropped on attackers. Gun-

Red Bridge, Southampton

ports can be seen in the surviving towers; artillery was an important factor in the effectiveness of the defences.

Westgate led directly to **West Quay**, which was for many centuries the only quay that could accommodate large ships. Henry V's army left from here in 1415 for Agincourt, and the Pilgrim Fathers set sail from here in 1620. In the gateway the grooves for the portcullis can be seen. Adjoining Westgate is the **Tudor Merchants Hall**, which formerly stood in St Michael's Square, when it was a fish-market and cloth-hall. It was sold in 1634 and moved to its present site for use as a warehouse.

The **Mayflower Memorial** commemorates the departure of the Pilgrim Fathers to America in 1620. Their ships, the *Mayflower* and the *Speedwell*, had to call at Dartmouth and Plymouth, where the *Speedwell* was left behind. Nearby is the less-familiar **Stella Memorial**, to a stewardess who gave her life in a shipwreck. Opposite is **Mayflower Park**, where ships can be seen passing on their way to and from the Western Docks; it is also the venue of the annual Boat Show. The **Royal Pier** was opened in 1833 and was for a long time the largest in the south of England. Its future is now uncertain.

At the corner of Bugle Street is the former **Yacht Club**, built in

1846, considered by some to be the most beautiful building in the city. Opposite is the **Wool House**, the only surviving medieval warehouse in Southampton, built by the monks of Beaulieu. Wool was the basis of Southampton's prosperity in the Middle Ages and was stored here for export. French prisoners were kept here during the Napoleonic Wars and several bone model ships in the museum inside may be their handiwork. The first aircraft built in Hampshire were made in this very building in 1910 by Eric Moon; they were called 'Moonbeams'.

The Wool House houses the **Maritime Museum**, with exhibits illustrating the history of the port. There are superb scale models of ocean liners and relics of the SS *Titanic*. Southampton suffered a tragic blow in 1912 when the *Titanic* sank on her maiden voyage, as most of the crew were from the town. Other exhibits include a large-scale model of the docks, and the history of the Royal Mail Steam Packet Company and Scott-Paine's British Power Boat Company.

Town Quay was an important commercial centre of medieval Southampton, handling cargoes from all over the world; it was also the place where warships were built for Henry V.

East of the Wool House in Porter's Lane is '**Canute's Palace**'. It has nothing to do with Canute but is in fact the ruin of a twelfth-century merchant's house, a rare example of a Norman upper-hall house. The remains of five other medieval houses have been exposed by excavations at the south end of High Street. On the corner of High Street are the remains of **South Gate** or Water Gate. Across High Street in Winkle Street (from the German word meaning 'angle') is **St Julian's chapel**, the only remains of St Julian's hospital or God's House, founded in the twelfth century. Later it was given to Queen's Hall, now Queen's College, Oxford, who still own it.

God's House Gate is at the south-east corner of the walled town, and adjoining it is God's House Tower, which was built in the early fifteenth century and is one of the earliest artillery fortifications in Europe. Guns were stored on the ground floor and the upper floor was a gun battery. **God's House Tower Museum of Archaeology** illustrates the history of Southampton, and has a large collection of post-Roman European pottery, together with finds from Saxon *Hamwic*, Roman milestones and an altar from *Clausentum*. The O.G.S. Crawford Memorial Room relates the history of Southampton illustrated by finds from excavations. Crawford was the first Archaeology Officer of the Ordnance Survey, whose headquarters are now at

Maybush. The Ordnance Survey moved to Southampton from the Tower of London in 1841-2. Nearby is **God's House Green**, which claims to be the oldest bowling green in England, first used in 1299.

From here one can make a diversion to the Hall of Aviation and Terminus station (see below) or continue the circuit of the town walls. Only a small part of the eastern wall remains. The southern arm of the Southampton and Salisbury Canal was constructed on the line of the ditch outside the eastern wall — hence the street here named Canal Walk. The ruined **Polymond Tower** is at the north-east corner of the walls and further remains can be seen between here and Bargate, which completes the $1^1/_4$-mile circuit. There is a public walkway along the whole length of the medieval walls.

About half a mile from God's House Gate, via Queen's Park, is **Terminus station**, which was opened in 1840 and is a classic piece of early railway station architecture. It was designed by Sir William Tite in an Italianate style with a ground-floor colonnade, and set a high standard for other L & SWR stations. Terminus station was Southampton's main station until the opening of Central station.

In Royal Crescent is the **Southampton Hall of Aviation** with the R.J. Mitchell Museum. Mitchell was the designer of the famous Spitfire fighter aeroplane, built at the Supermarine works in Southampton. He died in 1937 and this museum is his memorial. Exhibits include a Spitfire, a Supermarine S6A of Schneider Trophy fame, a Sandringham flying-boat, a Gnat, a Sea Vixen, a Vampire and two gliders. South of Canute Road is the Ocean Terminal, completed in 1950 (no admittance).

Nearby is **Ocean Village**, which promises to be the most exciting of all Southampton's post-war developments. Here, on 75 acres of the former Princess Alexandra Dock, a complex of buildings is nearing completion. The largest is Canute's Pavilion, an arcade of shops; others include the Heritage Theatre, with an audio-visual display of the history of Southampton's dockland and shipbuilding industry, and the Maritime Heritage Centre, a museum located in the former P&O booking office. Ships at the marina include the Calshot Spit lightship, which for 40 years guided ocean liners in the Solent, and the Thames sailing barge *Kitty* of 1895.

The other places of interest in the old town are not far from Bargate. At the junction of Castle Way and Castle Lane are the remains of the drum towers of Castle Gate, which were added to the medieval walls in the fourteenth century and were over 20ft high.

The Castle House tower block stands on the site of the medieval castle keep and mound.

St Michael's Square, to the west of Castle Way, is an old part of the town, the centre of the French quarter. **St Michael's church** was founded in about 1070 and is the oldest building in Southampton, the only survivor of the five medieval churches in the town. The lower part of the tower is the original Norman; there have been many alterations and additions over the centuries. The church was originally cruciform; it is now virtually rectangular, with the tower in the centre of the building. The Norman nave was the same size as the present nave. Aisles were added in the twelfth century and the chancel was then rebuilt; in the thirteenth century north and south chapels were built. The aisles and chapels were rebuilt and widened in the fourteenth and fifteenth centuries, absorbing the former transepts. Considerable alterations occurred in 1828-9 when the medieval nave arcades were replaced.

The church contains many treasures. The Tournai marble font is one of four such fonts in Hampshire. The carvings on it are much cruder than those on the Tournai font in Winchester cathedral; they represent eleven grotesque creatures and a man or angel. The tomb of Sir Richard Lyster (died 1553), the owner of the Tudor house opposite the church, displays both Gothic and classical decoration, and appears to be a compromise between the lingering Gothic style and the coming of the Renaissance. The chained books include a rare Bible, and the larger of the two brass lecterns is one of the earliest and most beautiful in England.

Opposite is the **Tudor House Museum**, a fine early Tudor town house with a handsome banqueting hall. There have been additions and alterations to it over the years, culminating in a careful restoration in 1911-12 when it became a museum. The house was built about 1500 by Sir John Dawtrey, utilizing parts of earlier tenements. The rooms depict domestic life since the eighteenth century, and there are many interesting bygones, including the town stocks. Among the exhibits are photographs and maps of old Southampton, a re-creation of a ladies' tea-party of 1888, a German Noah's Ark, a replica of a middle-class Victorian kitchen complete with kitchen range, domestic appliances and utensils, and a collection of Georgian and Victorian domestic needlework and craft tools.

At the rear is a Tudor-style garden with a mulberry tree, similar to those planted in the town by the French Huguenots to feed

Westgate and the Tudor Merchants Hall, Southampton

silkworms. The garden is a re-creation of the features found in Tudor ornamental gardens, ie not a facsimile garden but a collection of Tudor features, as in a museum. There are over 100 different plants, a selection of those common at that time. The garden gives access to the so-called 'King John's House', a well-preserved Norman house. Its ground floor, used for storage, opened on to West Quay, but was later incorporated into the town walls. The two gun-ports, inserted about 1360, are the earliest known in England.

In French Street is the **Medieval Merchant's House**, built about 1290 as the shop and home of John Fortin, a merchant of the town. Over the centuries the building has been put to many different uses, including a public house and a boarding-house. It has been furnished in medieval style to give an idea of domestic life in that period.

On the corner of Upper Bugle Street and Simnel Street (the street of the bakers) is the **Undercroft**, the lower floor of a fourteenth-century house. The house above the Undercroft is one of the three that have been preserved as examples of the first council houses in the town, built in 1903. In Bugle Street, the best preserved of Southampton's old streets, is The Duke of Wellington, a restored sixteenth-century house. Back in High Street, The Red Lion on the east side is the oldest inn in Southampton; the conspirators against Henry V were allegedly tried here in 1415. The ruined **Holy Rood church** was one of the five medieval churches and has many historical associations. It is now a Merchant Navy memorial; among others it commemorates the *Titanic*'s crew and Charles Dibdin, the poet and composer of sea-songs. Nearby is the **Dolphin Hotel**, rebuilt in 1775. The eighteenth-century winter assemblies were held here, and Jane Austen attended dances here when she lived at Castle Square. The **Star Hotel** was a coaching inn; a notice on the wall reads 'Coach to London (Sundays excepted). Alresford. Alton. Performs ten hours'. Coaches ran to London, Fareham, Oxford, Portsmouth, Bath and Bristol. Accidents were frequent, and highwaymen were a menace on the Common. Before the railway came in 1840 there were thirteen coaches each way daily to London, but by 1845 there were none.

The Tourist Information Centre is in Above Bar, the modern shopping precinct. Further on is the imposing **Civic Centre**, completed in 1939 and considered to be one of the best in the country. The **Art Gallery** here has a fine collection of twentieth-century British paintings, French Impressionists, European art of the seventeenth and eighteenth centuries, and ceramics and sculpture. The five parks immediately north and east of the city centre have been open for over 100 years, and were formerly the old common fields belonging to the town. In **Watts Park** there is a large war memorial by Lutyens, and by the statue of Isaac Watts, the famous hymn-writer who was born in Southampton, one can hear the tune of his hymn 'O God, our help in ages past', which echoes from the Civic Centre clock-tower four times a day. In **East Park** there is a large memorial to the engineer officers of the *Titanic*, none of whom survived the disaster.

The Avenue cuts through **Southampton Common**, a unique survival of medieval times — no other city in England has such a large area (365 acres) of public common within its boundary. It was purchased by the town from the manor of Shirley in 1228 for ten silver marks — surely one of the best bargains ever. In return the burgesses of the town relinquished their rights over Shirley Common. On the Common there are over 350 species of flowering plants, and over 100 species of birds have been identified. The Common Studies Centre organises guided walks (by day and by night). There is also a paddling-pool and a boating-lake. At the south-east corner of Bassett crossroads is an earthwork known as **Cutthorn** or Cutted

Thorn, the traditional meeting-place of the ancient Court Leet of Southampton. The Common once had a racecourse, first laid out in 1822; the last race was held in 1881. The Cowherds, the popular public house on the Common, was built in 1624 for the town cowherd; it was rebuilt in 1762 when he started to sell refreshments.

Eling is reached via the A35 Bournemouth road and a turning off the A326 Fawley road to a car-park opposite the church. The tide-mill ✳ at Eling is one of the only three in Britain in working order. Tide-mills operate by damming high-tide water behind a causeway, and then releasing the water to turn a mill wheel. There has been a tide-mill here since the Middle Ages, but this building is only 200 years old. The double high tide makes it possible for milling to be carried on for 8 hours each day (or night). A small display illustrates the history of the mill and there is a demonstration of milling on alternate weekends. Stone-ground flour produced in the mill is on sale.

On the causeway is the only surviving medieval toll in Hampshire; until recently it belonged to Winchester College. The toll has been in operation since at least 1418, the date of the earliest known lease. To avoid the toll a detour of 2 miles is necessary. Eling has been a small port for several hundred years; Henry I is said to have sailed from here to Normandy in 1130. Ships were built at Eling until the late nineteenth century. At Goatee Foreshore picnic park nearby one can watch ships unloading at Eling quay. At a certain spot on Goatee Foreshore one can see all seven crosses on the gables of St Mary's church, the one and only spot where this is said to be possible. The church up the hill is basically medieval; there is a sixteenth-century Venetian painting inside, and in the churchyard there is a remarkable collection of carved tombstones. The gravestone of William Mansbridge makes strange reading.

Totton, Eling's larger neighbour, once claimed the title of the 'largest village in Hampshire', but it is now officially a town. The seventeenth-century bridge over the River Test is isolated now on the north side of the modern road. At Totton the Test Way long-distance footpath starts at the end of Testwood Lane and crosses the lower Test valley. On this part of the walk one can see how conditions 🚶 gradually change from salt-marsh to freshwater-marsh. Birds to be seen here include wildfowl, waders, reed-warblers and snipe.

A minor road leads to **Nursling**, a once-quiet village now crossed by two motorways. In the church porch is a memorial to St Boniface. Winfrid (his real name) was born in Devon in 680, studied at

Places of Interest in Southampton

Town Walls
Impressive and interesting town
walls — original length $1\frac{1}{4}$ miles.
Four gateways survive. Walkway.

Bargate
Part Norman, one of the best
medieval gateways in England.

Southampton Maritime Museum
The Wool House, corner of Bugle
Street and Town Quay
The only medieval warehouse in
Southampton, now the Maritime
Museum. Superb models of
famous ships and relics of the
Titanic.

**God's House Tower Museum
of Archaeology**
Town Quay
Fifteenth-century tower, one of the
earliest artillery fortifications in
Europe. The museum has the
largest collection of post-Roman
European pottery in England, also
local archaeological finds.

**Southampton Hall
of Aviation**
R.J. Mitchell Museum
Albert Road South
Exhibits include a Spitfire, a
Supermarine S6A and a Sandring-
ham flying-boat.

Ocean Village
Shops, cinemas, museum, marina.
Heritage Theatre audio-visual
display of the history of the docks
and shipbuilding industry.

Maritime Heritage Centre museum
of maritime history.

St Michael's Church
St Michael's Square, off Castle
Way
Founded about 1070, the oldest
building in Southampton. Tournai
marble font and two medieval
lecterns.

Tudor House Museum
Bugle Street
Fine early Tudor house, carefully
restored, with banqueting hall and
rooms illustrating domestic life and
local history since the eighteenth
century. Tudor-style garden.
Remains of a Norman house at the
rear.

Medieval Merchant's House
(English Heritage)
58 French Street
Thirteenth-century house of a
medieval merchant, furnished in
the style of that period.

Art Gallery
Civic Centre
British and European paintings
including French Impressionists;
ceramics and sculpture.

Southampton Common
365 acres of public common,
woodland and park. Guided walks
on nature trails by Common
Studies Centre staff.
Boating-lake and paddling-pool.
Cutthorn — ancient earthwork.

Bugle Street, Southampton

Nursling monastery and later became the Apostle of Germany after many years missionary work in Europe. In the opinion of Sir Arthur Bryant, no Englishman has had a greater influence on world history. Andrew Mundy is commemorated in the church by three separate brasses. Two of them feature chronograms, in which the capital letters of the inscriptions are also roman numerals that add up to the year of his death (1632).

From here **North Baddesley** is reached via Rownhams. In 1365 Baddesley Manor became the headquarters of the Knights Hospitallers in Hampshire, who moved here from Godsfield. The church is a delightful little medieval building; from the churchyard there is an extensive view to the north. Close to the church gate are two unusual gravestones, both memorials to Charles Smith; one is sympathetic to him, one not. He was sentenced to death in 1822 for shooting at a gamekeeper, and was executed in spite of a plea for mercy from Lord Palmerston, whose game he had been poaching. The stone sympathetic to Smith is said to have been erected by William Cobbett.

At the A27 road junction turn left through Chandler's Ford to **Otterbourne**. This village was the home of Charlotte Mary Yonge, the prolific Victorian writer, throughout her long life. She lived at

Elderfield, the house opposite the church, and her grave is in the churchyard. Sir Isaac Newton often stayed at nearby Cranbury House towards the end of his life.

Eastleigh was a village in the parish of South Stoneham until 1894. It grew rapidly after the London and South Western Railway Company's carriage works moved here in 1889-90, followed by the locomotive works in 1909. The railway station and junction had been named Bishopstoke from the village on the east side of the River Itchen, Eastleigh then consisting of only a small farm.

The name of the town was decided by Charlotte Mary Yonge, who had to choose from Eastleigh, Barton and perhaps Bishopstoke. Most of Eastleigh was built between 1890 and 1939; most people worked for the railway or had jobs that served the railway employees.

Though there are no buildings of particular historical interest or architectural merit in the town there is a strange atmosphere of the past about Eastleigh, perhaps because it has a grid of late nineteenth- and early twentieth-century streets with a well-defined shopping centre.

There are two curious things in the park in the town centre. The bandstand of 1896 is a piece of Victoriana now quite rare, and the scented garden for the blind has descriptions of the flowers and shrubs in braille. Eastleigh Museum in High Street has a display of photographs of the town from the 1850s onwards to illustrate its history, and relics of the London and Southampton Railway (later the London and South Western Railway).

Most of Southampton Airport lies within the town's boundary. The airfield has many historical associations; it was here that the first Spitfire made its maiden flight in 1936. Opposite the airport, on Southampton Road, is Lakeside, a new leisure park.

A by-road opposite the airport leads to **North Stoneham**. The strangest object in the church is the tombstone of 1491 of a group of Venetian sailors. The reason for its being here is uncertain though it has been suggested that the stone came from St Mary's church in Southampton. The *Sclavoni* (Italian name for Dalmatians or Slavs) commemorated on the stone may have been members of one of the numerous Italian trading fraternities using Southampton at that time. Also in the church is a monument to Admiral Lord Hawke, who defeated the French at Quiberon Bay; he died at Swaythling not far away. The clock on the church tower is unusual in having one hand.

Further on, in a secluded corner of Southampton suburbia, is the church of **South Stoneham**; it has a Norman chancel and font. Stoneham House, now used by Southampton University, was designed by the great architect Nicholas Hawksmoor. The bridge at Woodmill marks the tidal limit of the River Itchen. On the east side is Riverside Park, with a recreation ground, free fishing and a pitch-and-putt course. At the Swan Garden Centre, a mile north-east on the A27, is Little Amazon, a replica of a tropical rain forest, and a mile north of this is Itchen Valley Country Park with footpath trails and woodland walks.

Botley is 6 miles east of Southampton via the A27 and the A334. Though not officially a town, its busy square, with the Market House of 1848, certainly gives it the appearance of one. Even so it is not as busy as in the great days of its market, when there were fourteen inns catering for the coach trade. Two of them survive, The Bugle Inn and The Dolphin.

Botley will always be associated with its most famous resident, William Cobbett, the great journalist-farmer. In 1805 he bought a house by the river, with four farms attached, and lived there until 1817 (apart from the 2 years he spent in prison). A memorial stone records the fact. Cobbett's house was destroyed soon after he left Botley, but a house and cottage still standing on the east side of Church Lane were once part of his estate. Cobbett described Botley as 'the most delightful village in the world'.

The mill is the only one in Hampshire listed in *Domesday Book* where flour is still made. Botley was once a small port at the head of navigation on the River Hamble, and boats came up here for corn and timber until the 1930s. The new church (1836) is on the main road; the old church, of which only the thirteenth-century chancel remains, lies a mile to the south, near the Hampshire Farm Museum. A memorial stone at the entrance to Botley station, beside the Victorian drinking-fountain, records the murder in 1800 of old Thomas Webb by a soldier from Botley barracks. The murderer was executed and his body hung on a gibbet on Curdridge Common.

From the Southampton road bear left through Hedge End to find the **Upper Hamble Country Park**. It is partly farmland where wheat and barley are grown on a 3- to 4-year rotation, and partly woodland that was formerly coppiced for timber for use in shipbuilding. In the nineteenth century the woodlands were used as game reserves. Today there is a return to coppicing to improve natural habitats. The

Hampshire Farm Museum

woodlands adjoining the river are in part inundated salt-marsh; trees include sessile oak and wild service. There are separate paths for walking and horse-riding, and a viewpoint on the river bank. The Queen Elizabeth Activities Centre for the disabled is here in the park. The Hampshire Farm Museum at Manor Farm has traditional farm buildings that illustrate the history of the Hampshire countryside, also vintage farm machinery. Manor Farm is more than a museum however; it is a working farm with all the sights, sounds and smells associated with livestock. The farmhouse dates from the fifteenth century and all its furniture, fittings and utensils have been carefully chosen to re-create the appearance of a country farmhouse of about 1900.

Bursledon, further down river, is a curiously scattered village, the newer part straggling along the main road, the older part secluded on wooded slopes overlooking the river. It was a busy shipbuilding centre from the time of Henry V until the nineteenth century. The *Elephant*, Nelson's ship at the Battle of Copenhagen, was built here in 1786 by George Parsons, whose memorial is in the church. Until 1800 the only crossing of the river below Botley was by ferry; then the first bridge (a toll) was opened and was not superseded until 1933. Warships were once built near The Jolly Sailor, a pleasant eighteenth-century inn on the waterside. The river is packed with pleasure-craft now and repair yards line the banks.

Daniel Defoe wrote about Bursledon in his book *Captain Singleton*; he mentioned two eighty-gun ships that had been launched there. The church has a fine thirteenth-century chancel arch, but much of the rest was restored in the nineteenth century. The memorial to John Tayler on the exterior of the nave depicts brickmaking tools, a reminder of another local industry.

On the way to Hamble turn off the road a short distance to **Hound** church. The simple Early English interior is quite unspoilt, but the surprise is the east window with its memorable stained glass by Reyntiens (1959). The figures of the Virgin and Child and Angels are representational and wonderfully coloured.

The river estuary at **Hamble** is one of the country's leading yacht harbours; there are over 3,000 craft here at any one time. Hamble was once famous for oysters; it was an active fishing port until World War I but very little fishing is carried on now. Before that it was, like Bursledon, a shipbuilding centre; now all is given over to pleasure. The tiny main street winds uphill with Georgian cottages and inns, rather reminiscent of a Cornish fishing village. The street named Rope Walk recalls the rope-making industry that was once here, and

Copperhill Terrace, Hamble

Copperhill Terrace is named after the coppers in which the tar for preserving the ropes was boiled. The Bugle inn is partly seventeenth century and it claims that its foundations were laid over 800 years ago ('when the Normans landed at Hamble-le-Rise'). The Royal Southern Yacht Club, a picturesque building with a sundial, was originally a row of four cottages (1818).

Beyond the square at the top of the street is the church, which is partly Norman. It was the church of the priory of Hamble-le-Rice, founded in the twelfth century, and its best feature is a fine Gothic east window. In the churchyard is the grave of Sir Alliott Verdon-Roe, one of the first Englishmen to fly and the founder of the aircraft firm of Avro here at Hamble in 1914.

From the quayside there is a ferry to Warsash and river trips in summer. There has been a ferry here for several hundred years. When the king's antiquary John Leland used it in the sixteenth century he described the estuary as 'a very fair rode for greate shippes'. On Hamble Common (car-park on the shore) an Iron Age bank and ditch cross the peninsula, fragments of St Andrew's Castle, one of Henry VIII's forts, can be seen on the shore at low tide, and there is a nineteenth-century gun battery.

Not far from Hamble is the **Royal Victoria Country Park** at Netley. It has been laid out on the site of the Royal Victoria Hospital, which was Britain's most famous military hospital until it was demolished in 1966. It was built in 1856-63, after the Crimean War, and was the longest building in Britain, stretching for 1,424ft parallel to the shore. Of 54,000 troops sent to the Crimea 18,000 died and 9,000 became invalids. Queen Victoria herself demanded a new hospital and she laid the foundation stone. Florence Nightingale did not approve of the design, accusing the architect of being more concerned with the appearance of the building than with the comfort of the patients. She was right, for the outward grandeur of the building concealed the great inconvenience of the interior. Each ward had nine beds and faced north away from the sea. Standards improved however; of the 20,000 patients admitted in World War I only 200 died. During demolition the prototype Victoria Cross was found under the foundation stone. Of the many other large buildings here only the chapel and the officers' mess survive. The chapel is now a centre for visitors, where the history of the hospital is illustrated by photographs and mementoes of the soldiers who were here. The tower is open to the public.

The park has a beach thick with shells and there are over 100 acres of open spaces with walks, a nature trail and a tea-room (in the wartime YMCA). Inland there is a contrast between the beech woods and the marshy areas where reeds and alders give shelter to birds such as reed-buntings and blackcaps. On the shore curlews and oyster-catchers are common.

The railway from Southampton originally terminated at Netley station, specially for the hospital, but it was later extended to Fareham. The original station survives; it was built in classical style like many on the L & SWR network. It was not until 1900 that the hospital had its own branch line; the railway cutting can be seen behind the Park Centre.

Netley abbey was founded in 1239 by monks from Beaulieu, and later supported by Henry III. The ruins are quite substantial, in a picturesque wooded site not far from the shore. The east window of the ruined church had four lights and bar tracery, a decorative motif also seen in Westminster abbey chapter-house, so the king's mason may have worked on both buildings. Though the cloister has disappeared, the ranges that once enclosed it are recognizable. Not much is known of its 300-year history. It was dissolved in 1536 and a year later the buildings and land were granted to Sir William Paulet, who converted the buildings to a private mansion. In the eighteenth century it came into the hands of a Southampton builder who began to demolish the site, but was killed by falling masonry from the church; the hint was taken and demolition ceased!

A castle, one of Henry VIII's forts, was built near the shore; it is still there but has been converted to a Victorian 'Gothic' folly. Netley church has a medieval effigy of a crusader monk, which was formerly in the wall of Netley Castle and must have come originally from Netley abbey. Netley village is a Victorian creation; there was nothing here until the building of the hospital and the railway.

The **Solent Way walk** traverses the whole length of the shore from Gosport, though a diversion has to be made through Southampton to avoid the docks.

Places of Interest Around Southampton

Eling Tide-Mill
near Totton, 4 miles north-west of
the city centre
One of the few working tide-mills in
England. Open to visitors.
Medieval toll bridge. Goatee
Foreshore picnic park.

Eastleigh Museum
25 High Street
The history of Eastleigh and its
railway.

Lakeside, Southampton Road, Eastleigh
Water-park for angling, bird-
watching and many other leisure
activities.

Little Amazon
Swan Garden Centre, Gaters Hill,
West End, Southampton
Birds, butterflies, insects, reptiles
and fish in a replica of a tropical
rain forest.

Itchen Valley Country Park,
Allington Lane, Eastleigh
Woodland and meadows between
Eastleigh and Southampton.
Nature trail, forest trail, Itchen
Navigation footpath.

Upper Hamble Country Park
1 mile north of Bursledon
Woodland and farmland paths for
walkers and riders. Hampshire
Farm Museum — buildings and
machinery.

Hamble
6 miles south-east of the city
centre
Yachting centre at the mouth of the
River Hamble. Ferry to Warsash
and river trips in summer. Interesting church.

Royal Victoria Country Park
Netley, 4 miles south-east of the
city centre
The wooded grounds of the former
Royal Victoria Hospital.
Nature study area, waterside and
woodland walks.

Netley Abbey
English Heritage
3 miles south-east of the city
centre
Substantial ruins of a Cistercian
abbey in a picturesque setting.

3

IN AND AROUND
PORTSMOUTH

Portsmouth is unique among English cities in being partly situated on an island (Portsea), which is connected to the mainland by bridges and causeways over a narrow creek. A large area on the mainland is also within the city boundary.

Portsmouth is not as old as Southampton and Winchester; the history of Portsmouth Harbour before the Norman Conquest is centred on Portchester. There had been small settlements on the island before the Conquest, and afterwards a larger settlement grew up on the south-west corner of the island at a landing-place at the mouth of the harbour.

The town was founded about 1180 by John de Gisors, a local landowner, who laid out streets and endowed St Thomas's church (now the cathedral). King Richard I seized the town from him and in 1194 granted the first charter to the inhabitants. This gave them certain privileges, including a weekly market and an annual fair, later known as the Free Mart Fair, which continued until 1847. In King John's reign Portsmouth became a ship-repairing centre and in 1212 the King ordered the 'docks' to be enclosed by a wall, which lasted only until 1228 (the 'docks' were little more than mud-flats). Foreign trade developed but Portsmouth was legally only a part of Southampton, which continued to exercise control over the collection of customs duties until 1835.

Even in the fourteenth century Portsmouth was no larger than an average modern village, consisting of little more than what is now High Street. Agriculture on the common fields adjoining the settlement was the main occupation. It remained a small place throughout the Middle Ages, but from 1295 it sent two Members to Parliament. At that time Portsmouth was unprotected and during the Hundred Years War was repeatedly sacked. Its first defences (in 1386) consisted of an earthwork and a ditch; an iron chain was used to protect the harbour mouth. In the fifteenth century its defences were improved; these improvements included the Round Tower and the Square Tower. When the world's first dry dock was constructed in 1495-6 Portsmouth became primarily a naval and military base.

In the early Tudor period Portsmouth was the chief English naval port, but then suffered a decline that lasted for over 100 years. In spite of this decline Portsmouth received its charter of incorporation as a borough in 1600. Decay and neglect continued throughout the Elizabethan period and the dry dock was filled in. There was no improvement until in 1649 the Commonwealth commissioned the first ship of any size since the *Mary Rose* (1509). Little is known of the size and wealth of Portsmouth before the late seventeenth century. A major reconstruction of the defences was undertaken in 1665-85 and again in the eighteenth century. Portsmouth became the best-fortified town in Britain, perhaps even in Europe. The old town remained much the same however, and indeed the street plan is much the same today as it was in the Middle Ages. King James II took a great interest in Portsmouth, perhaps because he thought of it as his port of escape from the country if necessary.

During the Napoleonic Wars, Portsmouth became the chief naval port, and has been so ever since. Most of the town's wealth in the late eighteenth and early nineteenth centuries resulted from wars, especially the Napoleonic Wars. In the period 1640-1815 Portsmouth prospered in times of war and declined in times of peace, a peculiar state of affairs not paralleled in any other English town of its size.

The population in 1801 was about 32,000 but by 1901 it had risen to 188,000 (more than in 1981 when it was 180,000). At the beginning of the nineteenth century the dockyard dominated the fortunes of Portsmouth; a large proportion of the population was dependent in one way or another on it. The dockyard was one of the largest industrial complexes in the country; in 1801 it employed 4,000 workers and in 1901 employed 8,000. Landport became the centre of the modern town. Southsea, at first a residential suburb, became a seaside resort after the coming of the railway in 1847. Fears of a French invasion caused the building of forts on Ports Down in the

1860s and soon afterwards the town walls, except those on the sea-front, were demolished. The town continued to cater for both the armed forces and the growing tourist trade, as evidenced by the number of cinemas (eighteen in 1914 and thirty in 1939) and public houses (995 in 1905!).

In 1926 Portsmouth became a city. In World War II the shopping centres, including High Street, were largely destroyed, as Portsmouth suffered terrible devastation from bombing. It has not been rebuilt with any imagination and it is spreading ever further on the mainland. The Tricorn, a strange concrete shopping complex in Market Way, was voted the ugliest building in Great Britain by the readers of one Sunday newspaper. There are not many buildings of architectural merit or historical interest, other than the defensive works, but there are several old streets, especially in Southsea and the old town, that are decidedly attractive.

There are no less than eleven excellent museums depicting various historical aspects of the Portsmouth area, as well as HMS *Victory*, HMS *Warrior* and the *Mary Rose*. It is best to visit the places of interest in and around the old town on foot, starting at the **City Museum and Art Gallery** in Museum Road. This is housed in a former military barracks and has a fine collection of furniture and decorative art, including glass, ceramics and paintings dating from the sixteenth century. One gallery has old kitchen and domestic ware, and another has a collection of antiquities from Cyprus.

Before turning into High Street a short walk along St George's Road leads to the **Landport Gate**, built in 1760, which was the chief entrance to the walled town and is the only one of the old town gateways to survive on its original site. In High Street is **Buckingham House**, named after George Villiers, Duke of Buckingham, King Charles I's favourite. He was murdered in the previous house on this site in 1628 by John Felton, an embittered Army officer.

The church of St Thomas became a **cathedral** in 1927. It was founded about 1185 and became a parish church in 1320. Unlike any other cathedral in England it is not only unfinished but is also of three distinct periods. First are the late twelfth-century choir and transepts, which were part of the medieval church, second the former nave and tower of 1683-93, and third the nave and transepts of 1938-9, when the old nave became the choir. The interior has an odd appearance; much of the old character has been destroyed by modern alterations.

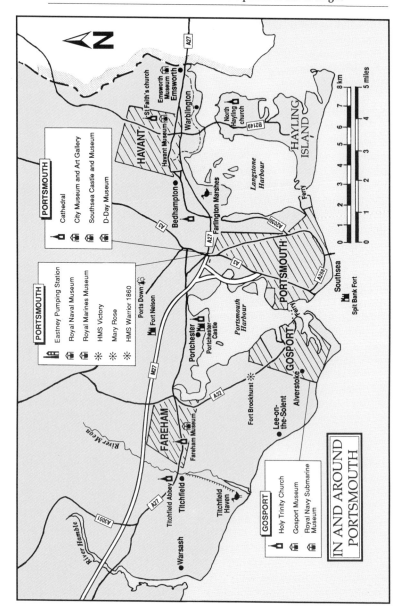

IN AND AROUND PORTSMOUTH

PORTSMOUTH

- Cathedral
- City Museum and Art Gallery
- Southsea Castle and Museum
- D-Day Museum

PORTSMOUTH

- Eastney Pumping Station
- Royal Naval Museum
- Royal Marines Museum
- HMS Victory
- Mary Rose
- HMS Warrior 1860

GOSPORT

- Holy Trinity Church
- Gosport Museum
- Royal Navy Submarine Museum

The church is known to have been under construction in 1185. The earliest part is the choir (the present sanctuary) and the architecture of this medieval choir is remarkably ambitious for its date. The nave and transepts followed the choir; the transepts are relatively tall and narrow, and in a recess in the north transept there is a wall-painting that is probably contemporary with the building. Unfortunately nothing remains of the medieval nave, which was rebuilt together with the tower in the seventeenth century. This rebuilt nave now serves as the choir, and before the extensions of the 1930s it must have had more character, when the old galleries were still in place and before the second aisles were added. The nave was extended in 1938-9 by Charles Nicholson in the Romanesque style. Only three of the six planned bays were completed; the temporary west wall of the cathedral still stands 50 years later. There are plans to complete the nave, adding one further bay and building a Gothic-style west front with twin towers. The cathedral's one treasure is the majolica plaque of the *Virgin and Child* of about 1500 by della Robbia. The weather-vane of 1710, which fell in a storm, stands on a plinth made of wood from HMS *Victory*.

The Victorian novelist George Meredith was born at the former No 73 High Street and went to school in Southsea. Grand Parade was the scene of military parades in the great garrison days and it still has many attractive Regency and Victorian houses. At its far end is the **Royal Garrison church**. This was formerly the church of the Domus Dei, or God's House, a hospital founded in 1212 that was dissolved by Henry VIII and later became the governor's residence. Here Charles II married Catherine of Braganza in 1662. The nave lost its roof in the last war but the chancel is still used for services.

Nearby are the impressive Long Curtain and King's Bastion, the only surviving parts of the ramparts and moat that enclosed the town. In 1665 Sir Bernard de Gomme, a Dutchman, was commissioned to reorganize the defences of Portsmouth. His aim was to increase the depth of the fortifications by means of extra moats and outworks. Over the next 20 years the ramparts and bastions were remodelled, a second moat was constructed and the eighteen-gun battery came into existence. Further improvements by 1750 made Portsmouth's defences the equal of any in the world. New thinking and new developments in warfare in the mid-nineteenth century resulted in the ring of forts further inland on Ports Down and at Gosport. The great defences of Portsmouth became redundant and were demolished (except those near the shore) in the 1870s, and the town then became primarily a naval port once again instead of a garrison town. At the seaward end of High Street is the **Square Tower** of 1494, built as an artillery fort and the governor's residence; it was later used as a magazine and as a semaphore station.

The sea-wall here was a part of the early defences and the **Round Tower** at the north end of it is the oldest defensive work in Portsmouth. It was built about 1418-26 to guard the entrance to the harbour. A chain was stretched between this tower and one on the Gosport side to prevent enemy ships from entering the harbour. The top is a splendid viewpoint from which to see ships entering and leaving harbour.

The Round Tower is in the area known as **Point**, which was outside the town walls and therefore outside the jurisdiction of the town. It was accessible on land only via a gateway from the old town and was for a time known as 'Spice Island' because of the exotic merchandise that was unloaded there. It flanks the small harbour known as the Camber, still used by fishing boats and the Isle of Wight ferries. With its narrow streets, Georgian and Victorian houses and waterside inns, Point is a picturesque place, especially around Bath Square. Quebec House on the waterfront here is a weatherboarded building built in 1754 as a bathing-house.

From the City Museum to the dockyard entrance is less than a mile via St George's Road. On the way, in Britain Street, beyond the small St George's Square, is a memorial stone to the great engineer I.K.Brunel, who was born here in 1806. **St George's church** (1754) was the first Anglican church to serve the new dockyard town and was the centre of the community in this area. The Hard (formerly the Common Hard) leads to the dockyard's Victory Gate and is a place of constant activity with the harbour railway station and the ferry to Gosport. In the nineteenth century it was known as 'Devil's Acre' from the unsavoury characters who frequented it, a place of robberies, brawls and drunkenness (there were thirteen public houses here in the 1890s).

Her Majesty's Naval Base is open only for visits to the Royal Naval Museum, HMS *Victory*, the *Mary Rose* and HMS *Warrior*. Everywhere else is out of bounds, except St Ann's church on Sundays. Of the original buildings in the dockyard those built of wood have not survived but most of the brick buildings built since 1761 are still standing, and the dockyard as a whole is perhaps the best complex of Georgian industrial premises in the country. Many of the best buildings date from the late eighteenth century, such as the three large storehouses of 1778 on the left of the road on the way to HMS *Victory*, and the Great Ropehouse (rebuilt 1776) in Anchor Lane, one of the longest buildings in the world (1,095ft). The latter was one of the buildings set on fire in 1776 by the notorious 'Jack the Painter'. The Portsmouth Royal Dockyard Historical Society have an exhibition that includes artefacts from the *Invincible* (1744-58), model ships and relics, and the story of block-making and the Block Mills, which are still standing.

HMS *Victory*, without doubt the most famous British ship in ❆ history, was launched at Chatham in 1765. She took 6 years to build and 3,000 oak trees were used in her construction. She is being restored to her appearance at the time of the Battle of Trafalgar, but the replacement timber is the longer-lasting Burmese teak. *Victory* had 100 guns and her crew at Trafalgar numbered 819; she saw 34 years of active service (1778-1812). After the Battle of Trafalgar, in which she was badly damaged, *Victory* eventually returned to Portsmouth. She lay at anchor in the harbour or under repair in dry dock for over 100 years; in the early years of this century her timbers were so rotten that she was in danger of sinking. She was put in her present dry dock in 1922 and after restoration was opened to the public in 1928. A guided tour of the ship should not be missed. After a sight of the cramped quarters in the ship it requires little imagination to appreciate the appalling conditions in which the crew lived.

The *Mary Rose*, a 700-ton carrack that carried ninety-one guns, ❆ was built in 1509-11 and rebuilt in 1536. It was the pride of Henry VIII's navy. One day in July 1545 the *Mary Rose* and other ships hastily put to sea to attack an approaching French fleet. The freshening wind caused the *Mary Rose* to heel over, water poured in through the open gun-ports and she sank quickly with the loss of nearly 700 men. The king watched the disaster from the shore. The wreck was located in 1836 and some guns were salvaged. It was found again in 1971 and after a long and costly rescue operation is on view near the *Victory*. The *Mary Rose* Exhibition displays thousands of articles salvaged from the ship. The *Mary Rose* itself has added greatly to our knowledge of early ship design.

The **Royal Naval Museum** is not only a memorial and tribute to 🏛 Lord Nelson and the *Victory* but also a repository for many things relating to Britain's naval history. It is the only museum devoted

Portsmouth Point

solely to the general history of the Royal Navy. It comprises five separate galleries. The *Victory* Gallery relates the history of that famous warship in detail, with many relics of Nelson and the Battle of Trafalgar. The battle is illustrated by seventy-three model ships arranged as they were just before the fight began. There are other model ships, figure-heads, and a panorama of Trafalgar with sound effects. The Lambert McCarthy Gallery contains personal relics of Nelson and furniture from HMS *Victory* and his house at Merton. The Douglas Morris Gallery relates the story of the Napoleonic Wars, the last days of sail, great navigations and explorations, and displays many medals and decorations of that period. The Wyllie Gallery deals with the Victorian Navy and has a replica of a royal yacht's deck-house. The Lewin Gallery brings the history of the Navy up to date with World Wars I and II.

✳ HMS *Warrior*, launched at Blackwall in 1860, was then the fastest, largest and best-armed warship in the world. Built completely of iron, she had sails as well as an engine. She was of revolutionary design, yet within 10 years she became obsolete. *Warrior* was never involved in battle, and for nearly 100 years was used for many

HMS *Victory*

purposes until finally restored at Hartlepool at a cost of £9,000,000. She has been refurnished in the style of the mid-nineteenth century, and visitors can again remark, as in HMS *Victory*, on the difference in comfort between the officers' and ratings' quarters.

The **Charles Dickens Birthplace Museum** at 393 Old Commercial Road, north of the city centre, is well worth the effort of finding. Charles Dickens was born here in 1812, the son of a Royal Navy pay clerk. He moved to London with his parents at the age of 2. The museum contains items relating to Dickens and his books and is furnished in the style of a middle-class house of the early nineteenth century. Near the Tricorn, in the Unicorn Training Centre, is the Museum of the Dockyard Apprentice.

Southsea developed rapidly in the nineteenth century. The Common, luckily, was not built on because it was needed for military training; it was owned by the Crown between 1785 and 1923. Southsea before development was mostly marshes; it grew not as a seaside resort but as a residential suburb for dockyard employees and retired people. The northward spread of Southsea catered for the working classes and the south-west for the wealthier, most of it inspired by Thomas Owen, a land and house speculator. In less than 30 years Owen built over a large area of Portsea Island, indeed much of what is now modern Southsea. His interest was in residential rather than business development, and it is to him that Southsea owes its distinctive architectural character, its terraces and villas having been built in a wide range of styles.

By about 1865 Southsea was becoming increasingly attractive to middle-class holiday-makers, and during the next 20 years most of Southsea's large hotels were built. By 1900 all available land had been used for building. A railway from a junction at Fratton to a terminus near South Parade Pier was opened in 1885; it ran until the outbreak of war in 1914 and became the first local railway in Hampshire to be closed. Evidence of its former existence is hard to find apart from the alignment of some streets.

A trail guide to the streets and buildings of Southsea is available from the Tourist Centre. Famous people associated with Southsea include H.G.Wells, who worked for 2 years in a local drapery store, Arthur Conan Doyle, who first set up in practice as a doctor in Elm Grove and wrote the first Sherlock Holmes story there, and Rudyard Kipling, who went to school in Southsea.

The 3-mile sea front between Clarence Pier and Fort Cumberland is one of the most lively and interesting in England with its gardens, museums and views across the busy water to the Isle of Wight. Clarence Pier was first built in 1861 and after extensions in 1882 proved to be a great success. There is a hovercraft service to the Isle of Wight from the pier. There are several memorials on Clarence Esplanade, including an anchor from HMS *Victory*, the splendid Naval War Memorial, a Crimean War memorial, one to HMS *Shannon's* Naval Brigade in the Indian Mutiny, and another to the men of HMS *Chesapeake* 1857-61. At the **Sea Life Centre** one can see many different ocean creatures including sharks, sting-rays, catfish, octopuses, conger eels and other exotic fish in a re-creation of their natural environment. A special feature is Europe's deepest tank.

Southsea Castle was one of the forts constructed by Henry VIII to protect the south coast from attack. It was built in 1539-44 to an advanced design, having a square keep and angle bastions, with large rectangular gun platforms on its east and west flanks. King Henry VIII came to see his newly completed castle in 1545, on the sad occasion when the *Mary Rose* sank before his eyes. It was enlarged in 1814 to provide extra accommodation, and later ramparts were built along the shore. The castle has had quite an eventful life. It changed hands during the Civil War, suffered at least two fires, was altered from time to time and was used as a prison. The lighthouse dates from 1828. Because it was in use by the military for over 400 years it remains one of the best-preserved forts in England. The museum in the keep has an admirable exhibition that explains the complex history of the Portsmouth defences — a fascinating story. The Tourist Information Centre is near the castle.

The **D-Day Museum** nearby opened on the fortieth anniversary of that momentous day in June 1944. The exhibition records the planning and operation of the Normandy landings (Operation Overlord) with sound and visual effects and examples of the equipment, weapons and vehicles used. The chief exhibit is the Overlord Embroidery, 272ft long, which took 5 years to complete and shows in detail the planning of the operation.

The 600ft-long South Parade Pier was opened in 1879 and rebuilt in 1908 after a fire. Though it no longer has a theatre it is a great attraction for visitors with its amusements, boat trips, bars and restaurant. The popular canoe lake near the pier was part of the 'Great Morass', a pond on the heath that once occupied this area.

Southsea Model Village is on the site of what was known as

Places of Interest in Portsmouth

City Museum and Art Gallery
Museum Road
Furniture and decorative art of the sixteenth to twentieth centuries.

**St James's Gate
and Landport Gate**
(English Heritage)
Two gateways of the old fortifications.

Portsmouth Cathedral
Features of the twelfth, seventeenth and twentieth centuries. Became a parish church in 1320 and a cathedral in 1927.

Royal Garrison Church
(English Heritage)
The ruined church of the Domus Dei (God's House), a hospital founded in 1212.

Portsmouth Fortifications
Round Tower is the earliest defensive work in Portsmouth (1418). Square Tower (1494). Long Curtain and King's Bastion, Saluting Platform and Eighteen-Gun Battery.

Point
Picturesque area of old streets and houses between the Camber and the sea. Ferries to Isle of Wight.

Portsmouth Royal Dockyard Historical Society
Her Majesty's Naval Base
Displays relating to the history of the dockyard.

HMS Victory
Her Majesty's Naval Base
Nelson's ship at Trafalgar, restored to her former glory. The only surviving battleship of the period.

**Mary Rose Exhibition
and Ship Hall**
Her Majesty's Naval Base
The *Mary Rose*, Tudor warship, on view in the Ship Hall. The museum displays many articles recovered from the wreck.

Royal Naval Museum
Her Majesty's Naval Base
Illustrates the general history of the Royal Navy. Collections of ship models, figure-heads and Nelson relics.

HMS Warrior 1860
Her Majesty's Naval Base
The fastest, largest and best-

Lump's Fort, one of Henry VIII's forts; the name was derived from Ralph Lumpee who leased some land here. The village is at a scale of 1:12 and other attractions include a model railway layout, a toy museum and an indoor railway.

Cumberland House Natural Science Museum and Aquarium has many interesting exhibits illustrating the geology and natural history of the Portsmouth area, freshwater and marine aquaria, and armed warship in the world in 1860 restored to its original appearance.

Charles Dickens Birthplace Museum
393 Old Commercial Road
The house in which Dickens was born, furnished in nineteenth-century style. Exhibits relating to his life and work.

Museum of the Dockyard Apprentice
Unicorn Training Centre

Southsea Common and Sea Front
Clarence Pier: hovercraft service to Isle of Wight. Amusement park.
Clarence Esplanade: monuments, canoe lake.
South Parade Pier: boat trips and amusements.

Sea Life Centre
Clarence Esplanade, Southsea
Marine life including sharks, octopuses and catfish. Europe's deepest tank.

Southsea Castle and Museum
Clarence Esplanade
One of Henry VIII's coastal forts, built 1539-44. Museum depicts the

history of Portsmouth defences.

D-Day Museum
Clarence Esplanade
The Overlord Embroidery depicts the planning of Operation Overlord. Maps, models, weapons and vehicles.

Southsea Model Village
Village on scale of 1:12. Model railway and toy museum.

Cumberland House Natural Science Museum and Aquarium
Eastern Parade
Exhibits illustrate the geology and natural history of the Portsmouth area. Freshwater and marine aquaria. Iguanodon model.

Royal Marines Museum
Eastney Barracks
The history of the Royal Marines and their campaigns, with collections of medals, uniforms and relics.

Eastney Pumping Station
Henderson Road, Eastney
Two 1887 Watt beam-engines and pumps seen in action, also three Crossley gas-engines.

a life-size model of an iguanodon. Particularly realistic are the displays of the flora and fauna of the local downlands and marshlands. There is a live butterfly annexe (open in summer), which includes the rare swallowtail species. Other exhibits in the museum include the history of the landscape over the last 225 million years, the formation of Portsea Island, and a cabinet of 'curiosities' (animals and birds).

The **Royal Marines Museum** in the former officers' mess in Eastney Barracks illustrates the history of the Marines from their origin in 1664 as the Admiral's Regiment, with details of all their campaigns. There is a large collection of uniforms and over 6,000 medals including ten Victoria Crosses. The history of the Royal Marines Bands makes an interesting display. In its presentation and detail this is one of the best regimental museums in the country.

Eastney Pumping Station in Henderson Road (open in summer) is an essential visit for those interested in Victorian technology. Here one can see in operation two 150hp Watt beam-engines and pumps, which pumped sewage into underground tanks for discharge at high tide.

Fort Cumberland (not open) was built in 1746 to protect the entrance to Langstone Harbour. It is the best example in Britain of an eighteenth-century defensive fort and one hopes that it will be preserved. There is a ferry from Eastney to Hayling Island.

Portsmouth has two types of beach, shingle as found at Eastney, where there are plants such as sea-holly and sea-kale, and rocks as found near Southsea Castle, with seaweeds and marine life.

The A2030 skirts the east side of Portsea Island and leads north out of the city. Those interested in canals may like to find at the end of Locksway Road at Milton the sea-lock where the Portsea section of the Portsmouth and Arundel Canal entered Langstone Harbour. The lock walls are still in good condition but the gates have long since gone. The canal was opened in 1822, the terminus being near the town centre, but it was not a success and this section closed for traffic in 1831.

Farlington Marshes (car-park off the roundabout at the junction of the A2030 and M27) is a nature reserve of international importance. It has been reclaimed from salt-marshes and here one can see many winter migrant birds and many rare species of plants. It offers the birds a sheltered expanse of water, plenty of food and freedom from disturbance. Over 230 species of birds have been recorded here and on any one day about eighty species may be seen. In winter the chief visitors are brent-geese from Russia (5,000 of them usually), widgeon and teal. The brent-geese feed on eel-grass, a submarine plant. There may also be as many as 20,000 waders in winter, chiefly dunlins, the commonest shore birds. Resident breeders (over fifty species) include redshanks, oyster-catchers, lapwings, shelducks, coots and herons. Over 300 species of plants are known here, many of them local and rare grasses. There is a footpath along the sea-wall giving good views of the birds. Langstone Harbour, at low tide an expanse of mud-flats and islands, is also a nature reserve; it was once famous for its oyster-fishing. The shore of the harbour is a good place for bird-watching, and wildlife in general thrives here. The flora includes salt-marsh plants such as golden samphire. The Solent Way walk follows the sea-wall on Portsea Island and then the north shore of the harbour and beyond to Emsworth. Some of the Mulberry Harbours used in the D-Day landings were built on the shores of Langstone Harbour before being towed to France.

Langstone village, the port for Havant in the Middle Ages, was used by ships until the nineteenth century. It is a picturesque little place, with a quay, an old tide-mill and windmill, thatched cottages and two inns. A plaque on the quay records that Langstone port furnished 'one shippe of war properly equipped for the defence of the realm'. The first bridge from Langstone to Hayling Island was opened in 1824; pedestrians paid a toll of a halfpenny! The present bridge, when opened in 1956, was the longest pre-stressed concrete bridge in England. The railway from Havant was opened in 1867 and ran for 90 years; part of its old embankment can be seen and the derelict wooden railway bridge can be seen at close quarters by walking along the old railway track from further down the island. Before the days of motor cars the railway was the chief means of reaching the island; the little tank locomotives used on the line were known as 'Hayling Billys'.

Hayling Island has been flooded many times over the years and has lost a lot of land to the sea; the highest point of the island is only 28ft above sea-level. It began to develop as a seaside resort in the late nineteenth century but became really popular only in the 1930s. Now at summer weekends it is very busy and it is advisable to visit the island during the week. A left turn over the bridge leads to North Hayling, where there is a holiday camp, a marina and a wind-surfing centre. The village is attractive and the old church well worth a visit. It mostly dates from the twelfth and thirteenth centuries; note the roof timbers with carved beams, the old font and pews, and the mass-dial, a rudimentary sundial scratched on the south wall, by means of which people knew it was time for mass. The three bells (not on view) are thought to be the oldest set in England.

The northern half of the island is farmland, whereas the southern half is largely built over. St Mary's church at South Hayling stands at the highest point of the island; it is a large thirteenth-century church restored last century. The oldest thing in the church is a Saxon font, one of the few in Hampshire; it was probably hollowed out of the base of a Saxon cross. The yew tree in the churchyard is thought to be almost 1,000 years old.

Facing the shore is Norfolk Crescent, a large early nineteenth-century block of houses dwarfing the modern houses near it. It was to have been part of a grand scheme of seaside development rivalling the crescents in Brighton and Bath, but only the eastern half and the Royal Hotel were completed. Early attempts to popularise South Hayling as a seaside resort came to nothing and it was not until the 1930s that development really began. Seacourt House, on the sea front, was the location of the British Mosquito Control Institute, the first anti-mosquito laboratory in Great Britain. Hayling Island had been infested with mosquitoes, perhaps another reason for its late development as a resort. Also at Seacourt House is the last full-size real tennis court to have been built in Europe (1910-11).

The sandy beach stretches for 5 miles from The Ferry Boat Inn to Black Point, a nature reserve where brent-geese live in winter. Eastoke Point, at the south-east of the island, is important for its dunes and heathland. The dunes, open sand, shingle and brackish hollows support acid grassland, heathland with lichens, salt-marsh and scrub, with many rare and local plants. The south-west corner of the island at Sinah Common has the best pure sand dunes on the Hampshire coast, and here there are tree lupines, marram-grass and clovers. On the ancient parts of Sinah Common there is a semi-coastal flora, with plants such as water-crowfoot, dotted sedge and creeping willow.

To find **Warblington** church turn right on the mainland on to the M27 and turn off at the first roundabout. St Thomas's church is one of the most interesting in Hampshire; its most arresting feature is the long steep roof, which sweeps down almost to the ground. The middle part of the tower is Saxon and the chancel is on the site of the Saxon nave. In the churchyard are two unusual 'watcher's huts', used in the nineteenth century by men guarding against body-snatchers who found this lonely but well-filled graveyard a tempting target for their evil trade. There are several old decorative tomb-stones, including one that shows HMS *Torbay* burning in Portsmouth Harbour. The ruined tower in the adjoining farm is all that remains of Warblington Castle, a moated manor house of the early sixteenth

Langstone

Old railway bridge, Langstone

century destroyed in the Civil War. Warblington village became deserted after Emsworth received its market in the thirteenth century, but the parish church of Emsworth remained at Warblington until 1840.

Emsworth, bounded by the River Ems on the east (the county boundary), was once the chief port in Chichester Harbour, famous for its oyster-fishing. Its prosperity at that time is reflected in the old streets of Georgian houses leading to the waterfront. A former tide-mill stands on the quay at the side of the mill-pond, which is enclosed by a breakwater. The square in the centre of the town is now happily bypassed by the main road.

When the Princess of Wales bathed in the sea at Emsworth in 1805 the town had ideas of becoming a royal watering-place but other than the building of a bathing-house at the end of Bath Road (now the Emsworth Sailing Club) nothing much happened. Perhaps the coming of the railway and the working classes who used it drove the gentry away.

King Street was named after John King, a shipwright. His house, The Hut (No 19), is said to have been built in just one day; it is mainly of wood so that is possible. Queen Street, formerly Dolphin Hill, was renamed after the visit of Queen Victoria in 1842. The Old Pharmacy in High Street has been a chemist's shop since 1812. The Emsworth Museum at the fire station has a collection of photographs, documents and artefacts relating to the town's history, also a model of the *Echo* (80 tons), the largest sailing fishing vessel to work from an English port.

Havant was until this century a small market town centred on the church at the crossroads. Its chief industry since the Middle Ages was parchment-making, which finally ended in 1936. The industry used water from the local springs, as did the other industries of tanning and cloth-making. Tanning survived until the 1950s but the cloth industry started to decline in the seventeenth century.

The name Havant means 'Hama's spring', probably referring to the one south-west of the churchyard. This spring was for hundreds of years the main source of water for the inhabitants. Two mills were recorded in *Domesday Book* so milling of one sort or another has always been important here.

Since the war the town has grown considerably and with Waterlooville is now a borough. Havant Museum in East Street has exhibits relating to local history, including the stocks and whipping-post that used to be in South Hayling churchyard. The main interest however is the splendid collection of firearms given by Cecil Vokes, the inventor of Vokes filters. There are many rare and strange guns here and also a display showing the history of local wildfowling. Other exhibits include machines used in the making of gloves and clay pipes, the old clock mechanism from the parish church, an aquarium of local fish and a replica of the Hayling Island waiting-room at Havant station. The Art Gallery houses temporary exhibitions.

St Faith's church is large and mainly Victorian but has a fine Early English vaulted chancel, an uncommon feature in a parish church, as are the aisled transepts. The exterior of the church looks old but it was all rebuilt in the nineteenth century. A few yards along South Street is The Old House at Home, dating from the sixteenth century. It is the oldest house in Havant and is now a public house.

Apart from the church and the museum there is little to detain the visitor in Havant. Tentative attempts have been made to exclude vehicles from the shopping streets but the traffic problem is still unresolved. Waterlooville, which is part of the borough of Havant, was named indirectly after the famous battle, from a public house on the Portsmouth road called The Heroes of Waterloo.

South of the Havant-Portsmouth road is the old village of **Bedhampton**, in this desert of suburbia a surprising oasis of large old houses. The church, restored about 100 years ago, retains its beautiful chancel arch of 1140. Of Bedhampton's two former corn-mills only Old Mill House survives, where it is said that John Keats finished his poem *The Eve of St Agnes* and in 1820 spent his last night in England.

The castle at **Portchester**, on a low promontory on the north side of Portsmouth Harbour, is one of the largest of the Roman 'Saxon shore' forts, which were built to protect the English Channel coast against invaders. It may have been the place known to the Romans as *Portus Adurni* but this is not certain. It was constructed about AD285-290 probably by Carausius, the rebel Roman ruler of Britain. It is the best-preserved Roman fortress in northern Europe and one of the most impressive ancient monuments in Britain. A walk round the outside of the walls, bounded in part by the water, is a sobering experience. The walls are 10ft thick and were originally 20ft high. The semicircular projecting bastions, of which fourteen of the original twenty survive, were a novel feature. They were designed for heavy artillery, the Roman ballista or catapult. Why these Saxon shore forts

Emsworth

Portchester Castle

were made so impregnable is still not clear, but with them Carausius ruled over an independent Britain for 10 years until his assassination. After the Carausius era the military buildings inside the fort seem to have been demolished, perhaps evidence that the threat of invasion was thought to have passed. About AD340 the caretaker garrison was replaced by a military garrison for some 30 years, and then by mercenaries. The fort seems to have been occupied by the Saxons throughout the Dark Ages and King Alfred used it as one of his strongholds in the defence of Wessex. In one corner of the fort the Normans built a massive castle keep, which is open to visitors and offers a spectacular view from the top. The Norman castle utilized the walls of the Roman fort on two sides; on the other two sides a moat was constructed, the entrance gateway being on the south. The lower two storeys of the keep were built about 1120-30 and later the keep was heightened. The ruined rooms round the walls of the inner bailey are those of Richard II's late fourteenth-century palace. Inside is a display showing the history of the coastal defences. The castle was refortified throughout the Middle Ages but its importance declined with the growth of Portsmouth. It was used as a prison camp in the Dutch and Napoleonic Wars.

The church of the Augustinian priory founded here in about 1128 stands inside the fort near the Water Gate or Water Port. Nothing else remains of the priory, which moved to Southwick 20 years after its foundation. The church is the parish church of Portchester and is an outstanding example of the Romanesque style, particularly the west front. Most of the original church remains intact, though the chancel has been shortened, and the Victorian restoration was fortunately not too drastic. The west doorway is a particularly splendid feature with its three orders and decorated shafts, and the whole of the west front exhibits work of high quality, restrained but quite beautiful. The nave has five bays but the chancel has been reduced to one bay of what was a vaulted chamber. Inside the church there is a hatchment commemorating the payment of money by Queen Anne towards a restoration, and the earliest Royal Arms in Hampshire (dated 1577). In the early seventeenth century busts began to replace effigies on monuments, and in this church is the earliest bust in Hampshire (1618), on the memorial to Sir Thomas Cornwallis.

In medieval times Portchester was a borough situated outside the castle gates; in 1294 it was granted a market and fair. However Portsmouth, at the mouth of the harbour, was in a much better position for trade than Portchester, and Fareham was in a better position for inland trade, so in course of time Portchester became a quiet backwater, as the old part of the village still is. The attractive village street leading to the castle has many eighteenth-century houses. They vary in size, scale and texture, giving Castle Street a good deal of character; much of it is unspoilt and full of surprises. Modern Portchester a mile to the north is an unpleasant contrast.

Two miles further on is **Fareham**. Thackeray, who spent his school holidays here, called it a 'dear little old Hampshire town'. He would revise his description if he saw it now, though he would recognise High Street, which is virtually unchanged since his day. Fareham has grown considerably since then and has a fine modern shopping precinct and entertainment centre (Ferneham Hall). High Street remains largely unspoilt and is undeniably one of the most attractive streets in Hampshire, with many splendid Georgian houses. Some of these houses are built of the local red bricks known as 'Fareham reds'.

The town was first mentioned by name in Saxon times and as a borough in 1261. In medieval times it was an active port and though it then declined, shipbuilding continued until the nineteenth century. The medieval town was centred on the church and High Street, but after the construction of the causeway over the river the East Street-West Street axis became more important commercially. Near the junction of High Street and West Street there was once a market-place (there is still a market on Mondays in West Street). There was a tide-mill at the east end of the causeway.

As shipbuilding declined other industries began to flourish — leather, corn, flour and timber were produced in and around the town. The brickmaking industry lasted until 1974; it produced the famous 'Fareham reds'. At Funtley, Henry Cort developed a new process for making wrought iron; the iron produced at his works probably saved Great Britain from defeat when foreign iron was unobtainable during the Napoleonic Wars. Very little remains of his ironworks, yet it was as important as the cast-iron industry at Coalbrookdale in Shropshire. There are still plenty of boats using the quay; the river is tidal as far as Fareham. At Fareham Museum the historical displays are linked thematically rather than chronologically; this gives a better idea of the relationship between the various industries and the social life of the town. Industries illustrated include bricks, strawberries, chimney-pots, tanning, brewing and shipbuilding. Other exhibits include a Victorian schoolroom, the history of local land-ownership, fairs and markets, and local transport, with a road-mending cart, a strawberry cart and an old milk-float. The church of St Peter and St Paul, a mixture of medieval, Georgian, Victorian and modern work, is interesting rather than attractive. The eastern part of the present Lady Chapel is all that remains of the chancel of the Saxon church; the junction of the Saxon wall with the thirteenth-century wall is clearly visible.

Fort Brockhurst, between Fareham and Gosport, is one of the five forts built across the Gosport peninsula in the mid-nineteenth century. Together with Fort Fareham and six more on the crest of Ports Down they were designed to protect Portsmouth and its harbour from attack by the French from landward, an exaggerated fear no doubt. They soon came collectively to be called 'Palmerston's Folly' after the Prime Minister who instigated the scheme. Fort Brockhurst is open to visitors and has a fine exhibition illustrating the history of the fortifications. A drawbridge over the moat leads to the keep and beyond is the large parade-ground, surrounded by ramparts on which cannon were placed. Of the other four forts in Gosport three are in official use and one has been destroyed.

Places of Interest Around Portsmouth

Farlington Marshes
North side of Langstone Harbour, south of the M27
National nature reserve with winter migrant birds and rare plants.

Hayling Island
Seaside resort with amusement park, golf courses and holiday camps. Two old churches at North and South Hayling.

Warblington
St Thomas's church
One of the most interesting churches in Hampshire.

Emsworth
Old port with picturesque streets leading to quay and mill-pond.

Emsworth Museum
Fire Station, North Street
Displays relating to the history of Emsworth and Chichester Harbour.

Havant Museum
East Street
The Vokes collection of firearms. Art Gallery.

Portchester Castle
(English Heritage)
The best-preserved Roman fort in northern Europe, a 'Saxon shore' fort of the third century AD. Norman castle keep of the early twelfth century. Romanesque church (1133) of Augustinian priory.

Fareham
Church — medieval to modern.
Ferneham Hall — entertainments and theatre.
Fareham Museum, West Street — displays illustrating the history of the borough.
Large shopping precinct.

Fort Nelson
Down End Road, Fareham
National Museum of Arms and Armour

History of the development of artillery.

Fort Brockhurst
(English Heritage)
One of the defensive forts constructed across the Gosport peninsula in the nineteenth century. Display illustrating the history of the defences.

Gosport Museum
Walpole Road
Exhibits relating to the geology, archaeology and history of Gosport.

Royal Navy Submarine Museum
Haslar
HMS *Alliance* and HM Submarine No 1. The exhibition illustrates submarine development and underwater warfare.

Spit Bank Fort
One of the forts built in the Solent in the 1860s. Ferries from Gosport, Southsea, Sandown and Cowes.

Lee-on-the-Solent
Seaside resort with amusements, swimming-pool, sand and shingle beach.

Titchfield Haven Nature Reserve
Bird sanctuary, open August to March by permit.

Titchfield
St Peter's church — the porch is the oldest piece of church architecture in Hampshire.
Titchfield Canal — the second oldest canal in England.

Titchfield Abbey
(English Heritage)
Ruins of abbey founded 1232, and Tudor gatehouse — remains of Place House, built by the Earl of Southampton.

Ports Down
The view over Portsmouth Harbour and the Solent is one of the finest views in southern England.

Little is known of **Gosport** in the Middle Ages; it became important only when it was fortified in the eighteenth century. In 1700 it
was only a small fishing village but by 1800 it was a town enclosed
by a wall and moat. In the eighteenth and nineteenth centuries
virtually the whole population was occupied in attending to the
needs of the Navy. When there was a war Gosport prospered, but in
times of peace things were not so good. Throughout this period the
population lived in very cramped and insanitary conditions within
the walls of the town. Gosport was still part of the parish of Alverstoke; in the village of Alverstoke, 2 miles away, living conditions
were quite different. There was a furious debate in the 1890s as to
whether the Local Board should be named Gosport or Alverstoke;
the latter was after all a much older place. Public opinion favoured
Gosport but as a compromise it was named the Gosport and Alverstoke Local Board. In 1894 the Gosport and Alverstoke UDC was
formed and in 1922 the new borough was named Gosport.

It has never been an attractive town, especially now with its car-
parks and tower blocks, but there are some surprising things to be
seen here. Probably the biggest attraction for visitors is the view
across the harbour and perhaps the ferry ride over to Portsmouth. A
floating bridge operated here from 1840 to 1959, but now all traffic
has to go round via Fareham.

Holy Trinity church is easily found by its belfry, a prominent
landmark. The plain brick exterior of the church leaves one quite
unprepared for the grand interior — a spacious nave of 1696 with
two rows of giant blue-and-white Ionic columns each made from a
single oak trunk. The treasure of the church is the organ, which is the
one used by Handel when he was director of music to the Duke of
Chandos at Stanmore; it was bought by the church at auction when
the duke died.

By the end of the eighteenth century Gosport was almost as well
defended as Portsmouth. Its ramparts and moats have been almost
entirely demolished, some as recently as 1965.

Near the church is a bastion that is the only part of the town's
defensive rampart open to the public. It gives some idea of what the
complete fortifications were like. All except one of the forts in
Gosport survive, but only Fort Brockhurst is accessible to the public.
Soon after the forts at Gosport and Ports Down had been completed
the political situation changed. Defensive works such as these, in the
tradition of Roman forts and medieval castles, became obsolete in the

age of modern warfare. In the mid-nineteenth century the great fear was the capture of Portsmouth and the British Navy by landward attack, so no expense was spared to ring Gosport and Portsmouth with impregnable defences.

The displays in Gosport Museum in Walpole Road illustrate the geology, archaeology and history of the Gosport peninsula from the earliest times to the present day. There are also collections of old sail-making and coopering tools and mementoes of World War II.

Railway-lovers will find, not far from here, the derelict Gosport station building, a classic of early railway architecture, looking for all the world like a ruined Greek temple. When the railway came to Gosport in 1841 passengers for Portsmouth had to alight here and cross by ferry (Portsmouth had no direct railway until 1847). An extension was built later to Clarence Yard where Queen Victoria embarked for the Isle of Wight from her own private station. Gosport now has the unenviable distinction of being the largest town in England without a railway station. Railway passengers making for Gosport have to alight at Portsmouth Harbour station, an ironic reversal of the state of affairs in 1841. Outside the old station is a very early Victorian pillar-box.

The Royal Navy Submarine Museum is at HMS *Dolphin* at **Haslar**. This unique museum has, in addition to exhibits illustrating the history of submarine development and underwater warfare, HMS *Alliance*, the Navy's oldest submarine, which was completed at the end of the last war. Also on display is HM Submarine No 1, known as Holland 1 after its designer; it was launched in 1901, sank in 1913 and was recently salvaged.

The Royal Naval Hospital at Haslar, when completed in 1762, was the largest brick building in England and unlike the Royal Victoria Hospital at Netley has survived intact.

Spit Bank Fort is the smallest of the four sea-forts constructed off the shore in the 1860s as part of the great defensive system that protected Portsmouth Harbour and Spithead. Spit Bank Fort mounted fifteen guns, the other three (St Helen's, Horse Sand and No Man's Land) forty-eight guns each. Spit Bank is open to visitors and can be reached by ferry from Gosport, Southsea, Sandown and Cowes. It must be Hampshire's most inaccessible and most unusual tourist attraction. The fort was built in 1867-78 on firm foundations set into the sea-bed; the depth of water here is about 9ft at low tide and 25-30ft at high tide. A tour of the fort reveals the ingenuity of its construction and its strength; it has 25in-thick armour-plating and provision for nine 38-ton guns and six other guns. Though not used against the French, their original purpose, these sea-forts proved useful in both World War I and World War II.

Alverstoke was a rural village until the mid-nineteenth century when it became a residential suburb of Gosport, mainly for naval officers. The old village near the church consists of a tiny triangular 'square' of old buildings, including almshouses and even a genuine thatched cottage. St Mary's church (1865-85) by Henry Woodyer is large and pretentious. Its medieval predecessor, of which nothing remains, was the parish church of Gosport; Holy Trinity church was its chapel-of-ease. The church kneelers, over 500 of them, depict aspects of the history of the parish.

The best thing in Alverstoke, in Crescent Road, is a curved nineteen-bay terrace of 1826. It was to have been the centre of a new planned marine town called Anglesey. To further this development there were bathing-machines, a hotel, a racecourse, a toll-bridge over Haslar Creek, a ferry to Portsmouth (the floating bridge), and much later (1863) a branch railway to a pier at Stokes Bay near the Crescent. But nothing much came of all this, and now all those amenities have disappeared with the exception of the Crescent. The line of the railway can be followed through the town as a footpath between the houses.

Lee-on-the-Solent was a late Victorian development, a marine health resort with a pier (demolished in 1958) and a branch railway (last used for passengers in 1930) whose station building, now an amusement arcade, still stands near the old pier-head. With the advantage of a railway Lee-on-the-Solent hoped to become another Bournemouth but it was not to be. The pier lasted longer than the railway (70 years) and its 120ft-high tower was a well-known landmark. Lee today is a popular seaside resort in spite of having nothing much more than a fine promenade and a good beach. The beach is the only one in Hampshire and the Isle of Wight to have received the Blue Flag Award for its high standard of water quality, good facilities and control of dogs (on parts of the beach dogs are not allowed). The Fleet Air Arm Memorial on the front lists all those members who died in World War II — about 1,800.

Beyond Hill Head is **Titchfield Haven**, a miniature harbour at the mouth of the River Meon, which flows into the sea through a sluice. The nature reserve here is open from August to March. It

Spit Bank Fort

Old Portsmouth from Gosport

Titchfield

Church Street, Titchfield

consists of freshwater marshes, reed-beds and islands on which migrant birds can be watched from hides. Much of it can be seen from the coast road.

A little further on, at a sharp bend, is a bridge that conceals the remains of the sea-lock at the south end of the former Titchfield Canal. A footpath follows the canal to Titchfield village. The canal was completed in 1611, thus making it the second earliest in England (Exeter was the first). It was also used for flooding the water-meadows on each side. At about the same time, on the orders of the Earl of Southampton, the river was sealed off from the sea by a wall, a move which enraged the villagers and eventually ended Titchfield's history as a port, because the canal was not a success.

Titchfield is one of the most interesting and attractive places in Hampshire. It was a medieval market centre and small port, and its prosperity rested on its commercial activities and the presence of the abbey nearby, but it never achieved borough status. After the dissolution of the monastery there was an inevitable decline, followed by a revival. Another decline followed in 1650-1750, during which time the canal became disused, but by 1801 the population had reached nearly 3,000. There was a regular weekly market; the old market-hall has been removed to the Weald and Downland Museum in West Sussex. Now designated a conservation area, happily preserved from suburban development, its picturesque streets have many attractive Georgian brick houses with a few earlier timber-framed ones, giving a pleasant homely atmosphere to the village. There are a few houses in the village dating from the fifteenth century (eg Nos 17-21 West Street and Nos 7-13 South Street) and more of the sixteenth and seventeenth centuries.

Not many churches of the early Anglo-Saxon period survive in England; most were destroyed in the Danish wars of the ninth century. The only certain survival in Hampshire of this early period is the lower part of the tower of St Peter's church at Titchfield, probably the oldest piece of church architecture in the county. The lower part of the church tower was the porch of the Saxon church and still serves as the porch. Western porches were a common feature of early Saxon churches; they were later replaced by western towers and the porches were moved to the south side of churches. Roman materials used in the construction of this porch also suggest an early date for it — probably late seventh or early eighth century. St Wilfrid was in west Sussex in AD681-6 and may have built it. The church was enlarged and altered throughout the Middle Ages, culminating in the beautiful north aisle. In the chapel is the grand monument of the Wriothesleys, the first and second Earls of Southampton; it was constructed in 1594 by Garret Johnson, a Flemish refugee. It is considered to be the best Elizabethan monument in the county. On the wall of the chapel is a display of photographs, maps and information on the history of Titchfield.

Titchfield Abbey is north of the village and the A27. It was founded in 1232 by the Premonstratensians (White Canons). Not much remains of the original abbey buildings — the entrance to the chapter house is the most important. Though the buildings have not survived to the same extent as those at Netley, the ground plan has been established. After the dissolution of the monasteries the Earl of Southampton converted some of the buildings into a mansion called Place House and what remains today is a spectacular piece of Tudor rebuilding, the shell of the gatehouse and its wings fashioned out of the abbey church nave. In 1445 Henry VI was married to Margaret of Anjou in the abbey church.

The third Earl of Southampton was a friend of William Shakespeare, who may have visited Titchfield. There is a legend that Shakespeare wrote some of his sonnets here, and that at least one of his plays was performed for the first time here. Near the abbey is a huge fifteenth-century tithe barn, timber-framed with a tiled roof.

Fishponds were introduced to England after the Norman Conquest and were an important factor in the medieval economy; they supplied fresh fish to palaces and monasteries. Over eighty fishpond sites have been located in Hampshire. Four large fishponds that were attached to the abbey can be seen from the public footpath on the west side of the ruins.

A mile south-east of Titchfield is Crofton old church, a pleasing mixture of architecture of various dates.

At **Warsash**, at the mouth of the River Hamble, a street of old houses leads down to a car-park and the quay, where a ferry crosses the river to Hamble and where one can buy fresh fish and crabs. Warsash, like Hamble across the river, once had a flourishing ship-building industry. George Parsons moved his shipyard lock, stock and barrel from Hamble and in 1808 the first ship from his yard at Warsash was launched. The largest ship ever launched at Warsash was HMS *Hotspur*, a thirty-six-gun frigate; there is a scale model of it in the parish church. A plaque on the Rising Sun inn records the sailing of 3,000 commandos to France on the eve of D-Day. South of the village is the College of Nautical Studies where ocean navigation is taught.

One can return to Portsmouth along the crest of the chalk ridge of **Ports Down**. This offers one of the finest panoramic views in the whole of England, from Sussex to Southampton Water, with the Isle of Wight in the distance, Butser Hill to the north, and Portsmouth Harbour at the foot of the hill. It is an incredible sight by day but perhaps even more so by night, with thousands of lights in all directions. The monument to Nelson at the west end of the down was erected by his officers and men.

The Palmerston forts on Ports Down, though similar in principle to Fort Brockhurst, are larger, with extensive earthworks, underground chambers and a deep dry moat on the north, from which direction they are wellnigh invisible, so well do they merge with the hillside. The forts on Ports Down were intended as a deterrent to enemy forces bent on capturing Portsmouth, which was the key to a successful invasion of England. These forts therefore had to delay the enemy until the British Army was fully mobilised. To capture any or all of them would have meant a long and costly siege; in the event they were never put to the test. Though their individual designs differed in detail they were all polygonal in plan; the traditional bastions were abandoned in favour of straight ditches flanked by caponiers, which provided cross-fire along the ditches. The main guns were on the ramparts to keep the enemy batteries out of range; the secondary guns were concealed and would have been used if the enemy had broken into the ditch. The bricks used in their construction were made at brickworks on the site. The underground tunnels, through which the ammunition was moved from the magazines to the guns, were cut by Welsh miners. Great precautions were taken to minimise the risk of an explosion, even to having wooden nails in the floor-boards in case of sparks from metal boots. The officers' quarters had protective shutters in case their men mutinied; after a tour of the men's primitive living quarters you will see why that was possible! Fort Nelson is open to the public and contains the National Museum of Arms and Armour; guided tours of the fort are included.

On Ports Down plants and insects typical of chalk areas can still be found, more especially in the less-disturbed spots near the forts. Plants commonly found include dogwood, orchids and kidney vetch. The great green bush-cricket is common, and about twenty species of butterfly have been recorded; corn buntings and jackdaws are birds often seen here.

Ports Down (the correct name for what is known locally as Portsdown Hill) has always been a popular place for picnics and recreation. Though the trees, windmill and tea-gardens that were here before the construction of the forts in the 1860s are gone the views alone make a visit well worthwhile.

4

THE SOUTH-EAST

From Bar End in Winchester a minor road skirts St Catherine's Hill and follows the course of a Roman road across rolling downland via Morestead to the hilltop village of **Owslebury**. Inside the medieval church is a serpent, an old and rare musical instrument, which once accompanied the hymn-singing.

Marwell Zoo, a mile to the south, is one of the largest in Britain. It is run by a charity whose aim is to breed animals threatened by extinction. The 800 animals in its 100 acres of parkland include many rare ones, such as snow-leopards and Asian lions (the only ones in Britain). Two species of particular interest are the scimitar-horned oryx, which has been chosen as Marwell Park's symbol because of its rarity and because this herd is one of the largest herds in captivity, and the Przewalski's horse, the only surviving species of wild horse in the world, which is already almost extinct in the wild. Guided tours and lectures on wildlife are available in the summer. Marwell Hall was rebuilt about 1816; an earlier house was owned by the brother of Jane Seymour, the third wife of Henry VIII. The hall is reputed to be haunted not only by her ghost but also by that of Anne Boleyn!

The A333 and a left turn leads to **Upham**, a small and attractive village which was the birthplace in 1683 of the poet Edward Young, the author of *Night Thoughts*; his father was the vicar. The name of the inn, the Brushmakers Arms, is evidence of a local craft that once flourished here.

South of Upham is **Bishop's Waltham**, which as its name indicates was held by the Bishops of Winchester from 904 to 1869. One of them probably laid out the town in the thirteenth century, as the street pattern suggests some form of planning. It has always been a market centre but has never attained the rank of borough. The narrow streets of Georgian and Victorian buildings give it an old country-town atmosphere, in spite of the restoration of some of its old buildings and the erection of new ones. The whole of the area bounded by Brook Street, Bank Street and Houchin Street may once have been a large market-place, and the narrow alleys in this area are intriguing and worth exploring.

Bank Street (formerly French Street) was renamed when the Bishop's Waltham and Hampshire Bank was founded in 1809 (the original building is opposite Malvern Close). This bank, later known as Gunner's Bank, was the last surviving private country bank in England when it was taken over in 1953. The east side of Basingwell Street, off Bank Street, consists of an almost continuous row of attractive seventeenth- and eighteenth-century houses, broken by the ugly Methodist church.

There is a small museum in Brook Street (open on Sunday afternoons in summer) with a collection of terracotta products from the nineteenth-century pottery works at Claylands, which at one time was the largest in Hampshire. Bishop's Waltham was once the terminus of a railway from Botley; the station was situated near the roundabout on the bypass, and one of the level-crossing gates and a section of the track have been preserved there.

The palace, first built about 1135 by Bishop Henry de Blois, was rebuilt two or three times. The moat that surrounded it, now mainly dry, was fed from the mill-stream. Much of the old brick boundary wall survives and enough remains of the fifteenth-century great hall to give some idea of what a splendid room it must have been. William of Wykeham died in the palace in 1404. It was captured by the Roundheads in the Civil War and reduced to its present condition, but enough of the palace survives to make it one of the most impressive ruins in Hampshire, testimony to the power and immense wealth of the bishops in the Middle Ages. The brick house adjoining the ruins was once the home of Admiral Cunningham, of World War II fame.

St Peter's Street, narrow and attractive, leads to the church, which has lost much of its old character through constant restoration. The tower (1584-9) and the aisles (1637-52) were rebuilt in the Gothic style, a late survival of that style. The gallery and its pews are eighteenth-century work and the pulpit dates from 1626. There are many interesting monuments in the church.

The Old Granary in Bank Street is a crafts centre where the work of many talented local people is on display; on Saturdays they can usually be seen at work.

South-east of Bishop's Waltham on the A333 is **Wickham**, where the market square is overlooked by fine Georgian houses. It was probably set out when Wickham was granted a market and fair in 1268. The village lies on the River Meon, on the line of a Roman road from Winchester.

The Square is one of the most impressive townscapes in Hampshire; though no individual house is outstanding the varying heights and sizes of the buildings give The Square a satisfying character. They range in date from medieval to Victorian, but Georgian predominate, many of them faced with unvitrified silver-grey bricks.

On The Old Barracks, one of the old houses in Bridge Street leading from The Square, a notice warns that 'vagrants will be punished with the utmost severity'! The Old Barracks probably derived its name from its use at some time as officers' quarters. At Queens Lodge opposite Queen Anne is supposed once to have stayed a night, when it was a coaching inn. Nearby is Chesapeake Mill, built in 1820 partly of woodwork from an American frigate of that name captured by the British in the war of 1812-14. William of Wykeham, famous as Bishop of Winchester, was born at Wickham in 1324.

Further on, south of the A333, is **Boarhunt**, a remote hamlet under the lee of Ports Down. Although it is apparently miles from anywhere, it is in fact only 2 miles from Fareham. The lonely church is a simple Saxon building, dating from about 1064, and is virtually unspoilt. One can imagine the villagers attending services in their new church, their familiar world soon to be taken over by Norman invaders.

The church was restored in 1853 and the Victorian furniture includes a three-decker pulpit, a squire's pew and a west gallery. In most churches at this time the Victorians were destroying such items in their pursuit of the Gothic Revival, but obviously the ideals of the ecclesiology movement had not penetrated to this remote little church. The Henslow monument (1577) is an example of the memorials with classical ornament that began to appear in the mid-sixteenth century.

At the pretty and peaceful village of **Southwick**, bypassed by the

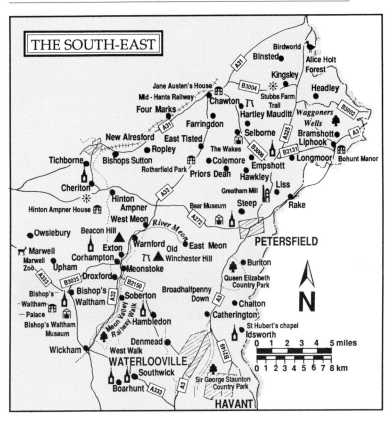

THE SOUTH-EAST

A333, the church dates from 1566, a rare date for church rebuilding. Its full name is St James-without-the-Priory-Gate and it is officially a 'peculiar', ie outside the bishop's jurisdiction. Once one of the best unrestored churches in the county, it still has its old pulpit, box-pews and gallery, which give it a feeling of character. Unfortunately the old pews had to be replaced by modern ones. Very little remains of the priory that moved here from Portchester in the mid-twelfth century. It was dissolved in 1538 and converted to a house. Recent excavations have proved that both the priory and the house were rebuilt more than once. Southwick House (1841), now part of HMS *Dryad*, the Navy's School of Maritime Operations, was the Supreme

Allied Headquarters at the time of the D-Day invasion.

In the nineteenth century a village public house often had its own brewery attached; later most of these local breweries moved to the towns. The Golden Lion at Southwick had its own brewery until 1956; the brewery buildings and machinery survive at the rear of the public house and can be visited by appointment. In 1900 there were over eighty breweries in Hampshire; now there are only two.

From Wickham northwards the A32 traverses the valley of the Meon, one of the most beautiful parts of Hampshire with some of its most unspoilt villages. A mile or two from Wickham is **West Walk**, a Forestry Commission wood of 900 acres. This is a small remnant of the ancient Forest of Bere, which once stretched from Romsey to the Sussex border. Most of the ancient forest has given way to agriculture but West Walk still has some old oaks, and some of the planted trees date back to 1800. The forest has in the past served the needs of Roman ironworking and Tudor shipbuilding, and now supplies wood to modern industry. West Walk provides a haven for birds and other wildlife, and there are picnic sites and two woodland trails.

Soberton, the first village along the Meon valley, has several large attractive old houses. Admiral Anson, the famous eighteenth-century seaman, once lived at the manor house, long since destroyed. The best part of the church is the south transept with its wall-paintings dating from about 1330. Outside is a Roman coffin found in the village. High up on the exterior of the tower there is a medieval carving of a skull, flanked by two heads, a key and a bucket or purse. There is a legend that the tower was originally built by a butler and a dairymaid, who are represented by the two heads. When the tower was rebuilt in 1881 money towards the cost was subscribed by servants from far and wide on the strength of this legend (see the inscriptions on the inside and outside of the tower).

Droxford, on the other side of the river, is equally attractive. The village street has many small Georgian houses; of the larger houses The Rectory and Manor House are outstanding. Izaak Walton often came here to fish in the river, which he considered the best in England for trout. His daughter married the rector of Droxford. The church, mainly Norman, has two good doorways of that period and four medieval mass-dials on the south side. The Wayfarer's Walk passes through the churchyard.

Across the river is the former Droxford railway station. Its most historic moment came in June 1944 when in a train standing at the station the Allied leaders planned the D-Day operations. The Meon Valley Railway from Alton to Fareham, one of the most delightfully rural in England, was opened in 1903 and finally closed to passengers in 1955. This railway, an ambitious project, was intended to provide a through route from London to Gosport. All five passenger stations on the line were of a high standard with first-class facilities. But such a thinly populated area could not be expected to give the railway much profit and it is surprising that the line lasted as long as it did. The 9-mile stretch between Wickham and West Meon is now a popular public footpath.

The church at **Meonstoke**, overlooking the river in one of the most beautiful spots in the valley, is Early English in style and has a Norman font. In 1830, for no known reason, its dedication was changed, a rare occurrence, from St Mary to St Andrew.

Across the road is Corhampton church, which, like Boarhunt, is a simple Saxon building, built about 1035. The 'long-and-short' stones at the corners are evidence of its Saxon origin. The church is a marvellous survival of pre-Conquest times.

The rare Saxon sundial on the south wall is divided into eight sections and not 24 hours as today; this is because the Saxons divided the day into eight 'tides' of 3 hours each. Norman mass-dials are usually marked in hours. The twelfth-century wall-paintings in the chancel and the nave are among the earliest and most important in the country; some of them depict legends from the life of St Swithun. There is a Romano-British coffin in the churchyard and also one of the largest yew trees in the county.

A mile further on is **Exton** with its pleasant riverside inn and medieval church. The most remarkable thing in the church is a headstone depicting the Angel of Death summoning a scholar from his books. From Exton a road winds uphill to Beacon Hill, a spur of downland open to visitors, 600ft above sea-level with beautiful views over the Meon valley and beyond.

Further north along the valley is **Warnford** where the exceptionally interesting church in the park can be visited on foot. There was a Saxon church here once; the sundial above the south door may have come from it. Notable features are the massive Norman tower, the timber roof and the extraordinary Neale monuments, one with nine children in a row. They are kneeling on cushions and four of them carry skulls to show that they died during their parents' lifetime. George Lewis's gravestone in the churchyard depicts a skeleton pointing to a branch of a tree. The story is that he was struck dead when sawing wood on a Sunday. Unfortunately for this story, the day of his death was a Friday! The thirteenth-century house known as King John's House, close to the church, has been a picturesque ruin for hundreds of years. Visitors will be reluctant to leave this peaceful and historic spot.

In **West Meon** churchyard lies Thomas Lord, forever famous as the founder of Lord's cricket ground; he retired here late in life and died 2 years later in 1832. Guy Burgess, the Englishman who defected to Russia, is also buried here, in the family grave. The most famous man born in West Meon was James Thorold Rogers, the nineteenth-century economist and the first man to legally withdraw from his clerical vows. His father, a doctor in the village for over 40 years, is commemorated by the cross in the village centre.

St John's church (1843-6) was George Gilbert Scott's first church in Hampshire, an early example of the 'second pointed' (Early English/Decorated) period of the Gothic Revival. The site of West Meon railway station can be found in Station Road. It has been derelict for 35 years and its platforms, partly under the road bridge, are enveloped in trees and vegetation, a sad sight for all railway-lovers.

The A272 from The West Meon Hut leads via Bramdean to **Hinton Ampner**. In the Middle Ages the manor here belonged to the almoner of St Swithun's Priory at Winchester, hence the strange name. Hinton Ampner House has been rebuilt several times, the last one having been gutted by fire in 1960. After this last fire it was refurnished with fine Regency furniture, pictures and porcelain. One of the previous houses was haunted so alarmingly that in 1793 it was demolished and rebuilt! At that date the old Tudor house was in a bad state of repair, deserted and uninhabitable because of the ghostly manifestations; it stood quite close to the church. The only remains of Tudor date are the walled kitchen garden and the stables. The house was occupied throughout World War II by the Portsmouth Day School for Girls, and in 1945 it was inspected as a possible home for the Royal Observatory. The garden is a combination of formal design and informal planting, with terraced walks giving charming views. The house and grounds now belong to the National Trust and are open to visitors. There was a Saxon church here — a doorway in the present church is Saxon, and there are several handsome monuments to the Stewkeley family.

*Gypsy church,
Bramdean Common*

*Hinton Ampner
House*

At the attractive and well-kept village of **Cheriton**, where the infant Itchen flows through the village green, the thirteenth-century church is said to be standing on a prehistoric burial mound. That is quite possible because churches were sometimes built on pagan burial and religious sites in order to affirm the supremacy of Christianity. Cheriton is thought to have been the last place in England where truffle-hunting was carried on. Truffles are rich-flavoured underground fungi esteemed as delicacies. They were tracked down by dogs and the industry supported several local families.

A monument to the Battle of Cheriton stands at a road junction north-east of the village, nearly a mile north of the main battle site, which was near Cheriton Wood. Here on 29 March 1644 the Roundheads under Sir William Waller routed a Royalist force when, to quote the inscription on the monument, '20,000 soldiers hazarded their lives'. The battle was a turning-point in the Civil War, throwing the king on to the defensive.

The village of **Tichborne** is famous on two counts, for the Tichborne Dole and the Tichborne Claimant. The Dole, now a gallon of flour for each adult, has been paid out since the twelfth century, sometimes in money, sometimes in bread. The custom arose when the dying Lady Tichborne made an agreement with her husband that the amount of land she could crawl around while a stick was burning would be set aside to grow corn for the poor — she managed to encompass 23 acres!

The Claimant was the central figure in one of the most celebrated trials of the nineteenth century. Arthur Orton, a butcher from Australia, claimed to be Roger Tichborne, a son of the local family, who had been presumed lost at sea. After the longest trial ever held in England Orton lost his claim and was convicted of perjury.

The church overlooking the village is happily unrestored and has many interesting features, including a Norman chancel and font and Jacobean box-pews. The Tichborne Chapel with the splendid alabaster monument of 1621 to Sir Benjamin Tichborne and his wife is a rare example of a Catholic chapel within an Anglican church.

New Alresford is not really 'new' because it was founded about 1200, when Bishop de Lucy of Winchester dammed the river and laid out a new market-place. New Market, later named New Alresford, was one of the bishop's six new planned towns (four in Hampshire and two in Wiltshire), founded not for military but for financial reasons, so that rents could be obtained from the building plots. The damming of the river created a large lake, which has now shrunk to 30 acres. The dam, which is crossed by the road between the two Alresfords, is one of the largest non-military medieval earthworks in England. It was thought at one time that this lake (Old Alresford Pond) was created in order to convert the river between Alresford and Winchester to a canal, but it has now been conclusively proved that it was a fishpond for the use of the Bishop of Winchester; it also provided water for the three mills on the river. The beautiful old thatched fulling-mill on the river dates from the time when Alresford had a flourishing cloth trade. Before that, in the fourteenth century, it had a large wool market.

The church has one of the few Saxon roods in the county. There are many attractive houses in Alresford but few earlier than the eighteenth century because of the frequent fires that ravaged the town, such as the one in 1689 that destroyed 117 houses. The tree-lined Broad Street is one of the most attractive thoroughfares in Hampshire. At No 27 Mary Russell Mitford, the author of *Our Village*, was born; she and her family moved when she won a £20,000 lottery prize at the age of 10!

In East Street and West Street there are several old bow-fronted houses and shops. The Old Sun was once the home of the cricket writer John Arlott, and the building which now encompasses Nos 56-60 West Street was formerly Perin's Grammar School, founded in 1697.

Alresford is a centre of the watercress industry; the beds occupy the river valley north and east of the town, some on the site of de Lucy's lake. The freshly-picked cress is highly recommended.

The industry was important enough to give the nickname 'Watercress Line' to the Mid-Hants Railway, now one of England's preserved steam railways. It runs from Alresford to Alton on the former Winchester to Alton line. The line was a major engineering feat with its cuttings and embankments and gradients of up to 1 in 60; locals referred to it as 'going over the Alps'. The line was opened in 1865 and most trains then ran from Southampton to Guildford, with one or two a day to Waterloo. The watercress trade was lost in 1963 when, faced with unreliable rail connections, the growers organized their own road transport.

The line was closed in 1973 in spite of strong local protest, but a dedicated private company has restored it and it is now one of the major tourist attractions in the county. Ropley station is a hive of

The Mid-Hants Railway (Watercress Line)

activity at weekends in summer with trains every half-hour and restoration work being carried out on the engines and carriages; the aim is to have sixteen locomotives in operation on the line. A trip on the railway can be recommended both to those who can remember with nostalgia the days of steam and to those too young to have enjoyed such delights.

From Alresford the A31 goes via Bishops Sutton, Ropley and Four Marks to Chawton near Alton. Jane Austen's House, where she lived for the last 8 years of her life, from 1809 to 1817, is now a museum. The house, then named Chawton Cottage, was bought by her brother Edward, who lived at Chawton House in the park. Originally an inn, the house has not changed much in appearance. In those days it was on a busy main road and is quieter today now that the village has been bypassed. In this house Jane Austen wrote *Mansfield Park, Emma* and *Persuasion*. The furniture includes her writing-table and there is a collection of documents and letters.

South of Chawton is **Farringdon**, an unspoilt village with a Norman church, the nave arcades of which are most impressive. Gilbert White was curate here for 24 years. From 1797 to 1919 there were only two rectors; the second of these, the Reverend

T.H.Massey, rector for 62 years, was a great builder. With the help of two or three workers he constructed the monstrous red-brick building opposite the church. Known as 'Massey's Folly', it took him 30 years to complete (1870-1900) and resembles no other building in Hampshire, or indeed in England. It has seventeen bedrooms and is decorated with terracotta panels of the type popular a hundred years ago. The original purpose of the building is uncertain; it was used for a long time as the village school. One of the yew trees in the churchyard is 3,000 years old. (The oldest in Great Britain is 3,500 years old.)

South of Farringdon, on the A32 at **East Tisted**, is Rotherfield Park, a house which is open to visitors. It was rebuilt in 1820-1 in a castellated Gothic style and further Gothicised in the 1880s with turrets and towers, including a huge red-brick stable tower. There are three other towers or 'follies': a square tower once housing the game-larder, a round tower with a stair-turret and a laundry chimney disguised as a slim tower. The outstanding feature of the interior of the house is the magnificent staircase in the hall. The house commands an extensive view and the gardens include a rose garden and a walled garden.

A left turn off the A32 leads to **Colemore**, where the little church

Fulling-mill, New Alresford

maintained by the Redundant Churches Fund has a Norman transept. In the chancel are buried Richard Pocock (died 1718) and James Cookson (died 1835); both had been rector for 59 years and both died at the age of 83! Narrow lanes lead to **Priors Dean** church, as delightfully rural as one could wish to find, facing an old farmhouse.

There is a lonely public house in the sparsely inhabited countryside south-east of Colemore. No signboard gives away its location — you have to know where it is! The White Horse was a favourite inn of Edward Thomas the poet; it inspired his first poem *Up in the wind*, in which he described the inn's isolation and how the signboard was stolen. Once having found The White Horse you will not regret the time spent in searching for it. One of the bars was once a smithy.

A road goes on via Hawkley to Empshott, the landscape changing from gentle farmland to steep wooded valleys as the chalk gives way to greensand, with the roads winding up and down through cuttings. These sunken lanes are a feature of this part of the county; in places they are 20ft below the top of the bank on either side and were worn down by traffic and water in the days before roads were metalled.

Hawkley church (1865) is in the Romanesque style, not a popular style at that time. It has a tower with a Rhenish helm spire, the only one in Hampshire, similar to the one of Saxon date at Sompting in West Sussex. In 1774 a huge landslip occurred a mile east of the village near Scotland Farm, when part of the sandstone escarpment slid down over the underlying clay. A cottage was almost destroyed and was rebuilt (now Slip Cottage); the landslip can be seen from the road above the cottage. **Empshott** has an unspoilt little early thirteenth-century church set in completely rural surroundings, memorable for its abundance of old woodwork, including its benches and choir-stalls.

Selborne is famous far beyond Hampshire, in fact all over the world, for its association with Gilbert White the naturalist. He was born at the old rectory, now gone, and lived at The Wakes from the age of 9 or 10 for the rest of his life. He was curate of Selborne four times but was never rector. The book on which his fame rests, *The Natural History and Antiquities of Selborne*, published in 1789, was based on his 40 years of observation of the birds, wildlife and plants in his garden and around the village, and consists of letters to Thomas Pennant, Daines Barrington and others. Gilbert White died in 1793 at the age of 72, his lasting legacy one of the most enduring works of literature in the English language.

In The Wakes are displays relating to his studies and the natural history of the parish that show the wide variety of flora and fauna resulting from the geology of the area. There is also a display of finds from Selborne Priory, which owned most of the village in late medieval times. The garden is also open to visitors. The Wakes was purchased by R.W.Oates and also houses the Oates Museum commemorating Francis Oates, the explorer of South America and Africa, and his nephew Captain Lawrence Oates, who accompanied Scott on the tragic expedition to the South Pole in 1911-12. Opposite The Wakes is a small building that was once a butcher's shop. Gilbert White planted four lime trees in front of it to hide 'the sight of blood and filth' from his windows.

Gilbert White is buried under a simple gravestone in the churchyard. The church dates from about 1180 and has many interesting features, including a Flemish painting of about 1510 and White's memorial window showing St Francis with eighty-two birds mentioned in White's book. Also in the churchyard is the grave of John Newland ('the Trumpeter'), who was the leader of the local agricultural workers in the riots of 1830; he summoned his supporters by means of a trumpet. His mob attacked the workhouse at Selborne (Fisher's Buildings in Gracious Street) and frightened the vicar so much that he reduced his tithes on the spot! Newland took refuge afterwards in the woods and so escaped arrest.

The little square opposite The Wakes is named The Plestor, a corruption of 'playstow', in medieval times a playground. It was a favourite resort of young and old on summer evenings; there was once a huge oak tree in the middle that was blown down in the great storm of 1703. Also at Selborne is the Romany Folklore Museum, the first gypsy museum in England. Gypsies (so named because they were thought to be Egyptians) originated in north-west India and were first recorded in Great Britain in 1505. They have suffered persecution in the past — Elizabeth I ordered all gypsies to be hung, drawn and quartered, but they survived. The museum has traditional Romany 'living-wagons' and an exhibition of gypsy history, crafts and wagon-building with many details and documents relating to the history of gypsies, examples of their clothes, and basket-making tools. The Mallinson Collection of Rural Relics at the Selborne Cottage Shop is a collection of old agricultural hand-tools, dairy and domestic bygones, and tools used in village trades such as blacksmiths, wheelwrights, thatchers, coopers and brickmakers.

Many delightful walks can be taken around Selborne, up the zigzag path to Selborne Common and Selborne Hanger (beech woods on slopes in Hampshire are known as 'hangers'), following in the footsteps of the man who has contributed so much to our knowledge of natural history. A short walk from the Common is **Newton Valence**, a tiny and remote village with an Early English church facing the manor house. The yew tree in the churchyard may be 1,000 years old; the yew grows so well in the county that it is known as the 'Hampshire weed'. Three miles south-east of Selborne is Greatham Mill, which has an attractive garden open to visitors.

The B3006 and then two right turns take one to **Hartley Mauditt** where the little Norman church stands picturesquely alone facing a pond. It is all that remains of the medieval village, the traces of which in the adjoining fields are now an ancient monument.

Quiet roads through rich farmland lead to West Worldham and East Worldham, each with a medieval church, **Kingsley** with a red-brick church of 1778, and **Binsted**, notable for its oast-houses, relics of the once-prosperous hop-drying industry in this locality. The large-aisled Norman/Early English church here has a crusader's tomb, his effigy in chain-mail, in the north chapel. Viscount Montgomery is buried in the churchyard; he spent his last years at nearby Isington Mill, a beautiful spot on the River Wey. Stubbs Farm Trail at Kingsley is at a working farm where visitors are welcome.

Alice Holt Forest, once owned by the Crown, is now managed by the Forestry Commission who have a research station here. The history of Alice Holt goes back to Roman times when there were important potteries here producing wares on a large scale for the London market. From about AD60 to the fifth century pottery was produced on a large scale at Alice Holt, reaching a peak in the mid-to late fourth century. The pottery made there and at other kilns along the present Hampshire-Surrey border was kitchen-ware of a coarse grey type, using the underlying Gault Clay as raw material for the pots and sand from the nearby heathlands as tempering material.

In the Saxon period and after the Norman Conquest Alice Holt was a royal hunting-forest; its name probably derives from 'Aelfsige's holt' (the wood of Aelfsige). He was Bishop of Winchester and owned land here. There were forest laws to protect the trees, the deer and other game, and infringements were punished by heavy fines.

Places of Interest in the South-East

Marwell Zoological Park
6 miles south of Winchester
One of the largest zoos in
England. Specialises in breeding
rare animals.

Bishop's Waltham Museum
Brook Street
History of Bishop's Waltham.

Bishop's Waltham Palace
(English Heritage)
Ruins of the palace of the Bishops
of Winchester.

The Old Granary
Bank Street, Bishop's Waltham
Crafts centre where local craftsmen display their products and can
be seen at work.

Wickham
Attractive village with the best
market square in Hampshire.

West Walk
2 miles north-east of Wickham
Forestry Commission woodland,
once part of the Forest of Bere.

Meon Valley Railway Line
Nine-mile footpath along the
beautiful Meon valley.

Hinton Ampner House
(National Trust)
House rebuilt in Georgian style
and formal gardens.

Tichborne
Village with beautiful unrestored
church — Jacobean pews and
Tichborne chapel.

Mid-Hants Railway
Preserved steam railway known as
the 'Watercress Line' between
Alresford and Alton.

Jane Austen's House
Chawton
Jane Austen's home from 1809 to
1817. A museum devoted to her
life and work.

Rotherfield Park
East Tisted

Victorian Gothic house and
contents. Gardens.

The Wakes
Selborne
Home of Gilbert White the
naturalist. Gilbert White Museum
and Oates Memorial Library and
museum.

Romany Folklore Museum
Selborne
The first gypsy museum in
England. Romany wagons and
crafts.

**Mallinson Collection of Rural
Relics**
Selborne Cottage Shop

**Selborne Common and Selborne
Hanger** (National Trust)
Nature trail and walks.

Greatham Mill
Greatham, near Liss
Attractive garden intersected by
mill waterways.

Stubbs Farm Trail
Kingsley
Working farm with lakes and
woodland walk.

Alice Holt Forest
Woodland walks and drives.
Arboretum and visitor centre.

Birdworld
Holt Pound, near Farnham
One of the largest bird zoos in
England (over 1,000 birds).
Underwater World is an aquarium
with fish from all over the world.

**Ludshott Common and Waggon-
ers Wells** (National Trust)
Near Grayshott
A series of ponds, former iron-
foundry reservoirs, south of the
common, a fine place for walks.

Bohunt Manor
Liphook
Beautiful garden with herbaceous
borders and a lake with waterfowl.

In more recent times its oak trees, which flourished on the clay soil, provided timber for the Navy. Gilbert White noted that 'Alice Holt abounded with oaks'. The first timber for the naval dockyards was taken in the early sixteenth century. In 1633 the *Warspit* was built with Alice Holt timber. Before this however, timber had been taken for buildings, notably for the Great Hall at Westminster. After neglect of the forest in the eighteenth century an Act of 1812 ordered the removal of the deer and soon afterwards 1,600 acres were enclosed and planted with oak trees. Modern management of Alice Holt dates from 1905 when a plan was adopted for clearing the scrub and poorer specimens of oak and replacing them with conifers such as larch, Douglas fir, Scots pine and Corsican pine. In 1924 the Forestry Commission took over the forest. Alice Holt is a real working forest, producing timber for various uses. About 25 acres (20,000 trees) are felled and replanted each year, mainly with oak and Corsican pine. Oaks are harvested when they are 120-150 years old, pines when 55-65 years old and Douglas firs when 50 years old.

Today visitors can enjoy Alice Holt's forest walks and picnic sites. There are five trails, each one between $1^1/_4$ miles and $3/_4$ mile long, and other attractions include an arboretum and Lodge Pond. There are about 120 roe-deer in the forest, and other animals sometimes seen include badgers, grey squirrels and snakes. Birds are plentiful, especially warblers, and the forest is noted for its butterflies and moths. There is a great variety of wild flowers, herbs, grasses, sedges and rushes. Much active conservation is carried out to provide the maximum diversity of wildlife habitats.

Birdworld at Holt Pound is one of the largest bird zoos in England, with over 1,000 birds ranging from tiny hanging parrots to ostriches, and including vultures, macaws, penguins, eagles and storks, and in the unique sea-shore walk many species of waterfowl. Underwater World, an aquarium with 1,000 fish, tropical, marine and freshwater, is also a great attraction.

A drive through the pleasant wooded country of heaths and commons near the Hampshire-Surrey border takes one via the A325, Broxhead Common and Lindford to **Headley**, where there is a picturesque old corn-mill on the River Wey. It is one of the few mills in Hampshire still producing flour and with the waterfowl on the adjacent mill-pond makes an attractive scene. **Ludshott Common** is a National Trust open space near Grayshott, and the delightful **Waggoners Wells** are ponds that were once iron-foundry reservoirs, in which fishing is allowed by permit.

The Fox and Pelican public house at Grayshott has an interesting history. It was built in 1899 by the Grayshott and District Refreshment Association to encourage the sale of non-alcoholic drinks; it sold alcohol as well but from under the counter! It was opened by the wife of the Bishop of Winchester and even had a library of books donated by George Bernard Shaw. Shaw rented a house in the village and was one of the famous writers who used the local post office in Crossways Road, where the postmaster's assistant, a young woman named Flora Thompson, was herself destined to become famous one day for her trilogy *Lark Rise to Candleford*.

Two miles south-west is **Bramshott**, where 330 Canadian soldiers are buried in the churchyard. They died at the camp on Bramshott Common during the two world wars, many as a result of the influenza epidemic of 1917-18. Also in the churchyard is the burial ground of King George's Sanatorium for Sailors. The church is mainly Victorian with a few Early English details; the 200 kneelers are each of a unique design and depict the flora and fauna of the Bramshott countryside. John Pym, the Parliamentarian, was married here in 1604. Hammer Bottom and Hammer Vale, as the names indicate, were the scene of ironworking at several mills on the River Wey. There was one named Pophole at the exact spot where the counties of Hampshire, Surrey and West Sussex meet — its remains can still be seen.

Woolmer Forest is partly heathland, partly forest. There are several footpaths leading into it (when it is not in use for Army firing). From the Passfield Common side you will come to the remains of the Longmoor Military Railway, where Royal Engineers were trained in the operation of a railway. The track can be seen in places, and there are one or two derelict bridges.

At **Liphook**, one mile on, the seventeenth-century Royal Anchor Hotel was a famous coaching inn once patronized by George III and Nelson. Coaches passed through Liphook every hour on the London to Portsmouth road, stopping to change horses. The whole journey cost £1 and took 8 hours.

The beautiful garden at **Bohunt Manor** on the Petersfield road is open to visitors in aid of the Worldwide Fund for Nature. Over fifty species of waterfowl can be seen on the lake.

The Flying Bull public house at **Rake**, between Liphook and Petersfield, is unique in that it stands partly in Hampshire and partly in West Sussex. A notice in the Two Counties Bar indicates exactly where the boundary is — you can buy a drink in Hampshire and enjoy it in West Sussex. It is said that the former kitchen oven was exactly on the boundary and that in 'beating the bounds' of the parish a small boy had to be pushed through it.

Petersfield is a little town at the junction of several main roads, especially busy on market days (Wednesdays and Saturdays). It was formerly a part of the parish of Buriton and became a borough sometime in the twelfth century. The early settlement was centred around the church, which was founded in the early twelfth century. From the sixteenth century the town became increasingly important because of its markets and industries. It had a Merchant Guild similar to the one at Winchester. A sheep market was held in what is now Sheep Street and there was a large cattle market, which helped the development of a leather and cloth industry. It was reported in the late sixteenth century that about 1,000 poor people were working in the clothing trade.

The best houses in Petersfield are Georgian, recalling its heyday as an eighteenth-century country town. The most attractive parts are The Spain, Sheep Street and The Square. The Spain, perhaps named after Spanish merchants who gathered here, is a charming little square with houses of various dates. John Goodyer the naturalist lived in one of them. In The Square is a statue of William III on horseback, incongruously dressed as a Roman.

The church was originally only a chapel of the mother church at Buriton. Founded about 1120, it is one of the best and most interesting Norman churches in the county, retaining its old character in spite of Victorian restoration. For a time it had a central tower and a western tower. The chancel arch is the former eastern arch of the central tower, which was never finished, and above it there are three tall openings separated by clustered shafts, a beautiful piece of work. The west wall of the central tower has been taken down. The aisles embrace the western tower — an unusual feature. There have been no burials since 1860 and all the gravestones except one have been set against the churchyard wall. The exception is that of John Small, who was the last survivor of the early Hambledon Cricket Club members — his epitaph is worth reading. On the east side of the town the boating-lake and golf course are popular amenities; on the heath are several Bronze Age barrows.

The poet Edward Thomas, who was killed in France in 1917, lived

Headley Mill

for a time at **Steep**, a mile north of Petersfield. He came here with his family in 1906 to a house at Ashford Chace (now Berryfield); they moved to The Red House in Cockshott Lane for a while and finally to a cottage in the village. His memorial is on Shoulder of Mutton Hill to the north, reached from Cockshott Lane. The view from the hill is superb; the scenery here is perhaps the most spectacular in Hampshire — with good reason the area has been called 'Little Switzerland'. There is also a memorial window to Edward Thomas in the church, engraved by Laurence Whistler. The church is partly Norman, partly Early English; the chancel floor is of York stone from London Bridge. The Harrow Inn at the foot of the village is a real old English country pub, serving beer from the barrel and home-made food. Bedales School, which moved to Steep in 1900, was the first co-educational public school in England.

There is an old track up the steep face of Stonor Hill, which incredibly was the coach road from Petersfield to Alton and Winchester before the zigzag road was built about 1826. From the top of the hill one can see how the village nestles on the lower slopes of the hangers, and it is not hard to appreciate why Edward Thomas loved this landscape.

South of Petersfield is **Buriton**, a pretty village where the ironstone Norman church overlooks a pond with weeping willows. Buriton Manor House near the church was the home in his younger days of Edward Gibbon, the author of *The Decline and Fall of the Roman Empire*. Here in his father's house he developed the taste for history and books which inspired one of the great works of English literature. After his father's death Gibbon sold Buriton Manor and lived in London and abroad. It is said that the idea for his history came to him one day while musing in the ruins of ancient Rome. He had at one time been an officer in the Hampshire Militia and thus came to know Hampshire well. The parish church has Norman nave arcades, an Early English chancel and a tower arch resting on projecting stone tables — an unusual feature.

Two miles south on the A3 is the entrance to **Queen Elizabeth Country Park**, a 1,400-acre park set in the magnificent landscape of the western end of the South Downs, of which Butser Hill (888ft) is the highest point. The park is managed jointly by the Hampshire County Council and the Forestry Commission and within its boundaries are two wooded hills and one open downland hill. Many countryside activities are carried on within the park without conflicting with the aims of conservation of the landscape and relaxation for the public. Here visitors can enjoy woodland trails and walks in Queen Elizabeth Forest or drive to the summit of War Down, which gives access to the higher parts of the forest.

Beech trees predominate because they tolerate the chalky soil. Before they were planted the only trees were yews, thorns and junipers and these can still be found among the beeches. Constant grazing through the centuries by rabbits and sheep has made the downland a habitat for a wide range of flowers and insects. The forest is an ideal habitat for roe-deer; other animals commonly seen are badgers, foxes, hares, rabbits, squirrels and bats. There are several car-parks, picnic sites and way-marked trails through the forest (booklets at the Park Centre).

The open downland part of the park centred on Butser Hill offers superb views over Hampshire and West Sussex. The hill is grazed by a flock of 200 sheep and in summer visitors can watch demonstrations of sheep husbandry. The marks of ancient man are visible here too — Iron Age field boundaries or lynchets on the lower slopes and defensive works on the summit. Evidence for human occupation of the area in prehistoric times is provided by tools from the neolithic period and the Bronze Age.

The Ancient Farm is a reconstruction of an Iron Age farm of about 300BC and is the most ambitious project of this type yet undertaken. The evidence from excavations and ancient writings has been used as the basis for research into prehistoric agriculture by means of this open-air laboratory. At the farm there are barns, houses, animals and crops that resemble as closely as possible those of the Iron Age, the houses built according to known Iron Age ground plans, the animals descendants of ancient species and the crops those that have been identified by carbonised seeds. The centrepiece is the large conical Iron Age house known as the Pimperne house after the place where an Iron Age site was excavated. The evidence for the shape and size of the house was provided by the post-holes in the ground. Most Iron Age houses would have been much smaller — this one may represent the equivalent of a medieval manor house.

Plants that were grown in the Iron Age are grown here; they include the two main types of prehistoric wheat, emmer and spelt. Though difficult to thresh, these have about twice the protein content of modern wheat, and experiments have shown that the crop yield per acre is almost the equal of today's yield. The herb garden shows

Iron Age Farm in Queen Elizabeth Country Park

the range of plants grown in Britain in prehistoric times that may have proved useful to humans — about 160 species. There is also a small vineyard that demonstrates the methods used by the Romans for growing vines. Animals here include Dexter and West Highland cattle, the nearest modern equivalents to Iron Age cattle, and Soay and Shetland sheep. The Soay sheep from St Kilda are the direct descendants of prehistoric sheep.

The A3 closely follows the old road that in 1710 became the very first turnpike road in Hampshire. Bottom Cottage, not far from the Park Centre, was once a popular inn on the road and is mentioned in *Nicholas Nickleby*.

A left turn off the A3 leads to **Chalton**, a tiny village in the downs, no larger than it was 500 years ago, with a church that is partly Norman, partly Early English. The Red Lion opposite is one of the few genuine old thatched inns in the county, perhaps even the oldest; it probably dates back to the sixteenth century.

On Church Down north of the village a remarkable Anglo-Saxon village was excavated in 1970-6. Few Saxon villages have been completely excavated in Hampshire and this one at Chalton produced some interesting finds. The remains of sixty-one timber build-

Places of Interest in and Around Petersfield and Hambledon

Petersfield
Old market town with fine Norman church (markets Wednesday and Saturday). Heath Pond boating-lake, adjoining the golf course.
Bear Museum, 38 Dragon Street
Doll Museum, 16a Chapel Street

Steep
1 mile north of Petersfield
Beautiful scenery of hills and steep combes. Memorial to Edward Thomas the poet on Shoulder of Mutton Hill.

Queen Elizabeth Country Park
Entrance on the A3, 4 miles south of Petersfield
Hampshire's finest country park, a designated Area of Outstanding Natural Beauty. Woodland and downland walks and trails. Butser Ancient Farm is a reconstruction of an Iron Age farm. Visitor centre with books, information and café.

Butser Hill
Highest point of the South Downs (888ft) in Queen Elizabeth Country Park. Superb views. Iron Age earthworks.

St Hubert's Chapel
Idsworth
2 miles south of Chalton
Isolated Norman church with the best medieval wall-paintings in Hampshire outside Winchester cathedral.

Leigh Park Gardens and Sir George Staunton Country Park
Havant
Beautiful landscaped park with artificial lake and rare Chinese plants. The Ornamental Farm has a collection of animals in a farm founded in 1821.

Denmead Pottery
Forest Road, Denmead
Large pottery works and reject shop. Workshops open to visitors.

Hambledon
Attractive village with an interest-ing church of various architectural styles.

Broadhalfpenny Down
2 miles north-east of Hambledon
A monument opposite The Bat and Ball inn marks the site of the cricket ground of the famous Hambledon Cricket Club.

Old Winchester Hill
National nature reserve, consisting mainly of beech woods, but also yews. Many species of flora and fauna. Iron Age hill-fort with extensive views.

ings were uncovered, and the artefacts found in them date the occupation to the seventh century. The site is in the field adjacent to the south-east corner of Queen Elizabeth Country Park, above the by-road that runs from Buriton to Rowland's Castle.

This seventeenth-century road from Petersfield to Portsmouth follows the east side of Chalton Down to **Idsworth** and St Hubert's chapel, standing in a field, which is thought to date back to Saxon times though the present building is mainly Norman. Disused in the nineteenth century, it escaped restoration, so it still has its old pulpit and pews. Its importance lies in its early fourteenth-century wall-paintings, the best preserved in Hampshire after those in Winchester cathedral. They depict scenes from the lives of St Hubert and St John the Baptist. But for the occasional passing train there would be no more peaceful spot in Hampshire than this.

Sir George Staunton Country Park lies between Rowland's Castle and Havant, on the west side of the B2149. It is one of the few landscaped parks protected as a conservation area, a fine recreational park with a terrace, artificial lake, woodland walks and rare Chinese plants originally introduced by Sir George Staunton, a Far East traveller. His aim was to produce a park with pleasure-grounds that would reflect aspects of the China he knew so well. Many species of plants from China were introduced to Great Britain at Leigh Park. The gardens were the result of many years of work to re-create an eighteenth-century-style landscaped park. The second Leigh Park House (1863) was demolished in 1959. Most of the estate had been bought by Portsmouth City Council to build Leigh Park, one of the largest council house estates in Great Britain. The present North Gardens or Leigh Park Gardens were begun in 1821 and took 15-20 years to complete; the site of the second Leigh Park House is near the terrace. The site of the first Leigh Park House is in the South Gardens; here also is the Ornamental Farm, which has one of the best collections of farm animals and poultry in England, with several rare breeds.

The B2149 goes north to **Horndean**, where Gale's old brewery makes the famous Horndean Special Bitter. A lane goes on to **Catherington** with its late twelfth-century hilltop church and tomb of Admiral Sir Charles Napier (1786-1860). He lived at Merchistoun Hall, on Portsmouth Road at Horndean. Also here is the family tomb of the Kean family — Charles Kean, actor son of the famous Edmund Kean, and his wife the actress Ellen Tree. Catherington House was the home of Admiral Hood. Catherington Down is of interest to plant students with its typical downland flora.

The A3 leads to **Waterlooville**, named after an inn called The

Heroes of Waterloo, and from there the B2150 leads to Denmead. Denmead Pottery factory, one of the most modern in Europe, is open every day.

Three miles on is **Hambledon**, famous for cricket. The village lies in a downland valley, its focus the short High Street leading to the church. Here in 1256 the first market was probably held and sometime in the early seventeenth century Hambledon became a market town. It is only a village now, but an attractive one with an old-world air about it.

The church is an amalgam of many periods, having been enlarged more than once through the centuries. In many ways it is one of the most interesting churches in the county, for it could well be used as a textbook example of how an English parish church has been altered and extended from Saxon to late medieval times. Evidence of its Saxon origin is provided by the pilaster strips on the outer faces of the arcade walls, which would then have been the exterior walls of the Saxon nave. On the hillside north of the village is one of the largest vineyards in England; it produces two well-known blended wines.

English cricket, after humble beginnings, came of age on **Broadhalfpenny Down** (Broadhalfpenny was the toll paid to the lord of the manor for setting up a booth at the twice-yearly fair). The Hambledon Cricket Club, formed about 1750, soon became the leading club in England and the sport's accepted authority, though surprisingly cricket remained an illegal sport until 1845. The club finally ended its days in 1796. Its greatest moment came in 1777 when it defeated All-England at Sevenoaks by an innings and 168 runs! A monument opposite The Bat and Ball public house, 2 miles northeast of the village, marks the site of the club's ground from 1750 to 1787, and shows the curved bats and two stumps in use in those days.

Three miles north is **Old Winchester Hill**, a national nature reserve extending over the chalk downland and its wooded combes. There are few areas of chalk grassland of comparable size that exhibit such a variety of habitats. To birds and plants it offers chalk downs, thorn scrub, juniper scrub, yew wood and beech wood. Two of the only three native conifers in Britain, the juniper and the yew, grow here naturally (the third is the Scots pine), and whereas the yew is widespread (the Hampshire 'weed') the juniper is comparatively rare in southern England. The scrub is of great interest because of its variety; hawthorn predominates, with buckthorn, dogwood and

St Hubert's chapel, Idsworth

whitebeam. The yews harbour goldcrests, Britain's smallest birds. Forty-five different birds are known to nest here; the skylark, kestrel and sparrow-hawk are commonly seen. Thirty species of butterfly and fourteen species of orchid have been recorded.

An Iron Age hill-fort crowns the summit of the hill, defended by a single rampart and ditch and guarded by entrances east and west. Dating probably from the second century BC it commands extensive views; it may have been the tribal centre of this region. The origin of the name 'Old Winchester Hill' is not known.

East Meon is beautifully situated near the source of the Meon, which flows through the village. The Norman church sited close to the hillside is one of the finest in Hampshire and has a splendid tower of about 1150. The font is one of the seven black Tournai fonts in England. The carvings on it include *Creation of Adam* and *Expulsion from Paradise*. The stained glass in the east window depicts the patron saints of all the Allied countries that took part in World War I. The north transept was once a day-school and a Sunday school and it is worth noting that 160 children attended the latter in the early nineteenth century. The old Court House opposite the church dates from about 1400. From East Meon one can return westwards to Winchester or eastwards to Petersfield.

5

THE NORTH-EAST

One would hesitate to recommend a visit to **Basingstoke** for there is nothing attractive about the town and very little of historical interest remains. Drastic redevelopment has completely destroyed the character of the former old country town with housing estates of depressing uniformity. Yet its museum is worth a visit and its traffic-free shopping centre is one of the best in Hampshire; the perceptive visitor will even find a few old buildings in unlikely places.

Evidence of settlement in the Basingstoke area in the Iron Age has been found at Rucstalls Hill and Winklebury, and remains of buildings of the Saxon period have been found at Cowdery's Down. The king himself held Basingstoke at the time of the Domesday survey, which recorded three mills and a market there. The mills would probably have been situated on the River Loddon, which rises at Basingstoke. Settlement was no doubt influenced by ancient roads, the Roman road from Winchester to Silchester passing to the west (it forms the limit of the present built-up area) and the Harrow Way passing to the south (that part of it still named Harrow Way is also the limit of the built-up area and its continuation is named Pack Way).

Basingstoke has been an important market centre since medieval times; it became a borough in 1622 when James I granted a charter that recognised it as a free corporate body and gave it a weekly market and a fair twice a year. In 1641 another charter gave the town a mayor, seven aldermen and seven burgesses, but although the system of government was changed power was still held by a small group of families. By the end of the seventeenth century Basingstoke was a prosperous and well-established market town. In those days its industry was centred on the wool trade; today, much varied light industry flourishes with the help of 'overspill' population from London. The town has been growing since World War I, but in the last 30 years it has become the fastest-growing town in Western Europe; its population rose from 17,000 in 1951 to 67,000 in 1981.

Most main roads in north-east Hampshire converge on Basingstoke. The visitor may be confused at first by the ring-road system but will find plenty of car-parks in the town centre.

The parish church of St Michael the Archangel is uncomfortably near the new shopping centre. Its oldest part is the fourteenth-century St Stephen's chapel and its chief treasure is a beautiful Flemish painting of 1549. There are few important Perpendicular parish churches in Hampshire and St Michael's is perhaps the best of them, even though it has been over-restored. The nave, aisles and tower date from about 1520, with typical four-light windows of that date; the two-storeyed porch is a little later (1539). The chancel is earlier, rebuilt in 1464-5, and has its original timber roof. Sir Charles Nicholson built the memorial chapel in 1920.

In the cemetery near the railway station stand the ruins of the thirteenth-century Holy Ghost chapel and the sixteenth-century Holy Trinity chapel, forlornly picturesque in their wooded setting. All that remains of the Holy Ghost chapel is its ruined flint tower with a later doorway. The Guild of the Holy Ghost was a religious body equivalent to a modern friendly society; its members built the chapel on the hill to the north of the town about 1214-44 after the burial ground there had been consecrated. The Holy Trinity chapel was built by Lord Sandys about 1520 adjoining the chancel of the Holy Ghost chapel; it is known to have had a fine painted roof and stained-glass windows. During the Civil War both chapels suffered much damage and became derelict.

Other buildings of note in the town are Deane's Almshouse (1608) in London Street, the Old Town Hall (1832) and the Corn Exchange (1864). All Saints church in Victoria Street is an impressive and richly furnished building of 1915 designed by Temple Moore, probably the best twentieth-century church in Hampshire and a great improvement on anything built in the late Victorian period.

The Willis Museum was founded by a local archaeologist and watchmaker; his fine collection of clocks is now part of the timekeeping display, which includes a rare sixteenth-century Nuremberg clock-watch. The exhibits in this horological collection include many early clocks and watches, longcase clocks, curious clocks, clock and watchmaking tools and the old clock mechanisms from Basingstoke and Stockbridge town halls. In the museum there are many fascinating items relating to Basingstoke's history, especially over the last 200 years. The displays depict the history of the local banks, police, fire brigade, trade and industry, education and the Salvation Army riots of 1880-2. In those riots the Salvation Army was subjected to assault and abuse and many of its members were seriously injured for preaching against alcohol. Other exhibits in the museum include embroideries and samplers dating from 1625, and what is thought to be the oldest post-box in the country. Other displays feature the natural history of the Basingstoke area, the Basingstoke Canal and the archaeology of the county.

The Viables Craft Centre in Harrow Way (left turn leaving the ✳ town on the A30 going west) is a community of workshops where one can watch craftsmen at work and buy their products. The crafts include gold, wood, pottery, textiles, glass, engraving and framing.

Cliddesden railway station, a mile to the south, was on the Basingstoke to Alton line, opened in 1901 and closed to passengers in 1932. Its overgrown site lies at the first bend of the left fork beyond the parish church. The station (renamed 'Buggleskelly') was used in 1937 for scenes in the classic film comedy *Oh! Mr Porter* starring Will Hay. The platform can be seen in the undergrowth; elsewhere much of this line has disappeared completely. This railway line was officially a 'light' railway, which meant that it could dispense with certain operating requirements. It was the first line to be sanctioned under the Light Railways Act of 1896. There were only three intermediate stations, at Cliddesden, Herriard, and Bentworth and Lasham. The line's short life was interrupted when the track was taken up in 1916 for use in the war in France. It was not reopened until 1924, so its working life was restricted to a total of 23 years. In 1928 near Bentworth and Lasham station a spectacular crash between a train and a lorry was staged for a scene in the film *The Wrecker*.

A right turn off the B3046 leads to **Dummer**; its name means 'mere or lake by a hill', but there is no water now on these chalky uplands. The interesting little church in this pretty village has a chancel dating from about 1200 and a gallery that overhangs very nearly half the nave. The rood canopy above the chancel arch is intact and is the only surviving example in Hampshire; there are very few in England. The pulpit of about 1380 is the oldest in Hampshire and is one of only six of fourteenth-century date in the country. Preachers who have used this pulpit include the famous George Whitefield, an early follower of the Wesleys. A charity board in the church gives details of the foundation of Dummer school in 1610; it was situated in Up Street and was closed down only in 1971. Near The Queen Inn is the village well with its extraordinary wooden tread-wheel.

A left turn at the A30 and a right turn at The Wheatsheaf, a famous old coaching inn on the London to Exeter road, takes one via North Waltham to **Steventon**, the birthplace of Jane Austen. The site of the rectory where she lived is marked by a water-pump in the field at the junction of the lane to the church. The pump probably stood outside the kitchen. The house, demolished in 1826, was bounded by one of the thatched mud walls that were once common in the county.

Jane Austen must have walked along this lane on Sundays to attend the services conducted by her father, the vicar. Her brother James, who succeeded their father as vicar, is buried in the church-yard; he died 2 years after Jane. Her nephew William Knight, who was rector for 50 years, is also buried there.

There is part of a Saxon cross in the church and several memorials to the Austen family including one to William Knight's three daughters, aged 5, 4 and 3, who all died of scarlet fever in the same year. Jane would undoubtedly recognise this lonely lane today, even though she might not recognize the village itself with its railway bridge and embankment. Jane Austen left here with her family to live at Bath; when she returned to Hampshire she lived at Southampton and then at Chawton.

At **Deane**, 2 miles north, there is a splendid Gothic Revival church, built in 1818. It will not be open, but a walk to the church gives one a close view of the beautiful seventeenth-century Deane House.

The River Test rises in a meadow on the north side of the Overton road at Ashe, at the start of its long journey to the sea. Overton was one of the Bishop of Winchester's new planned towns of about 1200 and was, like Alresford, separated from the old village by a river. It was an important sheep and wool trade centre; the present Winchester Street was the principal market street where the annual fair was held every July. Overton was famous for its sheep fair and as many as 18,000 sheep were once penned in the market on fair day. The main industry today is paper-making for Bank of England notes at Quidhampton; in the nineteenth century it was silk-making at the

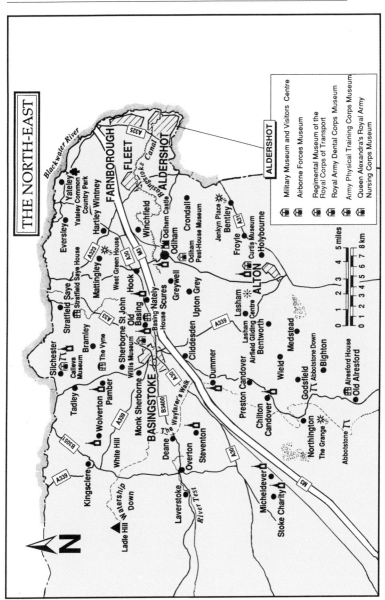

THE NORTH-EAST

N

ALDERSHOT

🏛 Military Museum and Visitors Centre

🏛 Airborne Forces Museum

🏛 Regimental Museum of the
    Royal Corps of Transport

🏛 Royal Army Dental Corps Museum

🏛 Army Physical Training Corps Museum

🏛 Queen Alexandra's Royal Army
    Nursing Corps Museum

local mills. Overton was on the London to Exeter coach road and the White Hart Hotel was a favourite stop for coaches. The church north of the river has Norman arcades and a thirteenth-century chancel. The Town Mill, mentioned in *Domesday Book*, was rebuilt in 1900. It cannot be said that Overton is as attractive or as thriving as it must have been in its old coaching days.

Further along the valley is **Laverstoke**, where Henri Portal, a refugee from France, established a paper-making mill on the River Test in 1712. This picturesque weatherboarded mill (Bere Mill) still stands on the river between Laverstoke and Whitchurch. The clear iron-free water of chalk streams such as the Test was ideal for paper-making. Portal was so successful that in 1719 he moved to a new mill in Laverstoke. Here the Bank of England notepaper was made from 1724 to 1950; it is now made at Overton. The present Laverstoke mill dates only from 1881.

Laverstoke church is Victorian; hidden away across the main road at Freefolk is the old church of St Nicholas, partly fifteenth century and restored in 1703. The curious half-thatched cottages on the main road are almshouses, built in 1939 by Portals in an Arts and Crafts style; they could be mistaken for much older houses. The wooded valley of the Test here is attractive.

White Hill, north of Overton on the B3051, is on the crest of the high chalk escarpment, where a superb view unfolds across the low-lying clay country to the Berkshire Downs in the distance. From here one can follow the Wayfarer's Walk west to Watership Down, the setting of Richard Adams's classic animal story of that name. Many places nearby on the downs and in the valley feature in his book. These downs have long been a training-ground for the horse-racing stables in Kingsclere. Seven Derby winners were trained here in the nineteenth century.

Further on is **Ladle Hill**, which has the best example in England of an unfinished Iron Age hill-fort. The uncompleted ditch and the piles of chalk dug from it have provided valuable evidence of the techniques used in the construction of hill-forts.

Kingsclere lies at the foot of the chalk scarp. Before the Norman Conquest it was an important royal estate, hence its name. By the twelfth century it had a market, probably at the junction of Swan Street and George Street. Swan Street has some attractive old houses, and The Old Brewery and The Old Mill in Pope's Hill recall former industries. There were once four mills on the small stream that flows through Kingsclere; three of them survive but are not mills any longer.

The spacious church is partly Norman, but Victorian restoration has not dealt too kindly with it. Its weather-vane is in the shape of a bed-bug or louse; legend has it that King John sent it as a gift after spending a night at the monks' unhygienic quarters. There is a splendid monument to Sir Henry Kingsmill and his wife (1670). This type of memorial, with recumbent effigies, was becoming quite rare by this date and was soon discontinued altogether until revived in the nineteenth century.

At **Wolverton**, on the road to Basingstoke, the red-brick church of 1717 is considered to be the best early Georgian church in Hampshire; few churches were built at that time. Its handsome tower dwarfs the nave; all the fittings inside are original and give the church a marked period atmosphere. Strangely the church is of cruciform plan, a reversion to medieval design, but the plain character of the building conforms with early eighteenth-century ideas of worship. The only unfortunate alteration was the restoration of the windows in 1872.

A recommended tour north of Basingstoke starts at **Monk Sherborne**, approached from the A339 or the A340. It has an early Norman church, but the 'Monk' in the village name comes from the priory or monastery at **Pamber**, 2 miles further on, which was founded in the reign of Henry I as a cell of Cerisy Abbey in Normandy. It was dissolved in 1414 and now belongs to Queen's College, Oxford. The remains of the priory church consist of the austerely beautiful chancel and the massive tower. The Early English chancel is perhaps the best of that period in Hampshire; it dates from about 1220 and has slender lancet windows. Pamber Forest was opened to the public in 1980 as a nature reserve. An ancient oak woodland, it is noted for its rare flowers and insects.

Tadley is Hampshire's newest town and consists mostly of large new housing estates. In the old village is the 'Old Meeting' United Reformed church of 1718-19, an early nonconformist chapel. The old church of St Peter is situated about one mile west of the old village; it has a tower of 1685 and a splendid unrestored interior, including a rare Commonwealth-period pulpit. The great industry in Tadley in former days was broom-making, using birch trees from Pamber Forest; at one time 100,000 were made annually.

Three miles east is **Silchester**, the Roman town of *Calleva Atre-*

Pamber Priory

batum. Soon after the Roman Conquest the tribal centre of the Atrebates was fortified and it became one of the most important towns of Roman Britain. The town was thoroughly excavated between 1890 and 1909 and the foundations of hundreds of buildings were exposed, including what was probably the earliest Christian church in Britain.

Unlike most other Roman towns in Britain *Calleva* was completely abandoned and never built over again, so the remains were not hidden by Saxon or medieval occupation. In the centre of the

The Vyne

town was a forum, an open square lined with shops on three sides, and a basilica, the equivalent of our town hall, on the fourth side. The earliest houses in the town were probably built of timber and daub, and later replaced by ones with flint and mortar walls, tiled roofs and glass windows. The building thought to be a Christian church had a nave and aisles with an apse on the west and a porch on the east, but it has features also found in pagan temples.

A footpath crosses the site but nothing of the town is visible now, though the lines of the streets can often be seen in summer as crop marks. They appear as yellow lines or as stunted growth, because crops or grass will not grow as high directly above walls and streets as above ditches and fields. Much of the late third-century wall that enclosed the town still stands and the amphitheatre, which had wooden seats for spectators, can be seen outside the east corner. The amphitheatre was built in the first century AD and was later reconstructed with a flint retaining wall. It could hold between 5,000 and 9,000 spectators and was used for sports and games, not as a theatre. The Calleva Museum at Silchester Common has a pictorial display of the history of the Roman town and is worth a visit, but most of the finds from the site are in Reading Museum.

The parish church stands just within the walls near the former east gate; it was built about 1180-1200 and is largely unrestored. Its plan is rather unusual — a long chancel and a short nave with aisles. It has thirteenth-century wall-paintings, a fourteenth-century tomb effigy and a magnificent old organ of about 1770, partially rebuilt. There were six rectors in 1349, an indication of the tragic consequences of the Black Death.

Three miles south is **Bramley**, a scattered village with a few good houses. Its exceptionally interesting church is noteworthy for its remarkable wall-paintings, which include a thirteenth- century depiction of the murder of Thomas Becket and a large fifteenth-century St Christopher. The furnishings include a gallery of 1735, ancient bench-ends and a fifteenth-century screen with five-light divisions. The medieval stained glass includes some English and some of the Liège school.

One mile south of Bramley is **The Vyne**, a graceful Tudor mansion considered by many people to be the most beautiful house in Hampshire. It was built between 1500 and 1520 for William Sandys, who became Henry VIII's Lord Chamberlain. In 1653 the estate was sold to Chaloner Chute, Speaker of the House of Commons in 1659. Chute altered the house to make each of the main fronts symmetrical, and the architect John Webb added to the north front a classical portico, the earliest example in England, which enhances the beauty of the Tudor building. Chute's descendants maintained the house in style and accumulated its tasteful paintings and furniture; it was bequeathed to the National Trust in 1956.

The house is open on certain days and should not be missed. On the ground floor is the late Gothic chapel, one of the finest private chapels in England; its contemporary stained-glass windows have no equal for brilliance of colour and clarity. The rare early sixteenth-century encaustic tiles were found in the grounds of the house. The tomb-chest of Chaloner Chute was designed by John Chute more than 100 years after the former's death; it is one of the best monuments of the late eighteenth century in England. Upstairs in the Oak Gallery the walls have sixteenth-century linenfold panels, beautifully carved. The park with its lake and gardens, though small, makes an attractive setting for the house.

At the village of **Sherborne St John**, named after the St John family, the church has many old furnishings and monuments. In the Brocas chapel is the imposing tomb of Ralph Pexall (1535), and the brass memorial to one of the Brocas family dated 1360 is the oldest brass in Hampshire. The sixteenth-century Dutch stained glass, depicting scenes on the theme of 'public humiliation', is the best of that date in the county. Note the memorial to George Beverly 'Erected in the 29th yeare of King Charles ye 2nd 1678' — put up by an ardent Royalist who refused to recognise the Commonwealth!

En route to Stratfield Saye on the A33 from Basingstoke a diversion can be made to Hartley Wespall. The church here has one extraordinary surviving feature, the massive diamond-shaped timber construction dating from the early fourteenth century exposed in the exterior west wall; nothing quite like it exists in any other church.

A left turn at the Wellington Arms Hotel on the A33 leads to **Stratfield Saye House** and passes the driveway to the parish church, which was built in 1754-8 in the shape of a Greek cross. Its original furniture gives it a genuine Georgian atmosphere; the Duke of Wellington used the manorial pew for over 30 years.

After the Battle of Waterloo a grateful nation voted the Duke of Wellington a large sum of money to purchase an estate, and in 1817 he chose Stratfield Saye. The house had been built in about 1630 and since then the interior has been remodelled several times. Wellington at first intended to pull the house down, but finally came to terms with it by installing central heating and water-closets and adding two outer wings. The house is full of priceless relics of the duke's life, his campaigns and his funeral, including his funeral carriage, surely one of the most remarkable vehicles ever manufactured. Many of the books in the library were acquired from Napoleon himself. An exhibition of the events of Wellington's life is in one of the stable-blocks. The pleasure-grounds contain many rare trees, most of them planted by the first duke; the Wellingtonias were named in his honour when introduced to England in 1853. Copenhagen, Wellington's horse at Waterloo, who died at the age of 28, is buried in the park.

East of Stratfield Saye is **Wellington Country Park**, centred on a lake where sailing, wind-surfing and fishing can be enjoyed. Among other attractions at the park is the National Dairy Museum, which has items illustrating the history of dairying.

The impressive **Wellington Monument** on the A33 at Heckfield Heath was erected in 1833. At Highfield House, near the church at **Heckfield**, Neville Chamberlain died in 1940, only 6 months after resigning as Prime Minister. Bramshill House, which was built in

1605-12 and is situated to the east, is occupied by a police college and is not open to the public.

A by-road north of Bramshill leads to **Eversley**, where Charles Kingsley, the famous author, was vicar from 1844 to 1875. He gave 30 years devoted service to his parish and yet found time to write many books, including such classics as *Westward Ho!* and *The Water-Babies*. He is buried in the churchyard; the rectory where he lived and wrote his books is nearby.

Kingsley spent much of his life trying to improve the lot of the poor and many of his books include ideas for social reform. He taught his parishioners to read, helped with the harvest and tended the sick. Many famous people from all walks of life attended his funeral. The wrought-iron gates of the Charles Kingsley school are a memorial to him; they incorporate figures of Tom in *The Water-Babies*.

Also buried at Eversley is John James, a leading architect of the early eighteenth century, who lived at nearby Warbrook and probably redesigned the church. The effigy of Dame Marianne Cope (1862) illustrates in detail the dress of that date and her monument has Renaissance-style ornament.

Yateley is now a town of some 20,000 people. It began to expand in the nineteenth century with the building of large houses near the village centre and these in turn have given way to post-war housing estates. The parish church suffered a disastrous fire in 1979 but the tower, one of the best timber towers in the county, fortunately escaped serious damage.

♣ **Yateley Common Country Park** straddles the A30 near the Blackwater River, which here forms the county boundary. This 500-acre common has many beautiful and colourful spots, especially in autumn when the heather blooms and the trees change colour. It does not lack variety either, with gorse thickets, oak and birch woods, ponds, bogs and Hawley Lake. It is a good place for bird-watchers; the Dartford warbler breeds here. There is a picnic area and a nature trail (round Wyndham's Pool), and fishing is allowed by permit. Wyndham's Pool is an artificial lake — an eighteenth-century fishpond reservoir — and is a favourite breeding place of dragon-flies. The cottages here, known as Brandy Bottom, may have got their name from smuggling activities on the common.

Beyond Hartford Bridge Flats and Blackbushe Airport is **Hartley Wintney**, important as a coach stop after the turnpike road was

Kingsley memorial gate, Eversley

opened in 1767. The railway killed the coach trade and now the M3 has taken through traffic away from the village. The commons and greens in and around the village, rather than its buildings, give Hartley Wintney its character. The rows of oak trees on The Common were planted by the lady of the manor after the Napoleonic Wars in order to provide timber for the Navy, but with the invention of iron ships the timber was not needed so the trees remain to enhance the beauty of the village. In St Mary's churchyard are the graves of two soldiers — Field Marshal Alanbrooke, Churchill's right-hand man in World War II, and General 'Hangman' Hawley, an eighteenth-century soldier of unenviable reputation.

The church at **Mattingley**, a quietly attractive village 3 miles north-west, is unusual in being completely timber-framed with brick infilling, which has given rise to unfounded suggestions that it was originally a barn or moot hall. There is much timber-work in the old houses in this area, stone in the past having been at a premium.

South of Mattingley via the beautiful Dipley Mill on the River Whitewater is the garden at **West Green House**, owned by the National Trust and open to visitors. A beautiful informal walled garden with lawns, flowering shrubs and herbaceous borders, it is well worth a visit. There are several 'follies' here, including a Doric lodge, a shell grotto and Chinese cowsheds. The house was once the home of the unloved General Hawley.

Winchfield church is found by crossing the A30 and taking a left turn on the B3016. One of the best Norman churches in the county, its most striking feature is the chancel arch, and it has an old pulpit and seats.

Odiham is one of the most attractive villages in Hampshire. Its name (from *wudiga-hamm*) means 'wooded land'. Its High Street, on a par with Alresford's Broad Street and Fareham's High Street, has many attractive Georgian and earlier houses, some with timber-framing, which was usual before the local bricks came into general use in the eighteenth century. The medieval street plan and some buildings in the town have remained unchanged for perhaps 400 years. Fortunately the whole of medieval Odiham has been designated a Conservation Area. Odiham has been an important settlement since Norman times; Parliament met here in 1303. In 1086 Odiham had eight mills and four churches and its population of about 250 was the second largest in Hampshire after Winchester. Its royal palace was superseded by the castle at North Warnborough.

The large Perpendicular church with its seventeenth-century tower dominates the village. Features of interest inside include brasses (the oldest dates from 1400), seventeenth-century galleries and pulpit, a hand-cart for coffins, a 'Breeches' Bible of about 1578 and a hudd (a vicar's funeral shelter).

In The Bury are the whipping-post and stocks, which in 1376 were ordered to be set up in every town and village. Nearby are the almshouses of 1623; the pest-house of about the same date, built to house and isolate those suffering from the plague, is now a small museum.

On Sundays at Colt Hill Bridge the narrow boat *John Pinkerton* takes visitors for $2^1/_2$-hour trips on the **Basingstoke Canal**. All profits go towards the current restoration of the canal; refreshments are available on board or at the old Water Witch public house by the bridge. The $37^1/_2$-mile canal was built between 1788 and 1794 from Weybridge to Basingstoke as part of a scheme to link London with Southampton and the Bristol Channel, but the vital connecting canals were never started. Hence the canal served only the small town of Basingstoke and it was never a commercial success. The last boat completed the journey in 1914. The tow-path walk with its constantly changing scenery and vegetation offers a rare opportunity for bird-watching and pike-fishing; the canal is an important freshwater wildlife habitat. It has become a slow-flowing river fed by springs inside the Greywell tunnel; as it flows east it passes over soils that become more acid, with consequent changes in its flora and fauna.

The picturesque village street at **Greywell**, 2 miles west, with its seventeeth-century brick cottages, looks down on the River Whitewater flowing close by the Norman church, which has a pre-Reformation rood-loft.

The collapse of the Greywell tunnel roof in 1932 finally sealed the fate of the Basingstoke Canal; the tunnel entrance can be seen from the tow-path in the village. The tunnel is the most important bat-roost in Great Britain; it has been estimated that there are about 2,000 bats of five different species living in the tunnel, including Natterer's bats and Daubenton's or water-bats, which feed on the canal insects. A half-mile walk along the canal is the ruined **Odiham Castle**, one of the only two octagonal keeps in England; its bailey was cut through by the canal. The castle was built in the thirteenth century for King John, who is said to have set out from here for his historic meeting at Runnymede. David Bruce, King of Scotland, was imprisoned here for 2 years. The castle became derelict in the fifteenth century and only the ruined keep survives.

A right turn at Up Nately, 2 miles north-west, takes one over the M3 to the tiny church of St Swithun at **Nately Scures**. This is the smallest church in use in Hampshire, the nave being only 30ft long, and is one of the very few Norman single-cell aisleless apsidal churches in England. The fine Norman doorway is a striking feature, and a grimly humorous note is provided by four memorial tablets in the nave in the shape of the suits of a pack of cards.

No ancient monument in Hampshire is more steeped in history than the ruins of **Basing House**. Here within the enormous earthworks of a medieval castle stood the largest private house in Tudor England, built by William Paulet, first Marquess of Winchester. Known as Old House, it had been rebuilt in 1531, and later New House was built adjoining it.

Basing House was besieged in the Civil War, but led by the fifth marquess the defenders managed to hold out for over 2 years in one of the longest sieges in English history.

The siege commenced in earnest in 1643; the house was defended

Places of Interest in and Around Basingstoke

Parish Church of St Michael
Fourteenth-century St Stephen's
chapel and Flemish painting of
1549.

All Saints Church
Victoria Street
Probably the best twentieth-
century church in Hampshire.

**The Willis Museum
and Art Gallery**
Old Town Hall, Market Place
History and natural history of the
Basingstoke area. Fine collection
of clocks, watches and sundials.

Viables Craft Centre
Harrow Way
Crafts centre where local crafts-
men can be seen at work.

Steventon
Site of the rectory, Jane Austen's
birthplace.
St Nicholas's church — memorials
to the Austen family.

Watership Down
2 miles south-west of Kingsclere
The setting of Richard Adams's
classic story.

Ladle Hill
1 mile west of Watership Down
Fine example of an unfinished Iron
Age hill-fort.

Silchester (English Heritage)
Site of the Roman town of *Calleva
Atrebatum*. Roman walls and
amphitheatre. Calleva Museum
with pictorial display.

The Vyne (National Trust)
Sherborne St John
Beautiful Tudor mansion with park,
lake and gardens.

Stratfield Saye House
8 miles north-east of Basingstoke
Seventeenth-century house bought
by the Duke of Wellington in 1817.
The rooms contain countless relics
and treasures of his life and
campaigns.

Wellington Country Park
2 miles east of Stratfield Saye
Lake with sailing, wind-surfing and
fishing. Adventure playground,
fitness course, farm, nature trails.
National Dairy Museum.

The Wellington Monument,
Heckfield Heath
Once stood at Hyde Park Corner;
re-erected here in 1885.

Eversley
3 miles north of Hartley Wintney
Charles Kingsley was vicar here
from 1844 to 1875.

Yateley Common Country Park
3 miles north-west of Farnborough
Picnic area, nature trail, fishing,
Hawley Lake. A good place for
bird-watching.

West Green House
(National Trust)
2 miles west of Hartley Wintney
Beautiful small walled garden with
lawns, flowering shrubs and
herbaceous borders.

Odiham
High Street, All Saints church,
stocks and whipping-post in The
Bury. Pest-house on the south side
of the churchyard is now a
museum.

Basingstoke Canal
Constructed 1788-94. Boat trips
available at Colt Hill Bridge,
Odiham, on Sundays.

Odiham Castle
North Warnborough
Ruined keep of a thirteenth-
century castle. Unusual octagonal
keep.

Basing House
Redbridge Lane, Old Basing
Ruins of the great Tudor house
besieged for over 2 years by the
Parliamentarians in the Civil War.
Tithe barn and Tudor garden walls.

The Basingstoke Canal at Crookham Village

Odiham Castle

by eleven mounted guns and 500 men armed with muskets. Over the next 2 years periods of heavy fighting alternated with periods of relief when parties of Royalists managed to get through with supplies. Many of the garrison deserted, including all the non-Catholics, and many died of disease. Finally in October 1645 the house was captured by Cromwell himself and many defenders were killed. The fifth marquess was imprisoned but later was allowed to go to France. Among those captured were Inigo Jones, the famous architect, and Wenceslaus Hollar the engraver.

After its capture by Cromwell the house was destroyed by bombardment and fire, but today one can get some idea of its former size and glory from a study of its extensive foundations. An exhibition at the Lodge House recounts the history of the house.

Fortunate survivals of the battle are the medieval tithe barn, one of the best in England, and the Tudor garden walls with their dovecots. In medieval times pigeons were a valuable source of food in winter.

The attractive village of **Old Basing** is worth a visit too; it was once a more important place than Basingstoke. Its only drawback is the noise from the main line railway, which crosses the village on an embankment. There are many old cottages and the former workhouse is near the church. There are four Paulet tombs in the church; those of the first marquess and second marquess have Renaissance details. There are remains of Norman work in the church, which was severely damaged in the Civil War and restored. One of the most handsome churches in the county, it is mainly early sixteenth-century Perpendicular, built in mellow brick with stone dressings.

Aldershot, in the far north-east of the county, is the 'home' of the British Army and the largest military camp in Britain. It should be visited even by those not particularly interested in military matters, for it provides a unique opportunity to study the history and activities of the Army at home and abroad.

Before the creation of the camp, the first military town in Britain since Roman times, Aldershot was only a picturesque village consisting of church, manor house and farms, on the edge of a vast expanse of wild heathland. The government of the day decided that this heath would be ideal for military training. In 1854 it purchased 10,000 acres and work began on the first permanent camp of wooden huts. Since then the camp has been continually developed and modernised; though the area is today about the same, the population has increased a hundredfold. A whole day can be spent in and around Aldershot; there are eight museums to visit including two just over the border in Surrey.

At the Aldershot Military Museum and Visitors Centre in Queen's Avenue, where details are available of all the museums and of the military town trail, there is a chronological display of the history of Aldershot camp and a reconstruction of a typical barrack-room of about 1900. The displays illustrate, with photographs and models, the development of the camp since it was first constructed in 1856-9. The first rebuilding took place in 1881-1900, when brick bungalows were erected; the museum occupies one of them. There is a section on military aviation and a Canadian gallery.

When visiting the museums in the barracks areas on foot or by car be prepared to produce evidence of your identity (eg driving-licence) or to complete a form with your name and address, to allow your car to be searched and to be escorted from the car-park to the museum. This part of Aldershot is subject to strict military security.

The Airborne Forces Museum depicts the story of airborne forces from 1940 to 1982, including German and United States forces, and covers all the major campaigns and battles, illustrated by documents, photographs and maps. It contains a large collection of model aircraft, memorabilia, weapons and medals. Special exhibits include World War II gliders, an Arnhem cameo, a diorama of airborne operations and a Dakota aircraft.

The Regimental Museum of the Royal Corps of Transport illustrates the history of Army transport from the Royal Waggoners of 1794 to the present-day Transport Corps. The exhibits include a Waterloo jacket worn by a soldier of the Royal Waggon Train and a collection of military train badges. There are special displays of the Battle of Rorke's Drift and of both world wars.

The Army Physical Training Corps Museum traces the evolution of Army physical training from its beginnings in 1860. It contains early equipment, items used in the Olympic Games and displays of physical training and 'tough tactics' centres.

The Royal Army Dental Corps Museum illustrates the links of dentistry with the Army. Soldiers once needed strong teeth in order to bite through paper cartridges when loading muskets. The Dental Corps was formed in 1921. The museum contains documents, uniforms, medals, dental chairs, the death-mask of Himmler and early dental instruments including a tooth-key that was used to extract

Napoleon's teeth.

Queen Alexandra's Royal Army Nursing Corps Museum, on the site of Queen Victoria's Royal Pavilion, outlines the history of Army nursing from its earliest days, with a medal collection and personal items from the Crimean War. There is also Florence Nightingale's Russian-built carriage, her silver communion service and letters written by her on the subject of Army nursing.

The Prince Consort's Library of 1859-60 with its marvellous collection of military books and maps is also open to the public.

Aldershot (the name has been spelt in nineteen different ways since 1248!) became a borough in 1922. The parish church, though enlarged in 1865, retains its twelfth-century Lady Chapel and sixteenth-century tower. Nearby is Manor Park House, built in 1670. In the Heroes' Garden in Manor Park is the Heroes' Shrine, the national memorial to those killed in World War II, and the rockeries are composed of stones from bomb-damaged buildings. The Basingstoke Canal can be followed all the way through Aldershot; about half a mile east of Gasworks Bridge you will be at the easternmost point of Hampshire. Aldershot town is largely Victorian; its High Street once had shops on one side and barracks on the other. The Aldershot of pre-Army days lies to the south-east of the railway station.

Aldershot and Farnborough together now form the Borough of Rushmoor, named after the arena where the famous military tattoos were held between the wars. First held in 1894, at the height of their popularity these annual displays were each attended by half a million people.

As Aldershot is the birthplace of the modern Army, so **Farnborough** is the birthplace of British military aviation. Here at Laffan's Plain in 1908 Samuel Cody made the first official powered flight in Britain. A metal replica tree commemorates the flight but can be seen only when the Farnborough Air Show is held. His Majesty's Balloon Factory was then responsible for the development of aircraft; it became the Royal Aircraft Factory in 1912 and the Royal Aircraft Establishment in 1918.

Farnborough is an unlikely place to be associated with French royalty but the Empress Eugénie came to live at Farnborough Hill in 1881; she died in 1920. The family mausoleum at St Michael's Abbey church is large and impressive; her tomb and those of her husband (Napoleon III) and son can be seen at certain times.

Places of Interest in and Around Aldershot and Farnborough

Aldershot Military Museum and Visitors Centre
Queen's Avenue
Chronological display of the history of Aldershot camp. Reconstruction of a typical barrack-room of about 1900.

Airborne Forces Museum
Browning Barracks
The story of the formation and operations of airborne forces since 1940. Exhibits include model aircraft, an Arnhem cameo and a Dakota aircraft.

Regimental Museum of the Royal Corps of Transport
Buller Barracks
The history of the corps from the Royal Waggoners of 1794, with collections of badges, models and weapons, and a display of the Battle of Rorke's Drift.

Army Physical Training Corps Museum
Queen's Avenue
The evolution of Army physical training since the first course in 1860 is shown by a pictorial display and a collection of equipment.

Royal Army Dental Corps Museum
Evelyn Woods Road
The history of Army dentistry since its early days, and the formation of the Dental Corps in 1921. Death-mask of Himmler.

Queen Alexandra's Royal Army Nursing Corps Museum
Royal Pavilion, Farnborough Road
Pictorial history of Army nursing in a building on the site of the Victorian Royal Pavilion. Exhibits include Crimean War relics and Florence Nightingale's Russian-built carriage.

Prince Consort's Army Library
Knollys' Road
Built 1859-60 by Prince Albert. Large collection of military books, maps and models. Open to visitors.

Heroes' Shrine and Rock Garden
Manor Park, Aldershot
The national memorial to those killed in World War II. A shrine with rockeries of stones from war-damaged buildings.

St Michael's Abbey Church
Farnborough
A mausoleum containing the tombs of the Empress Eugénie of France, her husband and son.

The parish church of St Peter retains many old features including two Norman doorways, a seventeenth-century timber tower and a

Jacobean gallery, and is happily situated in a quiet part of this busy town.

From Farnborough the B3014 takes one to Fleet, a large built-up area that is neither town nor parish nor village but just part of Hart District; it consists of modern housing estates and a long street of shops. Fleet Pond, a nature reserve, is Hampshire's largest freshwater lake. From 1650 to the early nineteenth century it served as a fishpond for the dean and chapter of Winchester cathedral, and from 1854 to 1972 was used by the Army. Its varied flora and fauna can be seen on a circular walk that starts at the car-park (entrance from the B3014).

South-west of Fleet is **Crookham Village**, where the former Basingstoke Canal wharf has been converted to a car-park. This is a convenient starting point for walks along the canal in either direction.

South of here, across the A287, is the picturesque village of **Crondall** with its many attractive houses, those in Church Street and The Borough being of particular interest. Much of the church is Norman but the chancel is Early English. The Norman tower was taken down in the seventeenth century and replaced by a brick tower modelled on a church tower in Battersea. In the church there is an anchorite's cell, two coffin trolleys, an ancient chest and one of the three oldest brasses in Hampshire (dated 1381).

Alton still has the air of an old country market town with its curving High Street and its small market square hemmed in by old buildings. Its new buildings have to a certain extent harmonised with the old so that the town retains something of its old character.

Alton's main industry since the eighteenth century has been brewing, using the hops that were once grown widely in the area, though the only native product now is the famous Harp Lager.

St Lawrence's church at the highest point of the town was the scene of a ferocious fight in 1643 when Royalist troops were cornered inside and their commander, Colonel John Bolle, refused to surrender and was killed. Bullet-holes are still visible in the old oak south door. The church was extended in the fifteenth century but retains its Norman tower.

Alton's most famous son was William Curtis, the botanist and founder of the *Botanical Magazine*, born at No 25 Lenten Street in 1746 (there is a plaque on the house). The Curtis Museum was founded in 1855 by another member of the family. Its main gallery illustrates the history of the town from prehistoric times. Artefacts from the Bronze Age and Iron Age, the excavations at the Roman posting-station at Neatham (a town of 30 acres occupied for 300 years) and the Saxon cemetery at Mount Pleasant are fully documented. The Alton Buckle is the finest piece of Saxon craftsmanship yet found in Hampshire. Other exhibits include a collection of mousetraps, Romano-British pottery from Alice Holt, a toll-gate board from Farringdon, fire marks and relics of the local brewing industry. The Gallery of Childhood has a good collection of toys — early wooden toys, tinplate toys, soft toys and a zoetrope, typical of the optical toys popular in the nineteenth century.

The Allen Gallery in Church Street has an extensive collection of ceramics representative of their manufacture since 1500, in particular blue transfer-printed ware and commemorative pottery. The displays illustrate the technical improvements in the last 500 years and the results of industrialisation. The collection includes Chinese, Japanese and European pottery, porcelain and stoneware to illustrate the influence of overseas wares on British production. There are also rare Staffordshire wares, pieces from nineteenth-century provincial potteries and earthenware tiles designed by Walter Crane.

In Church Street is the Quaker Meeting House of 1672. The oldest Quaker meeting-house in the world is at Hertford and dates from 1670, so this one at Alton may be the second oldest. The date is set into the boundary wall in darker bricks and can be seen to best advantage from the other side of the road.

In 1867 a horrible murder occurred in Alton, when a young girl named Fanny Adams was killed by a solicitor's clerk. She lived in Tanhouse Lane off Amery Street and her grave can be found in the cemetery. The phrase 'sweet Fanny Adams' was coined by naval ratings, who at that time were being issued with inferior tinned meat, and has passed into the language as a synonym for 'nothing'.

From Alton the A31 goes to Medstead via **Chawton Park Wood**, a Forestry Commission woodland that was once part of a medieval deer park, and has forest walks and a picnic area. Two miles north of Medstead is **Bentworth**, a quiet village with large attractive houses. It was once a royal manor owned by the Bishop of Rouen who evidently financed the building of the large church. Very little light penetrates the nave because of the enormous thirteenth-century arcades. In the churchyard is a tree grafted from the Holy Thorn at Glastonbury.

Grave of Fanny Adams, Alton

At **Lasham** airfield 2 miles north is the largest gliding centre in Britain. Here training is provided at all levels up to competition standard. Nowadays gliding is a very safe sport, with modern equipment and trained instructors. However, at weekends the visitor who prefers both feet on the ground will be fascinated by the skills displayed by the pilots of these machines. In one corner of the airfield the Second World War Aircraft Preservation Society has a collection of historic aircraft, open to visitors on Sundays. There are two Westland helicopters, a Hawker Sea Hawk, a De Havilland Vampire, a Hawker Hunter, a Gloster Meteor and other famous aircraft.

A right turn from the A339 goes via Weston Patrick to **Upton Grey**. This beautiful village is set in a valley and on the slope of a hill, on which stands the church. The curious internal appearance of the church was caused by the addition of a very large north aisle in 1715 to a narrow medieval nave and chancel. There are several interesting memorials and tablets.

From here quiet by-roads take one across the rich undulating farmlands of central Hampshire via South Warnborough and Long Sutton to **Bentley** on the A31. Lord Baden-Powell of South Africa and Boy Scouts fame chose to live here at the house named Pax Hill;

Places of Interest in and Around Alton

The Curtis Museum
High Street, Alton
Displays of local history and
industries. Geology and natural
history of the area.

The Allen Gallery
Church Street, Alton
Large collection of ceramics,
especially transfer ware and
commemorative pottery.

Lasham Airfield
Largest gliding centre in Britain.
Second World War Aircraft
Preservation Society's collection of
historic aircraft.

Chawton Park Wood
3 miles south-west of Alton
Woodland walks. Picnic area.

Jenkyn Place
Bentley
Beautiful garden with roses,

herbaceous borders and many
rare plants.

Alresford House
Eighteenth-century house once the
home of Admiral Lord Rodney.
'Pick your own' fruit and vegetables.

The Grange
(English Heritage)
Northington
Shell of the early nineteenth-
century house built in the Greek
style by William Wilkins. One of the
great neo-classical buildings of the
world, restored at great cost.

Abbotstone Down
Downland walks. Picnic area. Iron
Age hill-fort.

Micheldever Wood
Forestry Commission. Woodland
walks.

he designed for a village sign competition the curious wooden 'book'
at the side of the main road, which depicts points of interest relating
to the history of Bentley. The sign should certainly have gained an
award for the 'history' written on it; a stranger collection of 'facts' it
would be hard to find. It states for instance that the Romans were
here in AD41, 2 years before they invaded Britain! The beautiful
garden at Jenkyn Place is open to visitors; it has roses, herbaceous
borders and a large collection of rare plants.

The village of Bentley has moved downhill since the main road
became a turnpike. The church, now rather isolated, has an early
Norman chancel with a clerestory, an unusual feature in a chancel.
There are fragments of fifteenth-century stained glass in the windows.

The church at **Froyle**, 2 miles west, stands beside the medieval house that is now the Lord Mayor Treloar College. The chancel of about 1300 contrasts markedly with the late Georgian nave. The armorial glass in the east window is also of about 1300 and there is a rare Easter sepulchre.

At **Holybourne**, between Froyle and Alton, the novelist Elizabeth Gaskell bought a house (The Lawn, opposite the turning to the church) in 1865 for her husband's retirement. She had arranged to let it to a tenant until her husband was ready to move, but while staying at the house prior to the tenant moving in she died. The church has one of the largest charity boards in Hampshire. It records the details of the will of Thomas Andrews, who endowed a school in the village in 1719. The school stands set back from London Road, an early Georgian building of purple brick.

The first stop on a pleasant tour from New Alresford (see Chapter 4) is **Old Alresford**, across Bishop de Lucy's dam from the 'new' town. Alresford House, open in August, was the home of Lord Rodney, the eighteenth-century admiral. As an added attraction fruit and vegetables are on sale; visitors pick them from the garden. The Mothers Union was officially founded at Old Alresford in 1876 by Mary Sumner, the vicar's wife; from that small beginning it has grown to a world-wide organization. Admiral Rodney is buried in St Mary's church in the family vault in the chancel. His greatest achievement was the defeat of the Spanish fleet at Cape St Vincent in 1780. The memorial to his wife Jane, who died at the age of 27, is one of the largest funerary monuments in the county. In the churchyard there is a sundial with a plate explaining the mysteries of solar time.

Two miles east is **Bighton**, its late Norman church in a peaceful tree-shaded spot between the late seventeenth-century Bighton Manor and The Old Rectory. The fourteenth-century Godsfield Chapel on the road to Wield is now part of a private house but once belonged to the Knights Hospitallers.

Wield is a quiet village; its church, hidden away behind a cluster of old thatched cottages, has a fine Norman chancel arch and doorway and remains of early medieval wall-paintings.

Preston Candover, 2 miles north-west, has some fine houses, especially Preston House built about 1720. At **Chilton Candover** an underground Norman crypt chapel was discovered in 1927 by the vicar; he had been told of it by an old man who remembered it from his youth. A curious survival, it consists of an apse and a rectangular room, all that remains of the Norman church that preceded a late medieval church.

The Grange at **Northington** is approached by a driveway from the B3046. There was no building in Hampshire as majestic or in such a commanding position as The Grange. It was one of the first European country houses inspired by Greek architectural ideals. In the early nineteenth century the old house here was transformed by the young architect William Wilkins into one of the great neo-classical buildings of the world.

The house built in 1665-73, which forms the core of the present building, was sold in 1787 to Henry Drummond, then let to the Prince of Wales who is said to have kept a bevy of mistresses there. Drummond engaged Wilkins to remodel The Grange; rebuilding took place between 1809 and 1816, until Drummond lost interest in it and the original design was not completed. Wilkins placed a portico on the short east front based on the Temple of Theseus in Athens. By 1970 it had become a ruined empty shell, but the government has spent £500,000 on its restoration.

The features that made The Grange one of the most famous buildings of its day have been preserved and the seventeenth-century west front has been exposed and repaired. The house is still empty; its immediate vicinity is open to visitors and one can look down on the beautiful landscaped park. The conservatory (1824) nearby with its Ionic portico is an early glass and cast-iron building and is one of the earliest such structures in Great Britain. In the 1890s it was converted to a picture gallery and ballroom.

Abbotstone Down one mile on is a good place for a picnic and walks across the downland. The so-called 'Oliver's Battery' (see also Chapter 1) on the down is an Iron Age hill-fort. Roe and fallow deer are quite common in the woods; downland flora include fifty-six varieties of mosses and liverworts. There are three way-marked walks starting from the official car-park, of $2^3/_4$ miles (red), 3 miles (blue) and $5^1/_2$ miles (yellow) respectively.

South-west is **Abbotstone**, a meeting-place of trackways since early times. Here in the fields one can see the terraces and hollow-ways of a deserted medieval village, once a thriving community with a manor house, now an ancient monument.

Visitors who want to return to Winchester can go via the Itchen valley or through Northington on the Lunway, an ancient trackway, past Micheldever Wood with its woodland walks, to **Micheldever** village. This extremely attractive village, with its numerous old timber-framed thatched cottages, grew up at the junction of two trackways, one from Overton to Winchester, the other from Stockbridge to Alton. The church here was altered in 1808 by the insertion into the medieval nave of a unique brick octagon, giving a strikingly odd appearance. The architect George Dance had already designed something similar at the church of St Bartholomew the Less in London. The result here is memorable for its eccentricity rather than for its architectural quality. In the church there are monuments to the Baring family with baroque-style details.

North of the village is the early railway station building, opened in 1840. It was then named Andover Road and remained the nearest station to Andover until 1854. On 11 May 1840 a great celebration at the station marked the opening of the railway from London to Southampton, the section from Basingstoke to Winchester being the last to be completed; thousands of people came from all over the county. Micheldever remains the only station on this 19-mile stretch across the chalk downlands.

The church at **Stoke Charity** in the charming little valley of the Dever is a veritable treasure-house of brasses and monuments. The sculpture of the Mass of St Gregory of about 1500 is the only well-preserved example in England, and the fifteenth- and sixteenth-century tombs with brass effigies are the best of that period in Hampshire and of great historical interest. Stoke Charity was once so poor that William Cobbett said that the only well-fed families were those of the vicar and farmer! The village got its name from Henry de la Charité, who owned the manor in the thirteenth century.

6

THE NORTH-WEST

The history of **Romsey** is to a large extent the history of its abbey, for the town owes its very existence to the nunnery founded here about AD907 by Edward the Elder for his daughter Ethelflaeda. It was refounded as a Benedictine nunnery by King Edgar in AD967. There is evidence to suggest that a church existed when the nunnery was first founded; there was certainly a church here immediately prior to the present one, for the foundations of the apse of a Saxon church beneath the present nave have been exposed and can be seen by visitors. The fact that there was no parish church in the Middle Ages, the townspeople having to use part of the abbey church, suggests that the town was subordinate to the abbey. The abbey church was begun about 1120 and extended in the thirteenth century, and with the exception of Durham cathedral is considered the finest Norman building in England.

The interior is perfectly proportioned and the two styles of architecture, Norman and Early English, unite to form a richly satisfying whole. The rebuilding of the abbey church began about 1120 and continued well into the thirteenth century. The earliest parts of the church are the choir, transepts, ambulatory and tower, built about 1120-50, followed by the four eastern bays of the nave (1150-80) and then the three Early English bays (1230-40). At the Dissolution the church was spared the fate of most monastic churches, perhaps because there was no separate parish church, and in 1544 it was sold to the townspeople for £100, surely one of the best bargains ever; the bill of sale can be seen in the church.

Relics of Saxon times are the two roods or crucifixes. The one inside the church behind the altar in the south aisle dates from about

AD1000 and depicts Christ on the Cross with Mary and John on either side. The other one, a carving of Christ with arms outstretched and the hand of God appearing from a cloud, is on the outside west wall of the south transept. This much larger rood dates from the eleventh century and is a priceless artistic relic of that period. In the south transept is the grave of Earl Mountbatten, whose home was at Broadlands near the town. Also in the church is the tomb of Sir William Petty, a man of many achievements and a founder-member of the Royal Society, who was born in Church Street in 1623. On the memorial to John Sainte Barbe and his wife in the south transept there is a curious anagram of their names.

There are many other things of interest in the church. In the south transept is a thirteenth-century Purbeck marble effigy of a lady wearing a wimple; the canopy with its ogee arch, however, is four-teenth century. The magnificent Decorated windows at the east end of the church replaced the original Norman windows in 1270. Below is the high altar, with a bas-relief of the Madonna and Child; there are six other altars in the church. In the north transept is a rare painted wooden reredos of about 1525; it depicts a row of saints and Christ rising from the tomb. A window in the chapel commemorates the Reverend Berthon, a nineteenth-century vicar who was also a fa-mous inventor.

Romsey, which became a borough in 1607, is overshadowed in both senses of the word by its abbey. However there are other buildings of note, such as the dignified Corn Exchange of 1864 and The Dolphin Hotel, flamboyantly bow-fronted. The market-place with its statue of Palmerston also has its merits.

In Church Street is King John's House, an upper-hall house built about 1230-40. It was used as a guest-house by the abbey and is in a remarkable state of preservation; it was recognised as such an early house only in 1927. It was probably the main building in a group centred on a courtyard and was not, as previously supposed, the hunting-lodge mentioned in a document as belonging to King John. It still has its original roof timbers and window details. The graffiti on the walls may have been cut during the visit of Edward I in 1306 for one of them is a caricature of him. Its museum contains many items relating to the history of Romsey. Exhibits include a penny-farthing bicycle, instruments from a local band, pottery, relics and other memorabilia.

Wool was once the main trade of Romsey and several mills were sited on the streams of the River Test, but from the eighteenth century the town became famous for its brewing. In *Domesday Book* three mills were recorded in Romsey, probably two town mills and the abbey mill; milling has been important throughout Romsey's history. Before the Norman Conquest a small settlement was growing up in the shadow of the abbey and the present Market Place may have been its focal point. Several streams once flowed through the town. One of them, the Fishlake or Town stream, runs alongside Middlebridge Street to meet the Test; the iron railings where it emerges from underground near the bus station came from the Sainte Barbe memorial in the abbey church.

The manor of Broadlands belonged to Romsey Abbey before the Dissolution; the Jacobean mansion was remodelled in classical style in the mid-eighteenth century by 'Capability' Brown, who also landscaped the grounds. The house then belonged to the Palmerston family, and the third viscount, who became Prime Minister, stayed there whenever his duties permitted. It was the home of Earl Mountbatten until his death and is now the home of his grandson, Lord Romsey. Rooms open to visitors include the classical saloon, the beautiful Wedgwood Room and the Oak Room with the Coronation Book of Alexander II, one of the largest books ever printed. The Mountbatten Exhibition in the stables illustrates the life and career of Earl Mountbatten and the part he and his wife played in national affairs, especially during World War II.

The **Hillier Arboretum** at Ampfield, 2 miles north-east of Romsey, has one of the largest collections of trees and plants in Europe.

The grave of Florence Nightingale is at **East Wellow** church, 4 miles west of Romsey. She died in London at the age of 90 and in deference to her wishes was buried here in the family grave; she came to live at nearby Embley Park when a child. Her grave is marked by an obelisk with the names of her family — her own name is recorded simply as 'F.N.' The church has thirteenth-century wall-paintings, notably of St Christopher holding a child in his arms, the murder of Thomas Becket and a scene from the life of St Margaret of Antioch, to whom the church is dedicated. Unfortunately none of the paintings are very well preserved. Also in the church there are Jacobean stalls and a carved pulpit.

The road from Romsey to Stockbridge follows the Test valley, which rivals the Itchen and the Meon valleys for peace and beauty.

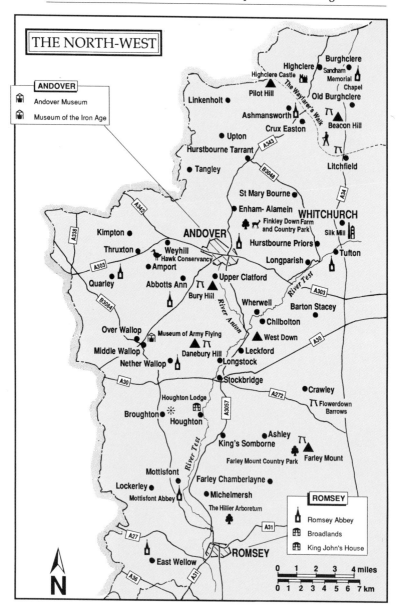

THE NORTH-WEST

ANDOVER
- Andover Museum
- Museum of the Iron Age

Highclere
Highclere Castle
Burghclere
Sandham Memorial Chapel
Old Burghclere
Pilot Hill
Linkenholt
Ashmansworth
Crux Easton
Beacon Hill
Upton
Litchfield
Hurstbourne Tarrant
Tangley
St Mary Bourne
Enham-Alamein
WHITCHURCH
Finkley Down Farm and Country Park
Kimpton
ANDOVER
Hurstbourne Priors
Silk Mill
Thruxton
Weyhill
Hawk Conservancy
Amport
Longparish
Tufton
Quarley
Abbotts Ann
Upper Clatford
Bury Hill
Wherwell
Barton Stacey
Chilbolton
Over Wallop
Museum of Army Flying
West Down
Middle Wallop
Danebury Hill
Leckford
Nether Wallop
Longstock
Stockbridge
Crawley
Houghton Lodge
Flowerdown Barrows
Broughton
Houghton
Ashley
King's Somborne
Farley Mount
Mottisfont
Farley Chamberlayne
Farley Mount Country Park
Lockerley
Mottisfont Abbey
Michelmersh
The Hillier Arboretum
East Wellow
ROMSEY

River Test
River Anton

ROMSEY
- Romsey Abbey
- Broadlands
- King John's House

0 1 2 3 4 miles
0 1 2 3 4 5 6 7 km

N

Broadlands

The former railway station at Horsebridge

The railway line through the valley followed the bed of the old Southampton to Andover canal, which had twenty-four locks in its 22 miles. The canal was completed in 1794; it mainly followed the east bank of the River Test. Boats carried coal and building materials from Southampton to Romsey and Andover and carried agricultural produce the other way, but the canal was not a financial success. The section from Romsey to Timsbury is still water-filled and can be followed on foot; the former Plaza cinema stands on the site of the canal wharf. The Andover and Redbridge Railway was opened in 1865, using about 14 miles of the canal bed; it became known as the 'sprat and winkle' line. The Kimbridge to Andover part of the line was closed in 1964. The old station buildings remain at Mottisfont, Horsebridge and Fullerton but Stockbridge station has vanished completely.

East of the road the church at **Michelmersh** has a massive and unusual detached weatherboarded tower of uncertain date; the church as a whole is difficult to date because of the extensive restoration in 1847. There are some interesting memorials in the church, including an effigy of a crusader knight with a stag at his feet. The one to Trustram Fantleroy (1538) is probably the earliest example in Hampshire of a memorial with detached kneeling figures. The field south of the church is said to have been the scene in 1415 of a large gathering of knights and archers on their way to the Battle of Agincourt.

West of the road the eighteenth-century **Mottisfont Abbey** has the most beautiful setting imaginable, among green lawns shaded by enormous trees, close to the peaceful River Test. The thirteenth-century priory was dissolved in 1536 and the nave of the church was transformed into a Tudor mansion before being altered again in the Georgian period. The north front of the house is in fact the north wall of the church nave. When the priory was dissolved it was given to Lord Sandys of The Vyne in exchange for the villages of Chelsea and Paddington. The Georgian south front is of mellow brick with stone quoins, perfectly complementing the beautiful grounds. It has been said that no house in England has a more harmonious setting than Mottisfont.

The outstanding feature of the interior is the drawing-room decorated by Rex Whistler, his last and greatest masterpiece. This and the monks' cellarium are the only two rooms open to visitors, who are admitted in strict order of arrival by timed ticket; at peak times there may be a considerable wait. There is a tea-garden in the village but not at the house.

In the eighteenth century most large houses had an ice-house in the grounds in which to store ice, and the one open to view here at Mottisfont is one of the best of the eighty or more in Hampshire. The famous rose garden is a show-place for the National Trust's collection of roses; in June the garden's brilliant display is an unforgettable sight.

The parish church, which became attached to the bishopric of York, dates from the mid-twelfth century. It has a fine Norman chancel arch and has more fifteenth-century stained glass than any other church in Hampshire. There is an Elizabethan monument of 1584 with Renaissance details depicting a kneeling family, an early example of this type of monument but unfortunately damaged.

At Mottisfont the Southampton and Salisbury Canal diverged from the Andover Canal and followed a course through Lockerley and East Dean towards Salisbury, which it never reached. Traces of the canal can be seen near the road through Lockerley and East Dean; it was in use for only about 4 years before the canal company became bankrupt. At East Dean there is an ancient little church, almost completely unrestored, with an old timber-framed doorway, rough tie-beam rafters and a tiny gallery.

At **King's Somborne** John of Gaunt, son of Edward III, is said to have had a palace. Excavations have been carried out near the church to try to substantiate the story, but apart from evidence of an Anglo-Saxon settlement nothing can be proved. His deer park, the banks of which remain in part, certainly lay between the village and the river. It is one of the best-preserved deer parks in the county — in one place the bank is nearly 12ft high. Of the many thatched cottages in the village one on the road to Ashley is a good example of the type known as a 'cruck'.

The school adjoining the church was once just about the most famous village school in England. It was founded in 1842 by the vicar, Richard Dawes, and soon became well known for the quality of its teaching; even the Prime Minister paid it a visit. The writing and reading of English formed the basis of the children's education. The war memorial in the village was designed by Edwin Lutyens. He also designed Marsh Court, the large house built of chalk ashlar overlooking the Test valley between King's Somborne and Stockbridge. The parish church is mostly Victorian but has a few earlier details.

Mottisfont abbey and rose garden

At **Ashley** the small Norman church (now redundant) stands within the bailey of a Norman castle, whose overgrown earthworks can be seen from the churchyard. A mile north of Ashley is **Little Somborne**, a tiny village with a whitewashed Saxon church (also redundant) on the miniature village green.

Nearer Winchester is **Farley Mount Country Park**, a large area of woodland and open downland offering a variety of scenery and walks. In West Wood the Roman road from Winchester to Old Sarum can be seen as a prominent 'agger' or raised roadway. A Roman villa has been discovered in West Wood; its mosaic floor is now in Winchester City Museum.

The curious pyramid on Farley Mount is a memorial to a horse, which in 1733 fell with its rider into a chalk-pit. Both were unhurt and next year even won a race, the horse having been renamed 'Beware Chalk-Pit'. Farley Mount Country Park has been designated a natural history site of special scientific interest; the woods are mainly of oak, beech and yew and orchids are plentiful. A 2-mile walk across Farley Down takes one to the remote village of **Farley Chamberlayne**, which derives its name from the owner of the manor who was chamberlain to William the Conqueror.

The Norman church here has been mercifully saved from drastic restoration. Its old tombs and its Georgian furniture and fittings are an essential part of its timeless character; the cresset beacon was used at the time of the Armada to pass on a warning. The ruinous building in the field near the church was a telegraph station on the projected London to Plymouth Admiralty semaphore line.

North of Farley Mount Country Park are the villages of Sparsholt, Littleton and Crawley. **Sparsholt** is best known for the Hampshire County Council's College of Agriculture. The church is Victorian, restored by William Butterfield. The Flowerdown barrows in **Littleton** recreation ground comprise a large disc barrow and a small bowl barrow. The former, a rare type of Bronze Age burial mound, is

Track of a Roman road, through Farley Mount Country Park

nearly 200ft in diameter. The church, which was rebuilt in 1884-5, has a Norman font. The attractive appearance of **Crawley** today is largely due to Ernest Philippi, who in the early years of this century created a model village by purchasing all the properties that came up for sale and placing restrictions on commercial premises. An unusual feature in the church is the nave arcade, which is constructed of wooden posts with arched braces. The Independent Broadcasting Authority occupies Crawley Court.

From King's Somborne a road crosses the Test at Horsebridge, not far from where the Roman road crossed it. The village of **Houghton** is in the heart of the Test fishing country. The beautiful garden at Houghton Lodge is open on certain afternoons.

Further west is **Broughton**, a large and attractive village between the main road and the Wallop Brook. The church dates from about 1200 but was restored after a fire in 1638. In the churchyard is a circular brick dovecot of 1684 — one of the best-preserved examples in Hampshire. Of the many thousands of dovecots or pigeon-houses that once existed in England few have survived. They were built in all shapes and sizes; this one is open to visitors. Also in the churchyard is the grave of Anne Steele, a well-known writer of hymns in the eighteenth century. Several houses in the village have names that recall former trades — The Old Malt House, The Old Coach House, Post House and others. The village well was constructed in the drought of 1921 by John Fripp in memory of his son, who was killed in World War I.

Stockbridge, where the London to Salisbury road crosses the Test, is a village of one long wide main street. It is situated where the river valley is crossed by a causeway. The eighteenth-century bridge over the river was rebuilt in 1963; the inscription that was on the earlier bridge of the fifteenth century is recorded on the present one. It was a borough as long ago as 1256 and was one of the Parliamentary 'rotten boroughs'. It sent two Members to Parliament from 1563 to 1832. One of the ringleaders in the bribery and corruption that attended the local elections was John Bucket, a local innkeeper. The epitaph on his grave in the old churchyard is worth reading. All that remains of the old church is its chancel, hidden away in the corner; the rest of it was demolished in 1863. There are a few attractive houses in the main street but only the Grosvenor Hotel arrests the eye. This was a popular rendezvous with riders when Stockbridge was a famous horse-racing centre in the nineteenth century.

On the road to Houghton is Drovers House, once a guest-house used by Welsh drovers; the inscription in Welsh on the front means 'seasoned hay, tasty pastures, good beer, comfortable beds'. Nearby is Hermit Lodge, named after the Derby winner of 1867, where the future King Edward VII often stayed when he attended the races at Stockbridge. His mistress, Lily Langtry, stayed at The White House across the river. Stockbridge Common Marsh is an ancient common now owned by the National Trust, as is Stockbridge Down, an open downland rich in plant and insect life.

The River Test, known as the 'queen of the chalk streams', is one of the most exclusive and expensive fishing rivers in the world and indeed is world-famous for its trout-fishing; one has to be wealthy or privileged to fish the Test, for unlike the Itchen there are no facilities for visitors. But even if one is not a fisherman the Test's tranquil beauty can be enjoyed from numerous vantage-points where it is crossed by bridges; there are few public footpaths along its banks.

Longstock, upstream from Stockbridge, is a quiet village of beautiful old thatched cottages, some timber-framed, and the Peat Spade Inn, whose name recalls the old days of peat-digging in the valley. **Leckford** on the opposite bank is not so attractive but has an old church of great character with a set of magnificent choir seats dating from about 1600, brought from an Italian monastery.

From **West Down** further on there are fine views of the Test valley and of the Anton valley in which lies Andover, and at its foot is **Chilbolton**, one of the loveliest villages in this area, with charming old houses in its long winding main street. Chilbolton Common, accessible by footpath from the village or from Wherwell, is a peaceful spot, an ancient common where over 100 species of plants have been recorded. The parish church is partly Norman with a thirteenth-century chancel and a fine early seventeenth-century pulpit.

Wherwell (pronounced 'Hurrell') was the site of a nunnery founded by the mother of Ethelred the Unready. Nothing remains of it today except a few pieces of stone on display in the church. Black-and-white thatched cottages cluster at the foot of a steep hill, which the road ascends by a zigzag over the old railway line.

At **Upper Clatford** near Andover an ironworks was opened in 1813; it had been founded at Abbotts Ann by Robert Tasker. It was later renamed Waterloo Ironworks, making ploughs and agricultural implements, and became famous for its traction-engines first

Crawley

made in 1869. During World War II it made some 19,000 trailers for the armed forces, including many of the large Queen Mary type. When the works closed many of its tools and machines were bought by the Hampshire Museum Service. Nothing remains of the old works, but the Workmens Hall in the village is now a chapel and Waterloo Terrace is a row of workmen's cottages.

On Bury Hill, overlooking Clatford, is a large and impressive Iron Age hill-fort with public footpaths.

Andover is now suffering the same fate as Basingstoke. Also once a quiet country market town, it has encouraged the migration of industry from London and its population has nearly doubled in the last 20 years. In 1974 it even ceased to be a borough in its own right. The loss of some of the town's old character is regrettable but the market-place survives with its Town Hall of 1825. The name of the town was first recorded in AD955 as *Andeferas*. The manor of Andover belonged to the king at the time of Domesday, when six mills were recorded. The medieval town grew up round a market near the church and priory; the wide High Street must have been the later site of the market. In 1175 the town was granted a charter, which gave the townspeople a merchant guild. A disastrous fire in 1435 destroyed

Broughton Dovecot

many buildings.

The parish church, which dominates the town from the hill, is the best Victorian church in Hampshire; its interior is a marvel of ingenuity. The architect was Augustus Livesay, who chose the Early English style; it was completed in 1846. Old inns in the town include the Danebury Hotel, which has a Tuscan porch, The Globe and The Angel Inn, which was owned by Winchester College when it was rebuilt in 1445 — it was known then as The College Inn. It claims to have served a meal to James II in 1688 when he was on the run and to have entertained at various times King John, Henry VII and Catherine of Aragon.

The Andover Museum has a wealth of information on the Andover area — geology, flora and fauna, local history, glass-working, archaeology, and weights and measures. There are exhibits illustrating the typical fauna of chalklands and chalk streams and the flora of ancient grasslands. Other items include a mayor's robe and a town- crier's coat.

The Museum of the Iron Age is a unique presentation of this prehistoric period. It depicts the history of the Iron Age with special reference to the hill-fort on Danebury Hill. From about 1500BC the population of this part of the country increased rapidly and permanent field systems came into use. After about 600BC the great hill-forts such as those at Danebury Hill and Quarley Hill appeared. The displays in the museum include a replica of the outer defences of Danebury fort and a replica of a round house. Daily life in the Iron Age is illustrated with tools, implements, weapons, querns and a replica loom.

Finkley Down Farm and Country Park, 2 miles north-east of the town centre, has a large collection of animals and a countryside museum.

As an alternative to the above route one can turn west at Longstock to visit villages and places of interest south-west of Andover. The Iron Age hill-fort at **Danebury Hill** was occupied by the Atrebates, a Celtic people, from about 550BC to 100BC. The chalkland in the area attracted prehistoric man because of its easily-worked fertile soil. The landscape around Danebury has one of the greatest concentrations of Iron Age sites in Europe. All the necessities of life were readily available in the area, with the exception of metal and stone. About 200-400 people lived here at any one time in reasonable security, protected by almost impregnable defences. The main entrance on the east was constructed to withstand almost any attack, yet there is evidence that it was burnt down about 100BC.

Excavations lasting 18 years have given archaeologists the most detailed picture of Iron Age society yet achieved in Europe; they revealed the layout of roads, houses, shrines and storage pits, and brought to light over 100,000 pieces of pottery. About half the interior was examined and the finds gave an unparalleled picture of life in the Iron Age. About 200,000 bones were found, 98 per cent of them from domestic animals, 2 per cent from wild animals. The bones gave an indication of what people ate in those days. The most numerous of the animals kept at Danebury were sheep, followed by cattle and pigs. By following the Danebury trail the visitor will be able to appreciate the natural and man-made history of this unique site.

A left turn beyond Danebury takes one to the three Wallops (disappointingly the name means only 'valley of the stream'). The most attractive of them is **Nether Wallop** with its brick and thatched cottages and a mill bordering the road that follows the Wallop Brook through the village. The church has many features of interest but is chiefly remarkable for its important wall-paintings. The earliest of these, above the chancel arch, is a figure of Christ in Majesty supported by flying angels, which dates from the late tenth or early eleventh century and may be the only Saxon wall-painting in its original position in existence. Christ in Majesty was a common subject above chancel arches before the Last Judgement superseded it. Other later paintings are of a sabbath-breaker and an enormous bell. The church is of Saxon origin, though the earliest visible details are Norman. The brass of Maria Gore (1436) is the only known brass memorial to a prioress. In the churchyard is the large pyramidal tomb of Dr Francis Douce (1760); his cousin Paulet St John also built a pyramid, the well-known one on Farley Mount.

Over Wallop is also strung along the valley — its church in contrast has been much restored. The Museum of Army Flying at **Middle Wallop** will be of great interest to students of military and flying history; it has a large collection of aircraft used in military aviation.

Rich farming country, sparsely inhabited, lies to the north. **Grateley's** station on the main line railway saved the village from obscurity; its church has a thirteenth-century chancel and tower. The lonely church at **Quarley** is partly Saxon, partly Norman, and to step inside is to be taken back a thousand years for it has been but little restored. It has two interesting features: the unique arrangement of its bells, which hang in a frame on the ground in the churchyard, and the east window of 1723, one of the earliest Palladian-style windows in England. The Iron Age hill-fort on Quarley Hill is one of the most impressive in the county, but there is no public access.

At **Thruxton** aerodrome motor and motor cycle race meetings are held regularly and are very popular. Thruxton and Kimpton are small and unspoilt villages with old churches and attractive houses.

At **Amport**, across the busy A303, RAF Maintenance Command had its headquarters during the war at Amport House. The almshouses and the school, both built in 1815, were paid for by Sophia Sheppard, a wealthy widow. The almshouses were for six poor widows, who in addition received £2 monthly. The church is in the Decorated style, which is quite rare in Hampshire. The nave was restored in 1866-7 but the chancel, tower and south transept are

Chilbolton Common

largely original, making this the most complete Decorated church in the county. In the church is a rare alabaster panel depicting the head of St John the Baptist, which is thought to have been an altar-piece in a wayside chapel. Beside the village green are some very attractive early eighteenth-century farm labourers' cottages with chalk walls.

At the **Hawk Conservancy** one mile north there are birds of prey from many parts of the world, including hawks, falcons, eagles, vultures, kites and owls. Flying demonstrations are given in dry weather and visitors are allowed to hold some of the birds.

Beyond Monxton, which has a large number of whitewashed thatched cottages, is **Abbotts Ann**, the only village in England which retains the custom of awarding virgins' crowns. This ceremony takes place at the funeral of an unmarried person (male or female) who was born and died in the parish and was of unblemished reputation! The crowns are made of hazelwood with paper rosettes and five white gloves (representing a challenge). Some of the crowns hanging from the church roof are nearly as old as the church itself, which was rebuilt in 1716. The Georgian atmosphere of the church is enhanced by its original pulpit, gallery and squire's family pew.

Weyhill, 3 miles west of Andover, was once famous for its fair,

158

one of the oldest recorded in England. Weyhill Fair was first mentioned in 1225 and was always one of the largest country fairs in England. It combined a sheep fair, horse fair, cheese fair and pleasure fair; people could buy almost anything there. The fair declined in the nineteenth century and finished in the 1950s. In its heyday it rivalled St Giles's Fair at Winchester and 140,000 sheep were known to have been sold in one day. Even in the eighteenth century it lasted for a whole week. It featured, thinly disguised, in Hardy's *The Mayor of Casterbridge* when Henchard sold his wife at auction for 5 guineas.

The village of **Enham-Alamein** on the Newbury road north of Andover was founded in 1919 for ex-servicemen. It was expanded to 150 cottages in 1945 with £250,000 donated by the Egyptian people. The new church contains the Alamein memorial chapel dedicated to those who took part in the famous battle. The medieval church of Knights Enham, the old village, lies hidden away on the road to Charlton.

Hurstbourne Tarrant was a favourite village of William Cobbett, who called it 'Uphusband' and thought it a 'sight worth going many miles to see'. No doubt he would recognise it still — the George and Dragon, the only remaining old posting inn, the old cottages and the church. This dates from about 1180 and has a wall-painting of the

The Mayfly public house, Wherwell

Three Living and the Three Dead, representing three kings meeting three skeletons! As much as he liked 'Uphusband' Cobbett was nevertheless saddened by the living conditions of the poor; he wrote that nowhere in England had he seen the labouring people so badly off. He used to stay with his farmer friend Joseph Blount at Rookery Farm (now Rookery House) on the main road; the trees around this solid Georgian house are still full of rooks.

Ibthorpe, adjoining Hurstbourne Tarrant, is one of the most unspoilt small villages in Hampshire. The River Swift, rising at Upton a mile or two away, trickles through the village past the old brick and thatched cottages and meets the Bourne Rivulet at Hurstbourne Tarrant.

This part of Hampshire, north-west of the Andover to Newbury road, is remote and sparsely populated. Its steep-sided chalk valleys, wooded hills overlooking scattered farms and narrow roads with little traffic seem worlds away from the built-up congested Southampton-Portsmouth area. A pleasant day can be spent touring and walking in this quiet countryside, visiting the villages of Hatherden, Tangley, Upton, Vernham Dean, Faccombe and Linkenholt. All of them have something to detain the unhurried traveller — an old manor house overlooking the road, an interesting church, a quiet inn for refreshment — what more can one ask?

At **Hatherden** there is one of the oldest schools in Hampshire, opened in 1727 in an old two-storeyed brick building and still in use. At **Tangley** the church has a lead font, the only one in Hampshire and one of only about thirty in England. Just north of the village of **Vernham Dean** is another of those spots where three counties meet, in this case at Rockmoor Pond, reached by a footpath from the road to Ham. The Boot Inn was once a shoemaker's shop; it has a collection of boots — glass, china and leather — from all over the world.

The beautiful old unrestored church at **Ashmansworth** is noted for its wall-paintings. They include some, sadly almost unrecognizable, of the twelfth and thirteenth centuries. Gerald Finzi the composer is buried here; his memorial window was engraved by Laurence Whistler and his tombstone by Reynolds Stone. The village of Ashmansworth is the highest-situated in Hampshire, 770ft above sea-level, and extends attractively along the summit of a ridge.

North-west of here is Pilot Hill, 937ft above sea-level, the highest point in Hampshire (not as is commonly supposed Butser Hill). It can be reached by an ancient track known as the Ox Drove, along which sheep drovers once brought their flocks to market. The track goes on to Walbury Hill, now in Berkshire but once the highest point in Hampshire. East Woodhay church (1823), late Georgian both in date and style, is dedicated to St Martin of Tours. Hollington Herb Garden has a wide variety of herbs for sale and is well worth a visit.

Crux Easton across the A343 was formerly Eston Croc (the village of Croc the huntsman). Its little Georgian church, so typical of that period, was connected by tunnels with the manor house and the school; their purpose has never been explained. The rector here was the father of the aircraft designer Geoffrey de Havilland, who made his early experimental flights from Beacon Hill nearby. During World War II the notorious Oswald Mosley was interned at the rectory.

Beyond Highclere a right turn leads to **Burghclere** across the A34. Here the Sandham memorial chapel (officially the Oratory of All Souls) was built in 1923-6 in commemoration of Lieutenant H.W. Sandham who died of an illness contracted during World War I. The mural paintings were executed by the late Stanley Spencer between 1926 and 1932 and represent scenes of military life in Macedonia, being the outcome of Spencer's experiences there in the war. They are considered to be the most important mural decorations in Britain and the foremost English expressionist paintings of the twentieth century. They leave an unforgettable impression of the impact on one imaginative mind of this most senseless of wars.

At **Old Burghclere** 2 miles south the church dates from about 1200, as witness the two Norman doorways. Burghclere Manor, by the church, was once a travellers' rest house administered by nuns. Nearby also is the old station on the former Didcot, Newbury and Southampton Railway.

Towering above the A34 is **Beacon Hill**, now a public open space, crowned by an Iron Age hill-fort. The climb to the summit is very steep but the reward is a splendid view over the north Hampshire downs. The grave at the top is that of Lord Carnarvon, who helped to discover the tomb of Tutankhamun in Egypt; his home was the great Victorian mansion of Highclere Castle below the hill.

Now open to visitors, **Highclere Castle** is the largest mansion in Hampshire. The previous house was completely rebuilt in Elizabethan style in 1839-42 by Sir Charles Barry, who designed the Houses of Parliament. The house is of three storeys, with an additional storey in each corner turret, and is surmounted by a strapwork balustrade.

Places of Interest in the North-West

Romsey Abbey

One of the most magnificent Norman churches in Europe, dating from about 1120. The abbey (a nunnery) was founded about 907 by Edward the Elder. Features of interest include two Saxon roods and the grave of Earl Mountbatten.

King John's House

Church Street, Romsey
Thirteenth-century upper-hall house, recognised in 1927. Local history exhibits and a 'penny-farthing' bicycle.

Broadlands

Romsey
Georgian mansion and grounds both designed by 'Capability' Brown. It is the former home of Prime Minister Palmerston and of Earl Mountbatten. Mountbatten of Burma Exhibition in the stable-block.

Mottisfont Abbey (National Trust)

$4^1/_2$ miles north of Romsey
Georgian house remodelled from a Jacobean mansion, incorporating the abbey church nave. Saloon decorated by Rex Whistler and monks' cellarium. Beautiful grounds by the River Test, and a rose garden with the National Trust's famous collection of roses.

The Hillier Arboretum

Jermyns Lane, Ampfield
One of the largest collections of trees and plants in Europe, it has the most complete collection of 'woody' plants — 10,000 species and varieties, in addition to 3,000 species of trees. It is most colourful in April and May. Conservation of endangered species is a priority.

Farley Mount Country Park

Downland open space of special scientific interest. West Wood and Crab Wood offer pleasant woodland walks. On Farley Mount is a monument to a horse that survived a fall into a chalk-pit. The remains of the Roman road from Winchester to Old Sarum can be seen on the southern edge of West Wood.

Flowerdown Barrows

(English Heritage)
Littleton
Bronze Age disc barrow and bowl barrow.

Houghton Lodge

Houghton
Beautiful grounds and walled garden by the River Test with glasshouses and a vinery. House not open.

Stockbridge Down

(National Trust)
Downland open space with Bronze Age barrows. Adjoining it is Woolbury Ring, an Iron Age hill-fort (no access).

West Down
Chilbolton
Downland open space with fine
views of the Test valley.

Andover Museum
Church Close, Andover
Local geology, flora and fauna,
archaeological finds, glass
exhibits, small aquarium, art
gallery and a special display
relating to Tasker's ironworks.

Museum of the Iron Age
Church Close, Andover
Exhibits illustrating the Iron Age
period and the history of Danebury
hill-fort.

Danebury Ring
3 miles north-west of Stockbridge
Iron Age hill-fort, one of the largest
in southern England, with complex
and formidable defences.
Danebury Ring trail.

Museum of Army Flying
Army Air Corps Centre, Middle
Wallop
The story of Army flying from
Farnborough balloon days to the
present day. Exhibits include a
large collection of aircraft.

Hawk Conservancy
Weyhill
Birds of prey from all over the
world, with demonstrations of flying
at certain hours.

**Finkley Down Farm
and Country Park**
1 mile north-east of Andover
Large collection of farm animals
and poultry. Countryside museum,
adventure playground and pets
corner.

Hollington Herb Garden
Woolton Hill
Herb garden with a great variety of
herbs, shrubs, roses and trees.

Sandham Memorial Chapel
(National Trust)
Burghclere
A chapel with unique wall-paintings
by Stanley Spencer, depicting
scenes in Macedonia during World
War I.

Beacon Hill
Burghclere
An Iron Age hill-fort crowns this
public open space.

Highclere Castle
Highclere
Victorian mansion designed by Sir
Charles Barry, with rooms in
various styles, set in a beautiful
park landscaped by 'Capability'
Brown.

Whitchurch Silk Mill
The only remaining silk mill in
Hampshire; it specialises in the
manufacture of silk gowns. The
looms can be seen working.

The richly decorated interiors range in style from Gothic to Moorish and rococo; the idea that each room should have a different style is a hallmark of the High Victorian rather than this early Victorian period. Treasures on view include Napoleon's desk and chair, Egyptian finds made by the fifth earl and a collection of paintings by European old masters. The rooms below stairs depict the servants' way of life in a stately home. The beautiful park was mainly the work of the great landscape designer Lancelot 'Capability' Brown. St Michael's parish church (1870) is an interesting design by George Gilbert Scott in the Early English style.

Whitchurch is very old; there was a Saxon settlement here with a church, possibly even a minster. After the establishment of a market and a borough in the thirteenth century the town grew up at the river crossing where two main roads met. It later became the first overnight coach stop out of London on the Andover road and The White Hart Hotel was one of the coaching inns.

The parish church was restored in Victorian times, having been almost entirely rebuilt in 1866. Three bays of the south arcade were retained however and are typical late Norman work. A rare feature is the fifteenth-century oak stair-turret within the tower. The church has one priceless relic, a Saxon gravestone of a woman named Frithburga with a carving of Our Lord holding a book, dating from the ninth century.

Lord Denning, famous Master of the Rolls, was born at No 5 Newbury Street (his parents' draper's shop). He attended school at what is now Old School House in London Street. This street has many old buildings surviving from the days when it was full of shops and inns. Town Mill on the River Test was once a flour-mill.

Whitchurch Silk Mill on the River Test is now powered by electricity, though its old breast-shot water-wheel has been restored to working order. It may be on the site of one of the four mills here mentioned in *Domesday Book*. It specialises in the manufacture of silk gowns. The present mill, one of the finest industrial buildings in the county, was built about 1800 and the clock was added in 1815 to commemorate the Battle of Waterloo. In 1816 the mill was sold and then used for the handweaving of wool, but it turned to silk production about 1830. Its recent purchase by the Hampshire Buildings Preservation Trust has safeguarded its future.

One mile south of the town is **Tufton** (mentioned in *Domesday Book* as *Tochiton*, owned by Wherwell Abbey). It consists of little more

than a farm and a perfect little Norman church, which has a large
wall-painting of St Christopher and a beautiful longcase clock of
1720.

North-west from Whitchurch a road follows the valley of the
Bourne Rivulet to Hurstbourne Tarrant via **Hurstbourne Priors**,
where the railway viaduct of 1854 on the Basingstoke to Salisbury
line is one of the most impressive pieces of railway engineering in
Hampshire.

At **St Mary Bourne** with its attractive old houses fronting the
long main street the church has the largest of the four Tournai black
marble fonts in the county, but only the bowl of the original font
survives. The carving of doves drinking out of cups is a rare piece of
Norman decoration. The Bourne Rivulet flows alongside the main
street; near the bridge in the centre of the village there is a cast-iron
lamp-post, a survivor from the days when the street lamps were lit
by oil.

A road from Hurstbourne Priors follows the Test valley downstream to **Longparish**, well named for it extends for nearly 2 miles
along the valley; its church is in the part named Middleton, the
former name of the whole parish, and is Early English (about 1210).
The set of stocks near the lich-gate is a replica of the original set and
the imitation Saxon cross nearby is dated 1867. Longparish was in the
news in 1986 when it won Hampshire's best-kept village competition and again in 1987 when its cricket team won the National Village
Knock-out Trophy. The village once had a station on the old Hurstbourne to Fullerton railway; the building survives (now Smallwood
Lodge). Here in 1927 the first of the three films named *The Ghost Train*
was made.

Harewood Forest, between the River Test and Andover, is
threaded by public footpaths, one of them being the Test Way. The
forest is noted for its moths and beetles — and for its bluebells. Near
one of the paths, but difficult to find, is the mysterious Deadman's
Plack, a monument recording the supposed killing near here in
AD963 by King Edgar of Earl Athelwold, who had secretly married
Elfrida, the intended bride of King Edgar. It is shown on the Ordnance Survey map as 'Monument'.

7

THE SOUTH-WEST

The New Forest, which forms a large part of south-west Hampshire, is the best known of our forests and a unique area of
England. Its varied and beautiful landscape of heath and woodland
results from its diverse soils. Over much of the forest the underlying
sands and clays are capped with gravel, which forms flat infertile
plateaux; where the gravel has been eroded by streams, the sands
and clays are exposed, giving rise either to well-drained slopes or to
low-lying marshes. There are thus three main types of vegetation
within the forest: Scots pine, birch, gorse and heather on the heathlands, beech, oak, yew and thorn on the well-drained slopes, and
alder, willow, bracken and moss on the marshes. Inhospitable as this
area must have been in prehistoric times there is evidence of early
man, for about a hundred Bronze Age barrows are known in the
forest and also remains of Iron Age and Roman occupation.

In 1079 William the Conqueror made it his own private deer park.
Domesday Book records the area as sparsely settled and there is no
evidence that William destroyed villages and churches. Much less
wooded than it is now, it was then largely open heathland with
scattered clumps of infertile woodland; the oaks and beeches so
much a part of the forest today were absent. He introduced harsh
laws to protect the deer. The King's Forest Law, as it was known,
prohibited any activity that would have interfered with the king's
hunting. Bows and arrows, animal traps, poaching and the enclosure
of forest land were all illegal. The peasants' own animals, however,
were allowed to graze in the forest but unfortunately these animals
and the deer did great damage to young trees and hindered the
natural regeneration of the woodlands. In later times trees were

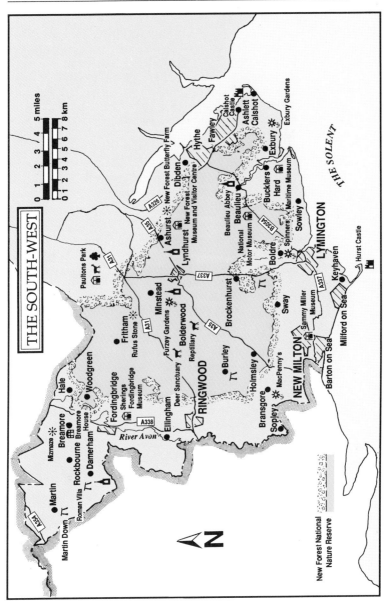

needed for the construction of houses and ships (the *Agamemnon* for instance required 2,000 trees) so in the later Middle Ages, when the dearth of new trees was becoming serious, parts of the forest were enclosed and animals were prohibited from those parts. They were thrown open again when the trees had matured; the first of these enclosure acts was in 1482. Long before this however the Forest Law had been relaxed so that death was no longer the automatic penalty for offences. Hunting gradually died out; James II was the last king to hunt in the forest.

Timber for the Navy was first required in the early seventeenth century and the amount supplied increased as Portsmouth dockyard developed, at least until the invention of iron ships. Today the Forestry Commission has a duty not only to supervise the replanting and growing of trees but also to conduct a forestry business at a profit. When an area has been felled it is replanted with seedlings or left to regenerate naturally, the favoured method.

Today there are about 1,500 deer in the New Forest, most of them fallow deer, and the number is controlled at about this figure in order to minimise damage to trees and crops. The forest ponies number about 3,000, and although ponies have roamed the forest since before the Conquest they are not strictly wild because they belong to the commoners.

Conifers were introduced to the forest 200 years ago; they are most suited to the infertile soils and have gradually changed the appearance of the forest besides affecting wildlife, for whereas an oak wood supports about 4,000 different species a coniferous wood supports only about 1,000. Some trees are absent or very rare — ash, elm, lime and hazel for instance. The oak is the traditional tree of the forest but beech, birch and Scots pine are now very common. About 700 species of wild flowers have been recorded, about a third of the British total, but most of these can be found only by diligent searching. Deer are not the only animals that one may meet in the forest. Grey squirrels and rabbits are numerous but are not welcomed by the foresters; foxes and badgers are sometimes seen. The adder is the only poisonous species of British snake and early spring is the time to be wary of them; grass snakes are harmless.

Conservation of the forest and its wildlife is of great importance today for the New Forest is a National Nature Reserve and with 7 million visitors a year it has to be protected. It has survived as a beautiful medieval landscape only because it is Crown land protected by special laws. There are certain rules that visitors should observe, such as not feeding the animals, not lighting fires, not picking wild flowers and camping only on official sites. Two words of warning — avoid the bogs (white cotton-grass is a danger sign) and do not get lost (it is quite easy to do so!).It is unwise to go for a long walk without a map — the New Forest is a large area. A compass can also be useful, and stout shoes, boots or wellingtons are advisable, even in summer. One final 'golden rule' — shut all gates behind you!

Lyndhurst, known as the 'capital' of the New Forest, has been the administrative centre since the Middle Ages. The Queen's House is the headquarters of the Forestry Commission and the official seat of the ancient Court of Verderers. The court came into existence in medieval times to enquire into all offences under the Forest Law. Its function now is to protect the rights of the commoners and it can make its own by-laws. The court is open to the public when in session — it meets six times a year in the Verderers' Hall at the Queen's House.

The parish church, whose spire is a familiar landmark, was rebuilt in 1860-9 by William White in a strange Early English style. The interior is striking with its polychromatic bricks and life-size angels in the roof. Lord Leighton's fresco of the *Parable of the Virgins* is said to have been the first fresco in an English church since the Reformation. Some of its windows are by William Morris and Edward Burne-Jones. In the churchyard Mrs Hargreaves, who was the original 'Alice' of *Alice's Adventures in Wonderland*, is buried.

The town is very busy with visitors in summer. Among the tearooms, antique shops and gift shops in High Street, John Strange's butcher's shop stands out. Here venison can be bought at any time of the year; note that before cooking it should be hung in a dry place for 7 to 10 days.

The New Forest Museum and Visitor Centre provides a useful introduction to the forest for visitors. Its displays illustrate the history of the forest over the last 900 years and prove that there is far more to it than just trees, deer and ponies. Here one can read about the unique customs and traditions of the New Forest and learn what is meant by such terms as 'verderer', 'estovers' and 'coppicing'. The film in the audio-visual theatre is entitled *The Changing Forest*.

Lyndhurst is a good centre for walking and Bolton's Bench, adjoining the A35 on the east side of the village, is a good starting-

New Forest Ponies

*White Moor,
near Lyndhurst
in the New Forest*

point for walks across White Moor heath. At Longdown near Ashurst, east of Lyndhurst, the New Forest Butterfly Farm and Longdown Dairy Farm are worth a visit.

South of Lyndhurst is **Brockenhurst** (meaning 'badger's wood'), a village which although only just within the forest boundary seems

The Queen's House, Lyndhurst

very much a part of the forest with ponies and cattle meandering through the village streets. The railway arrived here in 1847 and since then development has been largely restricted to the area north of it, leaving the south half of the village still pleasantly rural. On the north side the majestic Balmer Lawn Hotel overlooks a popular green with the Lymington River flowing by, and on the south side is the parish church, the only one in the New Forest mentioned in *Domesday Book*. Here many New Zealand soldiers of World War I are buried; they died at the Balmer Lawn Hotel when it was a hospital. The Snakecatcher public house (formerly the Railway Inn) was named after 'Brusher' Mills, who earned a living by catching snakes in the forest and selling them; his grave is in the churchyard. On **Setley Plain**, a mile to the south, those interested in archaeology will find two large interlocking disc barrows, a rare type of Bronze Age burial mound.

A road to the west leads to **Rhinefield Ornamental Drive**, the most popular route in the New Forest. Most of the trees bordering the road were planted in 1859 and several of them are the tallest of their species in Great Britain. Forest walks on each side of the drive are specially designed for exploration on foot. The shortest (half a mile) is at Brock Hill, an area of ancient oaks known for its badgers; the other two are the Black Water walk and the Tall Trees walk. Plaques along the way give information about the trees and natural history.

The drive is continued north of the A35 by the **Bolderwood Ornamental Drive**; those interested in reptiles should divert towards Lyndhurst and turn left to Holidays Hill, where a reptiliary has been specially created by the Forestry Commission to add to our knowledge of reptiles and amphibians and to breed them for release.

A short distance along Bolderwood Drive is the Knightwood Oak, a pollarded oak that is one of the oldest and largest trees in the forest. (Pollarded trees are trees that have been cut back in order to produce a thick growth of young branches.) The eighteen oak trees in the Monarch's Grove commemorate known visits to the New Forest by eighteen reigning monarchs from William I to Edward VII. A nineteenth oak outside the grove, planted by the queen in 1979, marks the ninth centenary of the founding of the New Forest. Near this oak is an example of 'inosculation' where the branches of an oak and a beech have united. Barrow Moor car-park is as far within the forest as it is possible to be, because it is the furthest point from any part of the New Forest boundary.

Further on at Bolderwood Farm is the **Deer Sanctuary**, where wild fallow deer are fed and protected and can with luck be seen from the observation platform. Five different species of deer live in the forest, by far the most numerous being fallow deer; the others are red deer (the largest British wild animal), sika deer, roe-deer and the very rare muntjacs. The roe-deer are found in family groups unlike the others, which roam in herds. Red deer, well established in England in Saxon times, became virtually extinct by the 1940s. In 1962 a small herd escaped from Burley and colonised the central part of the forest. Sika deer, introduced from Japan, are found only south of the railway line. Roe-deer were also extinct in the forest at one time but were reintroduced in 1830 from Dorset. The muntjacs, a small and elusive Asian species, hide themselves so well that visitors are unlikely ever to encounter them. In 1851 an Act of Parliament authorised the slaughter of all the deer in the forest to make them extinct. Fortunately this proved impossible but they were reduced in number to a few score.

Near the Deer Sanctuary is an arboretum, created in the grounds of Bolderwood Lodge soon after the Deer Removal Act of 1851. Many trees planted at that time can be seen in the arboretum today. A leaflet available there lists all the notable trees, which include redwood, blue gum and cypress.

The road passes under the A31 and then a right turn leads to **Fritham**, a small village in the heart of the forest and a convenient starting or finishing-point for walks. There was once a gunpowder factory at Fritham and the pond here known as Irons Well was the mill-pond that supplied water for driving the factory mill. The factory was established in 1863 by a German named Schultze; in its early days it made gunpowder for the Prussian Army, then turned to smokeless sporting powder and finally closed about 1921. At one time about 140 men were employed, working in two shifts. Four pairs of workers' cottages and a chapel survive in the village, which also has a pleasant old thatched inn, The Royal Oak.

A left turn off the A31 beyond Stoney Cross leads to the **Rufus Stone**, which commemorates the strange death of King William II in 1100. He was killed, accidentally it is said, by an arrow aimed by Sir Walter Tyrell, but it is more likely that he was deliberately assassinated because he was so unpopular.

At Ower, on the A31 beyond Cadnam, is **Paultons Park**. Reclaimed from a derelict lake and gardens that were part of the old Paultons estate, it offers adults and children a range of attractions unrivalled in Hampshire. In addition to many amusements for younger children, there are two museums, aviaries, gardens and hundreds of wildfowl (the largest privately owned collection of wildfowl in the south of England). The Romany museum gives a wealth of detail on the gypsy way of life and has a splendid collection of living-wagons. The village life museum has replicas of a wheelwright's shop, a blacksmith's shop and a dairy.

South of the A31 is **Minstead**, a village of thatched cottages in leafy lanes with one of the most unusual churches in Hampshire. Its unrestored furniture and fittings are excelled in England only by those at Whitby; they include two galleries, box pews (one with its own fireplace!), and an early three-decker pulpit. All these galleries and pews required windows and these give the church its odd 'cottage' appearance from the north. This curious and highly individual church is mainly Georgian in date. The parlour pew with its fireplace and own entrance is unique in Hampshire and the pulpit is one of only two or three of its type in the county. Two galleries in one church, one above the other, are also uncommon, but perhaps the most unusual feature is that the font stands near the pulpit, placed there so that the congregation could see and hear the baptism service. At Minstead one can see how it was possible to cram more than a thousand people into a small church.

Arthur Conan Doyle, creator of Sherlock Holmes, is buried at the far end of the churchyard; he died at Crowborough and was reburied here in 1955 in the village he loved. At The Trusty Servant inn the meaning of its name is explained on its signboard; the original is a picture in Winchester College that portrays the perfect servant.

Furzey Gardens at Minstead with its 8 acres of flowering trees and shrubs is a botanist's and gardener's delight, and for good measure the Will Selwood Gallery here displays a great variety of arts and crafts including pottery, pewter, wrought iron and paintings, all the products of local artists and craftsmen. At the sixteenth-century Ancient Cottage visitors can study the way of life of a forester of that period.

From Southampton the A326 via Totton leads to **Dibden**, overlooking Southampton Water but still surprisingly rural. The church here was the first in Britain to be destroyed by enemy action in World War II (in June 1940); it was restored in 1955, retaining its fire-blackened chancel.

Hythe is trying to modernise itself for it has pedestrianised its narrow High Street and constructed a seat-lined promenade on the waterfront. On the north side there is a new marina, consisting of a large yacht basin, terraced houses in the modern idiom and an attractive waterfront with pseudo-Victorian lamp-posts. The pier and The Drummond Arms are reminders of the past. The pier is over a hundred years old and is the longest on the south coast; its railway, which carries passengers to and from the Southampton ferry, is an interesting survival. The track was electrified in 1922 and uses two locomotives from a mustard-gas factory that have run continuously since that date. There has been a ferry here for over 400 years; the first paddle-steamer service began in 1830 but was not immediately successful. T.E. Lawrence was at Hythe in 1931-2 while in the Royal Air Force, testing high-speed air-sea rescue launches. He lodged at Myrtle Cottage, a house near the corner of South Street and Shore Road.

Fawley oil refinery, the largest in Britain and the second largest in Europe, was constructed on the site of Cadland House in 1920 and was enlarged to its present size in 1951. It has transformed the appearance of this side of Southampton Water, which at the turn of

Mulberry harbour construction site, Lepe

the century was a marshy stretch of coast echoing to the cries of wildfowl. Fawley church is partly Norman — its tower dates from about 1170.

Between Fawley and Calshot is **Ashlett** quay, a quaint little place to find between a refinery and a power station. There is a restored tide-mill and granary of 1816 and a convenient public house, the Jolly Sailor.

Calshot Castle was one of Henry VIII's coastal defence forts, built partly of material from the demolished Beaulieu Abbey. Completed in about 18 months (1539-40), it was intended primarily for use as a gun battery to sink enemy ships. In spite of alteration and modernisation at various times the original work is largely intact. Smaller than most of the other Solent forts, it consists of a central tower, a lower curtain-wall and a moat. The former barrack-room contains replica furnishings of the 1890s, and a display illustrating the history of the fort is on the second floor. There are spectacular views along Southampton Water and the Solent from the top of the fort.

A Royal Naval air station was opened at **Calshot** in 1913 and after sterling service in the two wars was closed in 1961. The old hangars are still here and the base is now used as a Council Activities Centre.

The famous Schneider Trophy seaplane races were held near here in 1929 and 1931.

This stretch of the Solent coast is now the **Lepe Country Park**. There is a good beach with safe bathing and offshore the water is a protected oyster-fishing area. There was a small port at Lepe in Roman times; in the eighteenth century shipbuilding, fishing and smuggling were the main activities. Some of the Mulberry harbours used in the Normandy invasion were constructed here and the remains of the construction site can be seen beyond Stansore Point, also some of the concrete blocks placed on the beach as a road for vehicles.

Inland is **Exbury**, famous for its rhododendrons. Here visitors can enjoy the beauty of one of England's most colourful gardens where Lionel de Rothschild has created within a natural woodland the finest collection of rhododendrons in the world, numbering many hundreds of species.

In 1205 a Cistercian abbey was founded at **Beaulieu** by King John; it was called *Bellus Locus Regis* (the king's beautiful place), a name no less apt today. The abbey is in ruins except for the refectory, which is now the parish church; it is unusual in that, as it was not built as a church, it is aligned north-south. After the Dissolution the abbey passed into the hands of the Wriothesleys, Earls of Southampton, and later to the Montagus. The present Palace House was rebuilt in the 1870s and incorporates the old abbey gatehouse.

The abbey church, the foundations of which can be seen, was the largest Cistercian church in England, built about 1206-46. Cistercian architecture emphasised simplicity of form and purity of line rather than decorative effect, as can be seen in the remains of the abbey buildings. The external stone used at Beaulieu came from Binstead in the Isle of Wight and the internal stone from Caen in Normandy. The monastic exhibition illustrates the daily life of Cistercian monks by means of models, dioramas and other displays. A set of accounts from the abbey dating from 1269-70 has survived; the various activities of the abbey recorded in this unique volume give a remarkable picture of life in a medieval monastery.

The parish church dates from about 1230; visitors should note that in the morning it is accessible from the village, but in the afternoon only by paying for entrance to the abbey/museum complex. The stone pulpit from which readings were given at meal times is a very early example; pulpits were used in monasteries long before they came into use in parish churches.

There was a settlement outside the abbey in the sixteenth century but little is known of the origin and development of the village itself. Today it is an attractive and tidy place with little of the commercialisation that mars so many popular places.

The **National Motor Museum** founded by Lord Montagu is the finest collection of veteran and vintage cars in Britain — over 200 of them from baby Austin Sevens to the famous 1960 Bluebird racing-car. Motor cars on display include the first Morris Mini-Minor (1959 — cost £537) and its predecessor the Minor of 1931 (cost £100), a 1909 Rolls-Royce Silver Ghost, a 1913 Argyll (an early car with four-wheel brakes), a 1924 Trojan in which the engine had only seven moving parts, a 1901 Columbia Electric (an almost silent car) and a 1907 Metallurgique with a 21,000cc Maybach engine taken from a Zeppelin airship. The racing-car section includes the Sunbeam that became the first car to attain 200mph, Segrave's Golden Arrrow of 1929 and Donald Campbell's Bluebird, which achieved 403mph in 1964. There are also large collections of commercial vehicles and motor cycles and a special display on the history of the Grand Prix racing-car. The house, gardens, abbey and museum together make Beaulieu a most popular attraction.

Bucklers Hard can be reached by road or by the Solent Way, which is also a nature trail here, starting at the Montagu Arms. The village was created by the second Duke of Montagu as a port (named Montagu Town) for unloading sugar from the West Indies. This venture proved unsuccessful but the village then became important as a shipbuilding centre. Today it is the only rural eighteenth-century shipbuilding site in the country not built upon by industry or houses.

The first ship built at Bucklers Hard was the *Surprise* in 1745; the most famous shipbuilder was Henry Adams, who lived at what is now the Master Builder's House Hotel. His first ship was the *Mermaid* (1749); the *Agamemnon*, one of Nelson's ships, was also built here. Shipbuilding was finished by 1840 however and the great days were over. Later in the nineteenth century Bucklers Hard became a fashionable pleasure resort, with steamer trips to Ryde in the Isle of Wight. Bucklers Hard was part of the manor of Beaulieu and therefore was not a typical village for the shops, church and school were at Beaulieu. In the late eighteenth century the village was a thriving community engaged in agriculture and shipbuilding. There were

The Beaulieu
River

Beaulieu
abbey

two inns, the New Inn and The Ship.

The wide picturesque village street leads down to the river where one of the old slipways can be seen. The Maritime Museum has created a realistic representation of Bucklers Hard in the 1790s, depicting the work and living conditions of the local people. There is a realistic reconstruction of the interior of the New Inn, with simulated conversation by the customers. The chapel of St Mary in those days was a cobbler's shop and later a school; under its floor was a smugglers' den. Services are still held in the chapel.

The Beaulieu River, which is privately owned, is still busy, yachts now taking the place of warships, and river trips by steamer are popular. Sir Francis Chichester set out from here on his record-

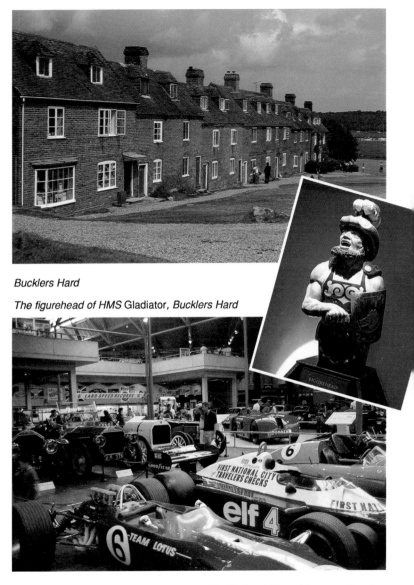

Bucklers Hard

The figurehead of HMS Gladiator, Bucklers Hard

The National Motor Museum, Beaulieu

breaking voyages. **Note** — the only car-parking available at Bucklers Hard is for museum visitors.

A by-road south of Bucklers Hard passes St Leonards Grange, where there are ruins of a grange and chapel once belonging to Beaulieu abbey and an enormous old tithe barn, the largest known Cistercian barn (222ft by 67ft). The present barn is about one-quarter the size of the old barn. Wool produced at Beaulieu was stored in the tithe barn before it was exported. Further on the road passes Sowley Pond, once a fishpond for the abbey and then a reservoir for an ironworks, the products of which were used by local shipbuilders.

Lymington is a very old town — it received its first charter about 1200 from Earl de Redvers and became a free port. Later it was a centre of the salt-refining industry and salt was its main source of revenue. The method of extracting salt was to channel sea-water into shallow ponds (salterns), then partly evaporate the water and boil the residue in a furnace. The industry reached its peak in the early eighteenth century when there were about 200 salt-pans on this coast; it died out because of the expense of bringing coal from a long distance and the imposition of a salt tax from 1694. Old salterns can be seen in the marshes between Lymington and Keyhaven.

The town became a fashionable bathing resort in the late eighteenth century. Boat-building has been carried on at Lymington for centuries; hundreds of boats are permanently moored here and it is a terminal for Isle of Wight ferries.

Lymington's attractive High Street is full of character. It displays a great variety of Georgian and Victorian first-floor façades — one should ignore the modern shop-fronts beneath them, although there are some splendid old bow-windows in Quay Hill, which leads down to the busy little harbour.

Inns feature prominently in the history of Lymington — there were once about forty-five in the town and even today there are plenty of them. Several former inns can be seen in Quay Hill and Quay Street (eg the Dolphin of about 1680). Pressgang Cottage in Bath Road was formerly the Harlequin Inn and the headquarters of the dreaded press-gangs. On the Southampton road adjoining the Tollhouse Inn stands the most picturesque toll-house in Hampshire. The Angel Inn in High Street has an old wrought-iron balcony and on the opposite side of the street General James Wolfe spent his last night in England at No 15 (now The Stanwell House Hotel).

The town's 700-year-old market is held on Saturdays. Successive alterations have destroyed the old character of the parish church but its galleries built round three sides of the nave are an unusual feature. A glass case contains the old roof bosses — a rare opportunity to examine these objects. In the churchyard is the grave of Catherine Bowles, the second wife of the poet Robert Southey.

At **Pennington**, a mile west of the town, the New Forest Brass-Rubbing Centre and Lymington Vineyard cater for specific interests.

Two miles north of Lymington is **Boldre** where the old parish church, away from the village on top of a hill, is of great interest; it dates back to Norman times, but has been restored since. There is a memorial to the sailors who died in HMS *Hood*, and a service for them is held once a year.

The vicar here from 1777 to 1804 was William Gilpin, who became an influential writer on travelling and the landscape, telling his readers how and where to look for the best features; his *Remarks on Forest Scenery* applied these principles to the New Forest. He paid for the building of a village school out of the royalties on his books. The old school is now Gilpin's Cottage, not to be confused with the house named Gilpins at Vicar's Hill, which was the vicarage. When Gilpin came to Boldre he found that the local people were more lawless than usual, so he set out to reform them by founding a village school and a poorhouse. Richard Warner, who wrote a history of Hampshire, was once curate here, and the poet Robert Southey was married to his second wife here in 1839.

The curious 218ft-high tower at **Sway**, north-west of Lymington, was erected a hundred years ago by Judge Andrew Peterson as an experiment, it is said, in the use of reinforced concrete. It has thirteen storeys and 330 steps and although apparently as solid as when it was built it has been declared unsafe. Trinity House refused permission for a light on the top because it would have been a danger to ships. Peterson's ashes were buried in a crypt beneath the tower. There are plans to convert the lower part of the building to a hotel.

Hurst Castle stands at the end of a shingle spit less than a mile from the Isle of Wight coast. This was another of Henry VIII's Solent defence forts, a twelve-sided central tower with three outer bastions. It was probably the strongest of the Solent defence forts, certainly after the massive and formidable wings were added in the 1860s. The Tudor castle and parts of the west wing are open to visitors. The defences of Henry's castle included seventy-one gun positions, and though it is unlikely that they were all manned at the same time they

Places of Interest Around Lyndhurst and Beaulieu

New Forest Museum and Visitor Centre
Lyndhurst
An introduction to the history and customs of the New Forest.

Rhinefield Ornamental Drive
An avenue of beautiful mature trees. The drive is continued north of the A35 by the Bolderwood Ornamental Drive.

Reptiliary
Holidays Hill, Lyndhurst
A collection of reptiles and amphibians that can be seen in their natural habitat.

Deer Sanctuary
Bolderwood
Here visitors may see wild fallow deer that come to the sanctuary for food and for its freedom from disturbance.

Bolderwood Arboretum
A way-marked walk directs visitors through the arboretum, where many of the trees were planted in 1860.

The Rufus Stone
Stoney Cross
Commemorates the mysterious death of William Rufus in the New Forest in 1100.

New Forest Butterfly Farm
Longdown, Ashurst
An indoor tropical garden with butterflies and moths from all over the world; the British species are kept in a separate area.

Paultons Park
Ower, Romsey
140 acres of gardens, aviaries and ponds. The village life museum recreates the atmosphere of bygone country life.

Furzey Gardens
Minstead
Eight acres of beautiful gardens of great botanical interest. The Will Selwood Gallery displays work produced by 150 local artists and craftsmen.

Longdown Dairy Farm
Ashurst
A working dairy farm with a wide range of farm animals.

Calshot Castle (English Heritage)
A coastal defence fort built for Henry VIII.

Lepe Country Park
A coastal country park, its chief feature being the shingle beach backed by low cliffs, with fine views across the Solent.

Exbury Gardens
The famous Rothschild collection of rhododendrons and azaleas, best seen in spring and early summer, in gardens of 250 acres.

Beaulieu Abbey and Palace House
The ruins of a Cistercian abbey founded in 1205 by King John. The former monks' refectory is now the parish church. Palace House incorporates the abbey gatehouse.

National Motor Museum
Beaulieu
England's leading motor museum, with a large collection of veteran and vintage vehicles illustrating the history of motoring from 1895 to modern times.

Maritime Museum
Bucklers Hard
Village famous for shipbuilding in the eighteenth century. The museum illustrates the history of Bucklers Hard, with a realistic representation of the village 200 years ago.

Boats moored in the harbour at Lymington

would have been a powerful deterrent to enemy ships. The castle was briefly the prison of Charles I en route from Carisbrooke to his execution in London. It can be reached by walking along the beach from Milford on Sea or by ferry-boat from Keyhaven.

Further along the coast is **Milford on Sea**, a small but popular seaside resort with an old village centre; it once had ideas of becoming another Eastbourne but nothing came of them. Its church, spacious and imposing, is mainly Early English in date. The oldest pillar-box in Hampshire stands at the corner of Cornwallis Road and Victoria Road; it dates from about 1856 and has a vertical posting slot. Keyhaven is a quiet little harbour; from here the Solent Way footpath follows the shore to Lymington via a nature reserve. On the west side of Milford, near the cliffs, is the graveyard of old Hordle church; many of the graves are of people washed ashore from shipwrecks.

Much new development has occurred further west at **Barton on Sea** and **New Milton**. Low cliffs and safe beaches along this coast attract many visitors. The Sammy Miller Museum at New Milton has a good collection of vintage motor cycles. Inland is **Hinton Admiral**; its name has no connection with the Navy but derives from the family of Aumarle or Albemarle who once held the manor. The Cat and Fiddle inn here is said to be very old. MacPenny's at Bransgore, north of Hinton Admiral, has a large woodland garden open to visitors.

The old railway station at **Holmsley** (now a tea-room) was on the Southampton to Dorchester line, which was known as 'Castleman's Corkscrew' because of its winding course via Brockenhurst, Ringwood and Wimborne. Holmsley, at first named Christchurch Road, was in 1847 the nearest station to Christchurch, which passengers reached by a 7-mile road journey. The main line to Bournemouth via New Milton was not opened until 1888.

Burley is a good centre for walkers and for horse-riders. The village is surrounded by many square miles of bracing open heathland and is always busy with visitors to its antique shops and tearooms. Castle Hill at Burley Street is an Iron Age camp and one of the best viewpoints in the New Forest.

Between the New Forest and the River Avon, which is the county boundary here, lies **Ringwood**, a lively town especially on market day (Wednesday) when it overflows with visitors. There is little of historic interest in the town other than Monmouth House in West Street, where the Duke of Monmouth is said to have been held prisoner in 1685 prior to his execution, and the Meeting House, built in 1729 as a Unitarian chapel. Ringwood's history goes back a long way however; it was recorded in *Domesday Book (Rincvede)* and its market dates from a charter of 1226.

North on the A338 is **Ellingham**; its quaint thirteenth-century church is full of old woodwork and furnishings. What appears to be a medieval chantry chapel is really a canopied family pew. The large ornate blue-and-gilt sundial on the porch is a striking feature; when checked in 1930 it was found to be surprisingly accurate. Dame Alice Lisle of nearby Moyles Court is buried here — she was executed in Winchester for harbouring Monmouth supporters.

The River Avon, famous for its fishing, is well stocked with coarse fish — pike, chub, dace, barbel and others. The salmon fishing is also among the best anywhere.

Fordingbridge has had a bridge over the Avon since early times. The earliest reference to one was in 1268; the present bridge is partly of the fourteenth century and is a designated ancient monument. It was once the boundary between the two royal chases of Cranborne and the New Forest.

There was a great fire in the town in 1702 and several houses have a rebuilding date of this time as evidence. Much of the parish church dates from the thirteenth century; its most notable feature is the hammer-beam roof of the north chapel, reminiscent of those in East Anglia; here the carvings are of prophets and kings and not of angels.

Sherings Museum in Church Street, open on Wednesday afternoons in summer, has an intriguing collection of rare and curious bygones, including old woodworking tools, household and motoring relics, toby jugs, dolls and World War I mementoes. Other exhibits include coffin trolleys, pre-World War II jars and tins, and pottery from excavations in Fordingbridge. Augustus John, the celebrated painter, lived at Fordingbridge for many years until his death. A commemorative statue stands in the recreation ground not far from the bridge.

Three miles north is **Breamore**, famous for its house and its church. The beautiful Elizabethan red-brick house was damaged by a fire in 1856 that ruined the interior, but the exterior has much the same appearance as when it was built in 1583. It was purchased in 1748 by Sir Edward Hulse, the King's physician, and remains in that family today. The house contains many valuable paintings, tapestries and pieces of furniture. The paintings include many of the

Fordingbridge

Dutch school and a unique set from Mexico. There are many other items of historical interest, including a James I pile carpet.

The church is the most important Saxon building in Hampshire; many features date from this period including the rood above the south doorway and the unique inscription over the south transept arch, which translated means 'Here the covenant is made plain to thee'. The church was built in the late tenth or early eleventh century and is one of the few Saxon churches of cruciform plan. The nave, tower and transept are part of the original Saxon church but the chancel has been rebuilt. The rood or crucifix resembles the one at Headbourne Worthy and has also been mutilated.

In the Carriage Museum in the stables is the *Red Rover*, the last stage-coach to run on the London to Southampton route. The Countryside Museum has a large collection of old farm tools, implements, vehicles and machinery that illustrate the changing pattern of agriculture over the years. The museum is designed to show the development of tools and machinery used at the various seasons of the year. Exhibits include traction-engines, tractors (the earliest 1917), ploughs, replicas of a blacksmith's shop, wheelwright's shop, brewery and dairy, and old and unusual farming implements.

Places of Interest Around Lymington and Ringwood

Lymington
Busy town and port with a yacht harbour and Isle of Wight ferry terminal. The attractive High Street has Georgian houses, and the church is interesting.

Lymington Vineyard
Pennington
Vineyard walk and free wine tasting.

New Forest Brass-Rubbing Centre
Pennington
Brass-rubbing from replica memorial brasses.

Spinners
School Lane, Boldre
Beautiful landscaped garden with many woodland plants.

Hurst Castle (English Heritage)
South-east of Milford on Sea
One of Henry VIII's forts, built to defend the entrance to the Solent. It can be reached by a $1^1/_2$-mile walk along the shingle beach or by boat from Keyhaven.

Sammy Miller Museum
Gore Road, New Milton
A collection of vintage motor cycles to delight the enthusiast.

MacPenny's
Bransgore
A large woodland garden, open in aid of the National Gardens Scheme.

Sherings Fordingbridge Museum
Church Street, Fordingbridge
Extensive and fascinating collection of bygones and relics, some relating to Fordingbridge and others of universal interest.

Breamore
Breamore House is a beautiful Elizabethan manor house with fine furniture, tapestries and paintings. The *Carriage Museum* has old coaches including the *Red Rover*, and the *Countryside Museum* has old farm machinery, tractors and implements.
Breamore church is Saxon and the most important of that period in Hampshire.
The *Mizmaze* on Breamore Down is a turf-cut maze probably of medieval date.

Roman Villa
Rockbourne
One of the largest Roman villas in Britain — over seventy rooms have so far been uncovered. Fine mosaic floors and the bath complex are on view. A museum displays finds from the site.

Martin Down
National Nature Reserve, mainly chalk grassland, with a wide range of plant species, animals, birds and butterflies. Many ancient monuments and earthworks, including Bokerley Ditch, Grim's Ditch and Bronze Age barrows.

A footpath near the house leads to the Mizmaze on Breamore Down, a turf-cut maze probably of medieval date, one of the only two in Hampshire. Turf mazes are peculiar to England and probably originated in the same way as the stone mazes found in churches on the continent of Europe. The maze at Breamore is circular and is similar in design to those in the cathedrals of Chartres and Lucca.

At the side of the main road in the village are the old stocks, and across the Avon a road passes the picturesque mill on the Test and leads to **Woodgreen** where the village hall has mural paintings of the 1930s, illustrating scenes of everyday rural life (look through the windows if the hall is closed).

A little further on is Hale Park, a house built in 1715 by the architect Thomas Archer. It is not open, but the church nearby is worth a visit; it was rebuilt by Archer and he lies buried in the family vault. The nave and chancel walls were retained in the rebuilding and transepts were added, but its Georgian character was destroyed by a Victorian restoration.

The village of **Hale** is centred on Hatchet Green, at one end of which is Windmill Ball, a Bronze Age barrow where perhaps a windmill once stood. Part of Hale lies within the New Forest; the rare Dartford warbler has been seen at Millersford Plantation.

West of Breamore is **Rockbourne**, an outstandingly beautiful village. The Manor House is a complex of medieval buildings including an Elizabethan range and a thirteenth-century chapel. The church adjoining it is said to have a 'ghostly' wall-painting that sometimes appears.

A Roman villa was discovered by chance at Rockbourne in 1942 and the museum at the site displays many of the finds from it. Over seventy rooms have so far been uncovered, proving the villa and its outbuildings to have been one of the largest Roman farmsteads so far known in Britain. The foundations of many of the rooms can be seen and some have mosaic floors.

Damerham, 2 miles south, is an attractive village with seventeenth-century cottages. The church of St George (an unusual dedication) has a massive square Norman tower.

In the far north-west of the county is the remote village of **Martin**, consisting mainly of one long street of old houses, as charming and peaceful as any in the county. The medieval church was described in 1851 as being in a state of 'indescribable dilapidation' — it has since been well restored.

Until 1895 Martin was in Wiltshire and somehow it seems more like a Wiltshire than a Hampshire village, perhaps because it is so remote. W.H. Hudson described the village in his book *A Shepherd's Life* — he called it Winterbourne Bishop. In the churchyard is the grave of William Lawes, who was the original of the character Isaac Bawcombe in the book. The old coach road from Salisbury to Poole can be followed over Toyd Down and through Tidpit; at Blackheath Down stands one of the old milestones.

The importance of **Martin Down**, a National Nature Reserve, lies in its variety of downland habitats and its wide range of chalk grassland species; it has been described as the finest area of chalk heathland in England and sheep grazing is vital to its successful maintenance. In addition to the usual chalk grassland species there are uncommon species such as dwarf sedge, field fleawort and early gentian. On the grassland upright brome and sheep's fescue are common and many types of orchid can be found. The northern part of the reserve was ploughed in World War II and consequently supports a less rich flora. The several types of scrub include hawthorn, dogwood, elder and gorse, and these provide cover for a variety of birds and animals including roe-deer and brown hares. The reserve is noted for its grassland butterflies, some of which are quite rare, such as the silver-spotted skipper and the Adonis blue.

Martin Down is worth a visit not only for its quiet beauty and for the opportunity to study plant and animal life but also for its many ancient earthworks. Bokerley Ditch, a massive bank and ditch extending for about 4 miles along the county boundary, was probably a frontier or boundary of the Romano-British period blocking an open stretch of downland between two extensive woodlands. Grim's Ditch on the other hand, a complex of banks and ditches enclosing about 14sq miles, formed some kind of local land division; it evolved over a long period, the stretch on Martin Down probably being of Bronze Age date. Also to be seen here are Bronze Age barrows and an Iron Age field system. North of the A354 a prominent section of the Roman road from Old Sarum to Badbury Rings can be seen; near here excavations by General Pitt-Rivers in the nineteenth century proved that Bokerley Ditch was later than the Roman road. Here also at the edge of the wood are the westernmost point in Hampshire (56 miles from the easternmost point at Aldershot) and the point where Hampshire, Dorset and Wiltshire meet.

8
THE ISLE OF WIGHT

Few areas of Great Britain comparable in size to the Isle of Wight have such a diversity of scenery and of fauna and flora, and few areas so close to large centres of population have remained so unspoilt. Though only half an hour from the mainland (less by hydrofoil) the island has retained a character and atmosphere all its own.

The Isle of Wight became an island only about 6-8,000 years ago when the sea-level rose and inundated what is now the Solent. Evidence of prehistoric settlement is provided by the neolithic long barrows on the downs near Mottistone and Afton and by the numerous Bronze Age round barrows (over 240 on the island) found mostly on the chalk downs. Many of the latter can be seen when walking along the Tennyson trail in the west of the island. Evidence from the Iron Age is more scanty; there is only one hill-fort, on Chillerton Down.

The Romans did not occupy the island in a military sense but several villas were built by local Romano-British landowners; remains of two of them can be visited at Newport and Brading. There were no Roman towns on the island and so far no metalled roads have been found. The island was colonised again by the Saxons; two of their cemeteries have been found on the downs at Bowcombe and Chessell. Christianity may have been quite late in coming to the island, perhaps not until about AD686.

The Normans left their mark with Carisbrooke Castle, Quarr Abbey and several of the island churches. The first coastal fortifications were erected by Henry VIII at Yarmouth, Cowes and Sandown Bay, of which only the castle at Yarmouth survives. The Victorians

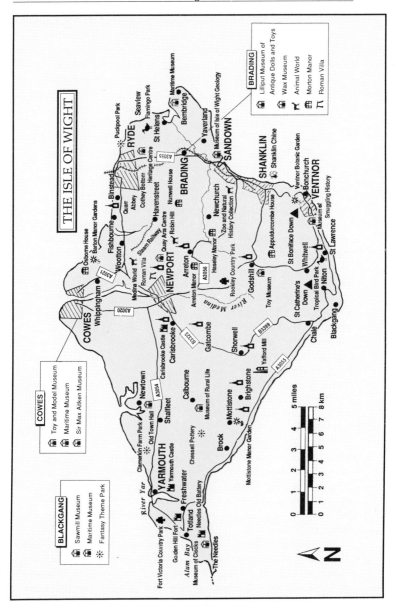

THE ISLE OF WIGHT

N

0   1   2   3   4   5 miles
0   1   2   3   4   5   6   7   8 km

were also concerned about the defence of the island and built several forts in the west and at Culver Down, Puckpool and Sandown.

No towns were mentioned in *Domesday Book*. Newtown, Yarmouth and Newport were early medieval planned towns, established in convenient situations for trade and communication with the mainland. Brading was established in 1280 by Edward I. The other towns, Ryde, Cowes, Ventnor, Sandown and Shanklin, developed rapidly after the Victorians discovered the island as a holiday resort. Ever since the visits of Queen Victoria the prosperity of the island has depended on the tourist trade. Its great advantage is that it can be visited throughout the year because of its mild winter.

That the Isle of Wight was prosperous in the sixteenth and seventeenth centuries is evident from the number of manor houses surviving from those times — over twenty remain of which Shorwell has three. Their weathered stones and beautiful grounds make no small contribution to the beauty of the island landscape; some of them are open to visitors.

As was so often the case on the mainland the growth of the seaside resorts was given fresh impetus by the construction of the island's railways. Only one of these, from Ryde to Shanklin, is still in use, apart from the restored stretch of steam railway from Havenstreet to Wootton. There were once thirty stations and 50 miles of track on the island. Some of the former tracks have been adapted for walkers and cyclists and provide some of the most interesting walks on the island (eg Newport to Cowes and Yarmouth to Freshwater). Other routes, such as Newport to Ventnor, have been lost for ever.

The first railway was that from Newport to Cowes, opened in 1862, but it aroused so little interest that only half a dozen passengers travelled on the first-ever train. The next line was from Ryde to Shanklin (1864), extended to Ventnor 2 years later. Ventnor was later to have a second station, the terminus of the line from Newport via Godshill. There was only one line in the western half of the island, from Newport to Yarmouth and Freshwater (1888); this was one of the first to close in the 1960s. It was a sad day for the island when the railways closed — they carried an estimated 3,000,000 passengers in 1951.

Just as the different geological strata have produced an extraordinary variety of scenery, so the soils have made possible a rich variety of flora and fauna. The two main areas of woodland are Parkhurst Forest, an ancient hunting-forest, where there are many different species of trees and wild flowers, and Brighstone Forest, which is now mainly beech wood. Spring flowers are a feature of the deciduous copses, and mosses, ferns and lichens are common in the older woods. Red squirrels, foxes, badgers and bats inhabit most of the woods.

The downland is mostly accessible to walkers (much of it is owned by the National Trust) and displays a different plant life to that of the woodland. The grass is often interwoven with myriads of tiny plants that have adapted themselves to the prevailing winds. Away from the sea, orchids are common and butterflies abound. The cliffs and chines, and especially the landslip areas, exhibit yet another range of plants. To see just what will grow in this Mediterranean type of climate a visit should be made to Ventnor Botanic Garden.

The shores on the north coast are more sheltered than those on the south, which are more often composed of sand, shingle or rocks rather than mud. The rocky shores (eg Freshwater Bay, Hanover Point and Foreland) are the best for marine life. The Duver at St Helens has probably a richer flora than any area of comparable size. Tidal estuaries are good places for bird-watching, as at Yarmouth and Newtown and between Newport and Cowes.

The island's great asset is the coast, where most visitors congregate, but inland there are many beautiful and unspoilt places and the visitor will find these, with one or two exceptions, surprisingly uncrowded even in summer.

Most of the villages are attractive, many of them having an ancient church and a picturesque manor house that add much to the charm of the rural landscape.

For a small island Wight is quite hilly; chalk downs form the ridge of its backbone and an outlier of chalk gives rise to the highest point of the island at St Boniface Down. Flat areas are found east of Brading, where the harbour has been reclaimed, in the south-west between Chale and Brook Bay, and in the north between Newport and Yarmouth.

Few counties are so well served with footpaths (over 500 miles of them!) and the island is a walker's paradise, covered by an intricate network of well-marked paths and nature trails. Visitors without a car will find good bus services and a railway from Ryde to Shanklin.

Newport is the county town of the Isle of Wight and a convenient centre from which to explore the whole island; there is much more of interest in the town than one might expect. It was founded about 1180 as the 'new port' for Carisbrooke (then the capital) at the tidal limit of the River Medina. Evidence of much earlier settlement is provided by the Roman villa in Cypress Road; here one can see the remains of a corridor-type house with a range of bathrooms.

In the narrow streets and wide squares of this old market town many fine Georgian houses remain from the days of the town's greatest prosperity and they give the place a good deal of character.

The most imposing and conspicuous building in High Street is John Nash's town hall of 1816, with its giant portico of Ionic columns. Near it is Watchbell Lane, a narrow alley of antique shops, where the night-watchman used to call out the hours; his bell is fixed high up on a wall.

In St Thomas' Square (the old corn-market) is God's Providence House (1701), perhaps the most attractive house in Newport, with its five bays and majestic shell-hood over the entrance. It was so named because the people who lived there survived the plague of 1584, unlike many other inhabitants who were buried in the plague grave-yard, now Church Litten Park.

Also interesting is the quay area at the end of Quay Street, a wide street with elegant old houses. Some of the streets near here are little changed since Victorian times. Small ships still come up to the harbour with cargoes of timber and heavy goods and there are several old warehouses, in one of which the Quay Arts Centre holds regular exhibitions. The Pirates Ship at the quay (open to visitors) was featured in the television series *The Onedin Line*.

St Thomas's church, which dominates the centre of the town, was rebuilt in 1854-6. Beneath the chancel is the grave of Princess Elizabeth, second daughter of Charles I; she died at Carisbrooke at the age of 14 in the year following her father's execution. Her monument in the north aisle was presented by Queen Victoria. The pulpit of 1637, the best of the many beautiful pulpits in the island churches, has panels with carvings representing the seven virtues and the seven liberal arts.

About a mile north of Newport is the famous Parkhurst Prison (no admission to law-abiding visitors!). A nature trail follows the east bank of the Medina downstream from Newport quay to Binfield Marina. Moored here is the *Ryde Queen*, an old paddle-steamer, now an inn.

Parkhurst Forest was recorded in *Domesday Book* and was one of

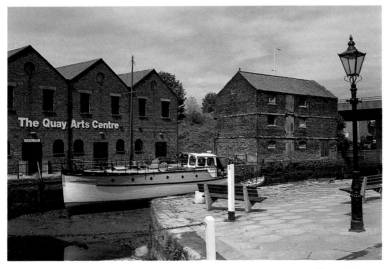

Newport quay

William the Conqueror's hunting-forests. In the forest there are two way-marked walks for visitors, one of $2^1/_2$ miles and one of $1^1/_4$ miles. The red squirrel is the animal most likely to be seen here — the island is one of its few habitats. The forest is a good place to search for uncommon wild flowers, but please do not pick them.

Carisbrooke, a mile from Newport, was for centuries the capital of the island. Its famous and much-visited castle is the only one of early medieval date on the island and its size and state of preservation make it one of the most impressive in England.

The castle built in the early Norman period was strengthened in the twelfth century by the present curtain-wall, in which archery loop-holes can be seen. The drum-towers of the gatehouse provide evidence of the change in medieval warfare — archery holes at the bottom and fourteenth-century openings for guns higher up. Increasing use of cannon necessitated the construction about 1600 of the outer wall and its bastions, nearly a mile in length. The castle was captured only once — during its first siege in 1136.

There are two medieval wells in the castle. One is inside the keep and is usually dry; the other is in the courtyard and can draw water from an underground stream. Both wells are about 160ft deep.

Charles I came here seeking refuge only to be held prisoner for a year until he was sent to London for execution. Relics of his imprisonment are in the museum in the Great Hall, together with some of Tennyson's possessions and the oldest organ in working order in Britain, dating from 1602.

The chief attraction in the castle, however, is the donkey-wheel constructed in 1587, now the only one in Britain, by means of which water is drawn from the courtyard well by a team of donkeys. The chapel of St Nicholas, rebuilt in 1904, is the official Isle of Wight War Memorial.

Overlooked from afar by the castle, the village itself is dominated by the parish church of St Mary, perhaps the most beautiful on the island with its great fifteenth-century tower. It was the church of a Benedictine priory dissolved by Henry V in 1415; later its chancel was pulled down by lord of the manor Sir Francis Walsingham. Inside is the fine stone tomb of Lady Wadham (about 1520), aunt of Jane Seymour, and the grave of William Keeling, discoverer of the Cocos-Keeling Islands.

On the Lukely Brook, which flows through the valley here from Bowcombe ('Beau-combe') to join the Medina, there were once six mills with their attendant mill-ponds. One or two of the ponds, reduced in size, can still be seen.

Arreton Manor, 3 miles from Newport on the Sandown road, is one of the most beautiful and historic houses on the island, rebuilt between 1595 and 1612. The manor once belonged to Alfred the Great and is mentioned in his will. The rooms are furnished in period style and the seventeenth-century panelling is of particular interest.

There are four museums in the house: the Museum of Childhood with toys, dolls and doll's houses from past centuries, the Pomeroy Museum with a famous Regency doll's house, the Lace Museum with a fabric and fashion collection, and the National Wireless Museum with many early radio and television sets that will delight the enthusiast. At Arreton Country Craft Village nearby nearly twenty different craftsmen have their workshops and display their products, which include pottery, furniture, metalwork, textiles and fossil ornaments.

Arreton church once belonged to Quarr Abbey; it was largely rebuilt in the thirteenth century and is one of the most beautiful churches on the island. In the churchyard are the graves of Oliver Cromwell's grandson William and Elizabeth Wallbridge, the heroine of *The Dairyman's Daughter*, the Victorian moral tale by Legh Richmond.

Only one mile distant is **Haseley Manor**, another fine old manor house, completely restored a few years ago from a ruin. The house dates from about 1550 and contests the title of oldest house on the island with the Wax Museum at Brading. Its twenty rooms contain period furniture and costume models illustrating the long history of Haseley. Here also is Haseley Pottery, the largest traditional pottery studio on the island.

Robin Hill Adventure Park, a mile north of Arreton, has about 100 different animals, nature trails, and an assault course popular with children.

The unusual and fascinating Medina World between Newport and Wootton incorporates Butterfly World and Fountain World. It has a landscaped tropical indoor garden with ponds, fountains and a waterfall, containing hundreds of colourful butterflies from all parts of the world. Adjoining it is the Medina Garden Centre, the largest on the island.

One of the saddest things to have happened on the island was the closing of the little branch railway lines that linked the towns and villages. However, at Haven Street station (Havenstreet on the Ordnance Survey map), south-east of Wootton, volunteer workers have restored a $1^3/_4$-mile stretch of the old Isle of Wight Central Railway, formerly the Ryde and Newport Railway, opened in 1875 and closed in 1966. Here visitors can enjoy a ride to Wootton and back; the line is now known as the Isle of Wight Steam Railway. There are also plans to re-lay the track from Haven Street to Smallbrook Junction on the Ryde to Shanklin line. The museum at the station has many interesting railway relics.

The name **Cowes** is synonymous with yachting and boats; the town lives by boats — making, servicing and selling all kinds from small yachts to hovercraft — and by entertaining the thousands of visitors who come every year for the yacht-racing.

Cowes is cut in half by the River Medina, which is crossed by a floating bridge. The two halves of the town are different in character, East Cowes industrial and unattractive, West Cowes full of shops and visitors in High Street and its continuation Bath Road.

Bird-watchers have their favourite spots; so do boat-watchers, and one of their favourites is the Parade at West Cowes. Here boats of all descriptions pass in an unending stream, summer and winter,

The starter cannons for the yacht races at Cowes

Arreton Manor

rising to a climax in Cowes Week in August when the annual regatta is held and everybody who is anybody in the yachting world throngs the town.

Cowes was a small fishing port until the nineteenth century when it grew rapidly into a great international yachting centre and the upper ranks of society descended on the town in Cowes Week. The Yacht Club, founded in 1815 with forty-two members 'of good social standing', became 'Royal' in 1820 and the Royal Yacht Squadron in 1833. In those days many of the members' boats were fully armed.

The headquarters of the Royal Yacht Squadron is at West Cowes Castle; the only part of the old castle surviving is the semi-circular platform on the promenade where the twenty-two brass guns that are used to signal the start of the races came from William IV's yacht *Royal Adelaide*. Half a mile beyond the castle is Egypt Point, the northernmost point of the island. Near here, at what is now the Grantham Hotel, lived George Stephenson the railway engineer.

High Street, long, narrow and winding, is full of surprises, an ever-changing succession of Victorian, Edwardian and modern shops and houses. Pascall Atkey is one of the oldest chandlers in the country (1799); note the early twentieth-century shop-front sign 'ship-smiths — galvanizers'.

Other attractions in Cowes are the Maritime Museum, the Cowes Toy and Model Museum and the Sir Max Aitken Museum. Thomas Arnold, the famous headmaster of Rugby School, was born at Westbourne House in Birmingham Road (see plaque).

A few years after their marriage Queen Victoria and Prince Albert felt in need of a country residence away from crowded London, and their choice fell on the Osborne estate. This decision materially affected the future of the island because it was thus brought to popular attention as a place to visit. The old house was demolished and the present house built between 1845 and 1851, designed jointly by Prince Albert and Thomas Cubitt in the style of an Italianate villa.

The pavilion was the first part to be completed and contains the formal rooms — drawing-room, dining-room and billiard-room; the private apartments on the first floor were more informal. The household wing was completed in 1851 but the Durbar room was not added until 1890. Though large, Osborne was designed as a house rather than as a palace. Its strange architectural style was imitated on a smaller scale all over the world. In front of the house there are mock Renaissance terraces with fountains and statues.

The prince died in 1861 and in the ensuing 40 years of her widowhood Victoria spent a lot of time at Osborne, and here she died in 1901. The rooms are little changed since her death, so that visitors have a unique opportunity to see the house and its contents as they were presented to the nation by Edward VII — a treasure-house of Victoriana. At the far end of the High Walk (mini-bus service) is the Swiss Cottage given to the royal children, a museum with the curios they collected and Queen Victoria's bathing-machine.

The most extraordinary church on the island, and perhaps one of the most bizarre in England, is at Whippingham. It was used by the royal family when they were at Osborne House and was rebuilt in 1854-62 in a curious Romanesque-Gothic style. The architect was Albert Humbert but the design is said to have been by Prince Albert himself.

The formidable tower with its pinnacles and spire is in the Early English style, as is the chancel, but the nave and transepts are in the Norman style; as a further architectural shock Gothic rose windows have been inserted in the transepts.

The massive marble tomb in the Battenberg chapel is that of Prince Henry and Princess Beatrice, Queen Victoria's youngest daughter. They were married in this church — probably the only instance of a royal marriage in an English parish church, certainly of the daughter of a reigning monarch. Henry died of fever at Ashanti in 1896. Victoria had nine children, eight of whom married foreign royalty or nobility. Outside the church are the graves of Prince Louis of Battenberg and Princess Victoria, parents of Earl Mountbatten, and of Uffa Fox the famous yachtsman, not far from his beloved River Medina.

Barton Manor has a longer history than Osborne House. The medieval house, whose predecessor was Barton Oratory, a religious house, was rebuilt by Victoria and Albert and the farm was used for scientific agricultural experiments. Today its beautiful gardens are open to the public and one of the island's vineyards is also here.

There was once a tide-mill near the Sloop Inn at Wootton Creek, one of several on the island; the main road bridge is the causeway of the dam that controlled the mill-pond. Corn was brought from Southampton and the flour produced from it was sent all over the island.

The church at **Wootton** has fortunately not been overwhelmed by the modern village. It has a Norman nave and an Early English chancel, and a good Jacobean pulpit. On the east side of Wootton Creek is Fishbourne, where the car-ferry from Portsmouth arrives, and beyond it is **Quarr abbey**. Visitors are welcome to the remarkable church of this Benedictine monastery, which was built in 1907-14 entirely of Flemish bricks and is considered to be a minor masterpiece of modern ecclesiastical architecture. The scanty ruins of the Cistercian abbey of Quarr, founded in 1132 and now incorporated in a farm, can be seen from the footpath that leads to Binstead.

Between Wootton and Havenstreet is **Firestone Copse**, a Forestry Commission plantation partly bounded by the former millpond, where herons can often be seen. There are three way-marked walks, one of 2 miles, one of 1 mile and one of a quarter of a mile. No less than 230 species of flowers and seventy mosses and liverworts have been recorded here, so those visitors interested in botany will be fully occupied.

Binstead church stands quite close to the shore; the Norman doorway re-erected in the churchyard has a grotesque carving above the arch. The quarries at Binstead supplied the building stone (an unusual type of limestone) for buildings such as Winchester cathedral and Romsey abbey. At Newnham Road is Brickfields Horsecountry, which includes the Isle of Wight Shire-Horse Centre and the Heritage Museum and Carriage Collection.

Ryde has the largest population of the island's towns (24,000). It has all the amenities of a modern seaside resort but away from its noisy and ostentatious front one will find a town of some character. The busy Union Street, first laid out in 1780, reminds one of its past elegance. The Royal Victoria Arcade in particular, with its Italianate front, harks back to the last century; its antique shops and underground market are worth exploring.

Ryde was becoming popular by about 1800 as a watering-place and soon large houses were being built for the wealthy as summer or permanent residences; many of them remain today as hotels. The building of the pier and the inauguration of the Portsmouth ferry service gave further impetus to this development.

Ryde pier, completed in 1814, was the first proper seaside passenger pier in Britain, built for the benefit of travellers who until then had to be transported across the mud and sands. Part of this early pier is incorporated in the present structure. The tramway and railway piers were added later. This unique triple pier affords an interesting insight into Victorian transport history.

Places of Interest in and Around Newport and Cowes

Roman Villa
Cypress Road, Newport
The remains of a Roman villa of corridor type with a range of bathrooms.

Quay Arts Centre
Sea Street, Newport
The island's arts centre, with regular exhibitions and educational events.

Pirates Ship
Newport Quay, Newport
The history of pirates with sounds and music displayed on board a 160-year-old ship that was featured in the TV series *The Onedin Line*.

Parkhurst Forest
$1^1/_2$ miles west of Newport on the Yarmouth road
Two way-marked walks traverse this old forest recorded in *Domesday Book*. One of the few habitats of the red squirrel.

Carisbrooke Castle
(English Heritage)
One mile south-west of Newport
The extensive ruins of a Norman castle, with later defences, on the site of a Roman fort; Charles I was held prisoner here. The Isle of Wight Museum in the castle has the oldest working organ in Britain, and the donkey-operated wheel for drawing well-water is the only one in Britain.

Arreton Manor
3 miles south-east of Newport
Historic seventeenth-century manor house with period furnishings.
Museum of Childhood (dolls and toys), *National Wireless Museum*, domestic and agricultural bygones, *Lace Museum* and *Pomeroy Museum*.

Arreton Country Craft Village
Arreton Manor Farm, near Arreton Manor
Craft workshops in a delightful rural setting.

Haseley Manor
Arreton, 4 miles south-east of Newport
A sixteenth-century house with twenty rooms furnished in period style. Haseley Pottery is the largest traditional pottery studio on the island. Lake, island and railway for children.

Ryde is now very busy with day-trippers from Portsmouth. Its attractions include Puckpool Park, Flamingo Park and Cothey Bottom Heritage Centre, which houses a splendid collection of veteran and vintage cars (including five Hispano-Suizas!).

Though hemmed in by new housing development the quiet little resort of **Seaview** manages to retain a little of its Victorian and Edwardian flavour. Its narrow streets slope down to the sea and its nineteenth-century villas and shops give it a certain charm. Its

Medina World
Staplers Road, Wootton
Butterfly World: a landscaped
tropical indoor garden with
hundreds of butterflies from all
over the world.
Fountain World: fountains,
waterfalls and garden pools, with
Italian and Japanese water-
gardens.

Isle of Wight Steam Railway
Haven Street Station, 4 miles east
of Newport
Restored steam railway on a
section of the old Isle of Wight
Central Railway. Museum and
booking-office at the station.

Robin Hill Adventure Park
Downend, $2^1/_2$ miles south-east of
Newport
A 10-acre animal enclosure with
100 different species, assault
course, water-gardens, walks and
nature trails.

Maritime Museum
Public library, Beckford Road,
Cowes
Models of steam-yachts and ocean
liners, and displays illustrating the
Spanish Armada and the battle off
the Isle of Wight.

Cowes Toy and Model Museum
95 High Street, Cowes
Thousands of model warships, old
Dinky and Corgi toys, model
soldiers, electric ships and trains.

Sir Max Aitken Museum
The Prospect, Cowes
Nautical instruments, paintings and
artefacts.

Osborne House
(English Heritage),
One mile south-east of Cowes
Built for Queen Victoria and Prince
Albert in the style of an Italianate
villa; the state rooms remain
virtually unaltered since the queen
died in 1901, with all the relics and
treasures of the royal family.

Whippingham Church
Strange Romanesque-Gothic
creation, allegedly by Prince
Albert. It has a profusion of royal
monuments and memorials.

**Barton Manor Gardens
and Vineyard**
Whippingham, $1^1/_2$ miles south-
east of Cowes
20 acres of beautiful gardens
originally laid out by Prince Albert
and Queen Victoria. Vineyard and
winery with a display of wine-
making equipment.

picturesque chain-pier was swept away in a storm in 1951. Salterns
Cottage, Old Salterns Gate and Rope Walk are reminders of
Seaview's former industries. The salt-works used ponds that were
formed by building an embankment across the harbour mouth.

Further along the coast at **St Helens**, all that remains of the old
priory church is the ruined tower right on the shore; the rest of the
church was carried away in the great storm of 1703. When the priory
was dissolved in 1414 its lands were given to Eton College. Some of

its gravestones are in the present church, which strangely is situated well inland a long way from the village it serves.

The houses of the village surround a long rectangular green. There are buildings of all dates and descriptions — old cottages, chapels and Victorian villas. A plaque on one house records that Sophie Dawes, daughter of a local smuggler, was born there; she ran away to London to become the mistress of the Duc de Bourbon.

The Duver (a local name for a low-lying sandy area), a wide expanse of grassy sand-dunes owned by the National Trust, guards Bembridge Harbour from the sea. St Helens was an important port in the Middle Ages; it finally gave way to Cowes and resorted to fishing and smuggling in the nineteenth century. These 40 acres exhibit a rich flora, the grassland in particular being of some interest; here thrift, sea campion (rare on the island), fescue and ten species of clover can be seen. The Duver is also the habitat of the mining wasp, which preys on worker honey-bees.

Bembridge is mainly a residential area, not as crowded in the summer as more accessible places; its harbour is one of the yachting centres of the island. At Bembridge Point, near the site of the railway station, is the unique Pilot Boat Inn, built in the shape of a boat.

Bembridge was a little fishing hamlet until the Victorians discovered it. When in 1878 the embankment across the harbour was built to carry the road and railway it put paid to Brading's history as a port and haven; before that the only road between the two places was via Yarbridge. There is still a passenger ferry from Bembridge Point to the Duver. At the lifeboat station on the shore, one of 200 on Britain's coasts, visitors can see a modern unsinkable lifeboat; this one is called out about forty times a year.

Foreland is the easternmost point of the island and the Crab and Lobster inn here is well known for its seafood. This is the best rocky shore on the Isle of Wight; the limestone pavement supports one of the best collections of seaweeds in the country and the sheltered channels contain large beds of eel-grass, a plant that survives under water.

Bembridge Windmill is the only one remaining on the island. It is one of England's oldest tower-mills, built about 1700 and last used in 1913. Once derelict, it has been expertly restored and its early machinery is of great interest. The sails were once covered with canvas and had to be faced into the wind. The cap or roof of the mill could be turned by pulling on a chain.

Bembridge Maritime Museum features the history of diving equipment, the history of deep-water sail and the discovery of the submarine *Swordfish*, and has a large collection of ship models.

The visitor is strongly recommended to take the road up to Bembridge Down and Culver Down, for the view from the top is one of the best on the island; a direction-indicator plate helps to identify distant points. The monument to the Earl of Yarborough, who founded the Yacht Club, was erected in 1849. Bembridge Fort (not open), part of the Solent defences, was constructed in 1862-7 as the main stronghold of the south coast of the island.

The hamlet of **Yaverland** lies at the foot of the down. Its Norman church was built about 1150 as the private chapel of the old manor house; the present house was built in 1620.

Over the south doorway of the church is a 'grinning' head, known locally as the 'monk'. The church was used for a long time as a garrison church for the troops who manned the forts along this coast.

Brading was once known as 'The King's Town of Brading' and relics of those times, including its charter of 1547, can be seen in the Old Town Hall museum. On the ground floor of the building is the old gaol with the stocks and whipping-post.

Brading was a port with a quay until the estuary was reclaimed in 1878-80, and soon after this it ceased to be a borough, though it has now regained town status. The site of the old quay and sea-wall is at the far end of Quay Lane; from here footpaths cross the marshes to Bembridge and St Helens. After several abortive attempts the sea was drained when the embankment at Bembridge was completed; the reclaimed land consists of tidal silt and sand and is used for grazing cattle. It is an important breeding area for birds such as lapwings, herons, warblers and coots. Many aquatic plants not found elsewhere in the island can be seen here.

At the road junction in the centre of the village there is a bullring, a relic of the days when the sport of bull-baiting was popular. The governor of the island provided a bull and the mayor and corporation attended in full regalia to watch this barbaric sport.

St Mary's church, one of the most interesting on the island, has a Norman nave and an unusual thirteenth-century tower built on to the nave. The Perpendicular Oglander chapel contains effigies of members of that famous island family. The one of Sir John Oglander (1655) depicts him with crossed legs and carrying a sword and shield

Brading

as if he was a crusader knight, a romantic touch but quite anachronistic.

Plant-lovers will be interested to learn that over 100 different species have been recorded in the churchyard.

Legh Richmond, curate of Brading from 1797 to 1805, wrote about the people of the island in his famous book *Annals of the Poor*, which sold about 2,000,000 copies. His stories were based on the lives of real people, such as Elizabeth Wallbridge (*The Dairyman's Daughter*) and Jane Squibb (Little Jane in *The Young Cottager*). Jane's grave is in the churchyard and her cottage can be seen in Down Lane. A memorial to Legh Richmond is in the church. In his book he describes the scenery of the Isle of Wight as well as the lives of the villagers.

Other attractions for the visitor include the Lilliput Museum of Antique Dolls and Toys, Animal World and the Wax Museum (in a house claimed to be the oldest on the island).

The Lilliput Museum contains one of the finest collections of dolls in Great Britain. There are over 1,000 of them, ranging in date from an Egyptian 'Answerer' doll of about 2000-1500BC to one of the present Princess of Wales. Of particular rarity are pedlar dolls of about 1820-30, an American circus of 1905 and old Punch and Judy

Places of Interest in and Around Ryde and Brading

Quarr Abbey
East of Wootton Creek
Twentieth-century Benedictine
monastery.

Firestone Copse
Between Havenstreet and Wootton
Bridge
Forestry Commission plantation
with three way-marked walks.

Brickfields Horsecountry
Newnham Road, Binstead
Includes the Isle of Wight Shire-
Horse Centre, and the Heritage
Museum and Carriage Collection.

Puckpool Park
Ryde
Incorporates Puckpool Mortar
Battery. Bowls, tennis, putting-
green, aquarium and aviary.

Flamingo Park
Springvale, Seaview, Ryde
Flamingoes, cranes and hundreds
of waterfowl to delight bird-lovers.

Cothey Bottom Heritage Centre
Adjoins the Westridge Leisure
Centre at Brading Road, Ryde
Exhibition of veteran and vintage
cars, motor cycles, bicycles,
stationary steam-engines and local
history.

Bembridge Lifeboat Station
An opportunity to see a modern
unsinkable lifeboat and its method
of launching.

Bembridge Windmill
(National Trust)
The only remaining windmill on the
island.

Bembridge Maritime Museum
Displays the history of sail,
navigation, shipwrecks and diving
equipment and has a large
collection of ship models.

Bembridge Down (National Trust)
Magnificent views with direction
indicator. Bembridge Fort (1862-7)
is not open to the public. Yarborough Monument (1849).

Old Town Hall
Brading
Museum with interesting collection
of relics of Brading town.

**Lilliput Museum of Antique Dolls
and Toys**
High Street, Brading
The Munday collection of dolls,
one of the largest in Britain.

Animal World
Brading
A collection of realistic animals,
birds and reptiles from all over the
world displayed in colourful
dioramas.

Wax Museum
Brading
An intriguing museum of wax
figures, housed in what is possibly
the oldest building on the island.

Roman Villa
Brading
Remains of a villa of about AD300
with remarkable mosaic floors.

Morton Manor
Brading
A house of 1680 furnished in
eighteenth- and nineteenth-century
style. Beautiful landscaped
gardens. Vineyard.

Nunwell House
One mile north-west of Brading
Seventeenth-century house, home
of the Oglanders.

Adgestone Vineyard
Upper Adgestone Road, one mile
west of Brading
Vineyard and winery open to
visitors.

puppets. The museum won a 'Come to Britain' Certificate of Merit in 1983, one of only two in the south of England.

The Roman villa has some of the best mosaic floors in Britain, remarkable for their wealth of pictorial representation. In Roman times the sea would have been only half a mile away.

Morton Manor is a beautiful old building. Its history dates back to 1249, though the present house was rebuilt in 1680; it is furnished in eighteenth- and nineteenth-century style. The landscaped gardens include a formal rose garden and ornamental ponds. Adgestone Vineyard, a mile west of Brading, has won many awards for its wine.

Nunwell House, north-west of Brading, has been the home for centuries of the Oglanders, one of the most famous island families. Henry VIII stayed here, as also did Charles I while a prisoner on the island. The present seventeenth-century house, in a fine park under the downs, contains good period furniture and collections of military and literary relics.

A road from Brading that follows the ridge of the chalk downs to Newport, passing the Ashey sea-mark of 1735, is recommended for its excellent views over the island. South of the ridge lie the unspoilt villages of Alverstone and Newchurch (the church was 'new' in Norman times when it was first built).

Alverstone is an unspoilt little village through which the railway from Sandown to Newport once ran; the station building is now a private house. The track of the railway provides a delightful walk east or west of the village; to the west it incorporates a nature trail. This area is noted for its wild flowers. On the way from Alverstone to Newchurch is Borthwood Copse (National Trust), an ancient oak woodland.

Newchurch is also an attractive little village and was once the centre of one of the largest parishes in the island. Its church has an unusual white weatherboarded tower and stands dramatically high above the Yar valley. Inside there is a fourteenth-century rose window, a Royal Arms of 1700 and a pelican (or eagle?) lectern.

The twin resorts of Sandown and Shanklin remain uncomfortable partners, the former brash and noisy and given over uncompromisingly to pleasure, the latter striving to retain some of its former character. Sandown is at sea-level, Shanklin is more than 100ft above the sea; they both regularly come top of the British sunshine tables.

Not as old as Ryde and not nearly as attractive, **Sandown** did not exist before 1800. There had been a fort here built by Henry VIII and another by Charles I, both now washed away. The Museum of Geology at Sandown public library has a large collection of rocks and fossils typical of those found on the island, and the partial skeleton of a recently excavated iguanodon from Atherfield.

Sandown is an ideal place for a family holiday, for young or old; it has a long sandy beach, a pier, boat trips, a zoo with rare animals, bingo, discos, theatre, canoe lake, golf course and leisure centre. There are no buildings in the town worthy of a second glance, except perhaps the Rivoli, an Art Deco cinema of the 1930s, the pier (1878) and the new pavilion (1934).

Shanklin has more character than Sandown. The picturesque thatched houses, now souvenir shops and restaurants, in the old village are much photographed by visitors. Shanklin was not really developed until after the coming of the railway in 1864 and its better houses date from soon after this. John Keats stayed in 1819 at Eglantine Cottage, now part of No 76 High Street. Like Godshill, Shanklin old village appears quite attractive at those times, early in the morning or late of a summer evening, when it is deserted and quiet.

Shanklin provides a similar sort of holiday to Sandown but has fewer entertainments, though it does have two theatres and of course Shanklin Chine, the oldest tourist attraction on the island. The Chine, 300ft deep, is one of many steep-sided ravines in the cliffs, called 'chines' in the Isle of Wight and Dorset; when opened in 1817 it was instrumental in the expansion of the tiny fishing village to a busy seaside town. The Victorians came in great numbers to see it and reckoned it far superior to Blackgang Chine, though the latter is now much more popular. It is noted for its flora, particularly the many species of mosses, ferns and liverworts. Of historical interest is the section of pipeline (PLUTO), which during World War II carried petrol down the chine and across the Channel to Normandy.

South along the coast from Shanklin are Luccombe Chine, less visited than Shanklin Chine, and the Landslip. One of the most attractive short walks on the island is that which crosses the Landslip to Luccombe Chine. From Nansen Hill car-park turn left at the tea-room and go down the cliff steps. Turn right and descend to the lower Landslip, then left on the footpath signposted Luccombe and Shanklin.

The path here crosses the wild and beautiful undercliff, where

The sea-front, Ventnor

old oak trees grow amidst the tangled undergrowth, with honey-suckle, clematis and hydrangeas running wild. At the far end of the Landslip continue straight on to Dunnose Cottage, then left up a narrow road (to the right is Luccombe Chine). At Luccombe Farm turn left and at the farm cottages follow a steep footpath back to the car-park.

The Victorians praised the village of **Bonchurch** in no uncertain terms; some said it was 'heaven on earth'. Many literary people came here to live or to stay awhile — Dickens, Tennyson, Thackeray, Macaulay. It still has something of a peaceful Victorian atmosphere — large houses set among trees, a village pond converted from a swamp, given by H. de Vere Stacpoole, author of *The Blue Lagoon*, and unexpected views of the sea.

Bonchurch rests on terraces above the shore with steep flights of steps connecting them. The area was once noted for its stone quarries and a pyramidal stone erected near the pond in 1773 is an example of the local stone. Horseshoe Bay lies at the foot of the village, a delightfully secluded little place where one can sample fresh sea-food.

The church of St Boniface, Bonchurch

The Winter Gardens, Ventnor

The beautiful old church, dedicated to St Boniface, is a simple nave-and-chancel building of the thirteenth century standing within sound of the waves below. Higher up is the new church of 1847-8, where in the churchyard is the grave of the poet A.C. Swinburne; he lived at East Dene from 1841 to 1865. Dickens wrote part of *David Copperfield* at the house named Winterbourne (now a hotel).

Ventnor is without much doubt one of the steepest towns in Britain for it is built on terraces on the cliff-face, inviting the inevitable comparison with the French and Italian Rivieras; it has been called 'the English Madeira'.

With its sub-tropical climate it is also one of the most sheltered towns. In summer the sun rises and sets behind the hills but in winter the town receives the maximum possible sunshine. The Victorians soon realised the climatic advantages of what was then a tiny fishing village, decided that it was an ideal place in which to live and built their villas and hotels on the cliff-face.

The town was eventually served by two railways, the first in 1866 from Ryde, approaching the town through a tunnel from Wroxall to a terminus in Mitchell Avenue. The second line was from Newport and Godshill, through a tunnel south of Whitwell, emerging dramatically on to the Undercliff at St Lawrence high above the sea, ending at Ventnor West station. Both lines are sadly now closed and their demise has had a marked effect on the prosperity of the town.

Another sad loss was the demolition in 1964 of Steephill Castle, the romantic Victorian Gothic edifice built in 1835. Of its gardens Sir Joseph Paxton himself said that he had never seen any more beautiful. Demolished in 1969, the Royal National Hospital for Consumpton and Diseases of the Chest was one of the longest buildings in Great Britain. It was not such a sad loss as Steephill Castle because it was replaced by Ventnor Botanic Garden.

Ventnor Botanic Garden is one of the best sub-tropical gardens in England, with over 10,000 plants of some 3,500 species. Rare trees, shrubs, alpines, perennials and succulents from all over the world flourish here in the open air. In the garden is the unique underground Museum of Smuggling History, which illustrates the history of smuggling through the ages with many relics of this fascinating occupation. Ventnor was the chief smuggling port of the island.

Ventnor is a combination of seaside resort down by the shore and busy town higher up connected by steep zigzag roads; it has a more sophisticated and elegant character than the other island towns.

There is just enough room on the shore for the usual seaside amenities including the Winter Gardens. In the town Hurst's ironmongers has its original Victorian façade and Burt's old brewery still produces quantities of Ventnor Ales. Visitors interested in the history of Ventnor and the coast should on no account miss the Longshoreman's Museum on the front and the Ventnor Heritage Centre in the town.

Above Ventnor and Bonchurch towers **St Boniface Down**, culminating in the highest point of the island (787ft above sea-level); from here on a clear day the views are magnificent.

The Undercliff forms one of the most distinctive pieces of coastal scenery in Great Britain. It is an area of ancient coastal landslips extending from Luccombe to Blackgang, about 7 miles long and up to half a mile wide. The landslips consist of massive blocks of the Chalk and Upper Greensand strata sliding on the underlying clay strata. Deep clefts or chasms mark the boundaries of the slipped blocks. The landslips are of prehistoric date but movement still occurs from time to time and is most active at the extremities. One of these movements in 1928 destroyed a section of the main coast road at Gore Cliff near Blackgang and 2 miles of new road had to be constructed via the village of Niton.

The town of Ventnor has been built within the complex of landslides and has the largest urban landslide problem in Great Britain. Occasional movements necessitate constant repairs to some roads and buildings, but no deaths have been recorded since 1799.

The woods on the landslips have a distinctive character; though some have been planted, some are older natural woods. Open land survives near St Catherine's Point and this is rich in rare and local plants. Stone walls were made from the rocky debris when the land was cleared for farming. The whole area is rich in wildlife and migrant birds make this their first port of call.

St Lawrence is well wooded, its large houses partly hidden by sub-tropical vegetation. Uphill from the main road is the tiny twelfth-century church, which until its chancel was extended in 1842 was the smallest church in England. A little further uphill is the old railway station building, now a private house; the line was closed in 1952.

Old Park on the Undercliff was one of the three hunting-parks on the island; the estate was once the property of Sir Richard Worsley, governor of the Isle of Wight. It was bought in the late nineteenth

Places of Interest in and Around Sandown, Shanklin and Ventnor

Museum of Isle of Wight Geology
Sandown public library, corner of High Street and Victoria Road
The geology of the island illustrated by its rocks and fossils.

Isle of Wight Zoo and Natural History Collection
Sandown
Tigers, pumas, monkeys, reptiles and birds, and a tropical house with snakes, housed in an old fort.

Sandown Pier
Pavilion Theatre, amusements and bingo.

Shanklin Chine
The town's most famous attraction, noted for its flora, especially mosses and ferns. A section of the wartime PLUTO pipeline can be seen.

Ventnor Botanic Garden
A sub-tropical garden of 22 acres with rare and exotic trees, shrubs and plants from all over the world — over 10,000 plants of about 3,500 species. Temperate House.

Museum of Smuggling History
Botanic Garden, Ventnor
The only museum in Britain that illustrates the history of smuggling over the last 700 years.

The Longshoreman's Museum
Esplanade, Ventnor
The nautical history of Ventnor as recorded in antique engravings, old photographs and models, including shipwrecks, baths and bathing, and paddle-steamers.

Ventnor Heritage Centre and Local History Museum
Spring Hill, Ventnor
Comprehensive collection of prints, drawings, photographs and maps relating to the history of Ventnor, models of railways and mementoes of wartime Ventnor.

Tropical Bird Park
Old Park, St Lawrence
'Walk-through' aviaries enable the visitor to get a close look at over 300 exotic birds. Woodland trail, lake and Tropical House.

Isle of Wight Glass
Old Park, St Lawrence
A glass-working studio where the skills of this craft can be seen.

St Catherine's Lighthouse
Niton
An 1840 lighthouse with the most powerful light in southern England. Open to visitors most afternoons.

century by a German, William Spindler, who unsuccessfully tried to build a port and town there; the broken-up promenade can be seen on the shore.

At Old Park is the Tropical Bird Park where special 'walk-through' aviaries give visitors a close look at the many species of birds, which include macaws, humming-birds and flamingoes.

Isle of Wight Glass was founded in 1973 by Michael Harris and at

Blackgang Chine
A fantasy theme park which includes a Wild West town, dinosaurs and a smugglers' cave; the most popular attraction for children on the island. *Blackgang Sawmill Museum* displays woodland crafts and the world of timber and has a working sawmill. *St Catherine's Quay Maritime Exhibition* illustrates the history of lifeboats and smuggling and has the skeleton of a whale on show.

St Catherine's Hill
From here there are extensive views over the west of the island. A curious fourteenth-century lighthouse stands on the site of a medieval oratory (English Heritage).

Appuldurcombe House
(English Heritage)
Half a mile west of Wroxall
The ruined shell of a mansion built about 1710 for the Worsleys, in a beautiful situation in grounds landscaped by 'Capability' Brown.

The Model Village
The Old Vicarage, Godshill
Large-scale model (one-tenth size) of a village, which visitors can walk through.

Godshill Toy Museum
A wonderful collection of toys of all dates in a picturesque old cottage.

The Old Smithy
Godshill
Attractions include a garden shaped like the Isle of Wight. Opposite is The Cottage Herb Garden.

Natural History Centre
Godshill
Tropical marine aquarium, 30,000 sea-shells, minerals, semi-precious stones and a water-garden.

Nostalgia Toy Museum
High Street, Godshill
Large collection of post-1945 toys, including Dinky, Corgi, Matchbox, Triang and other makes.

Rookley Country Park and Leisure Centre
2 miles north-west of Godshill
A landscaped park with an adventure playground, pitch-and-putt course and lakes; ideal for children.

the works visitors can see handmade articles being produced by ✳ skilled craftsmen. The glass articles made here, many using gold and silver in their designs, have won several awards.

The village of **Niton**, with its church dating back to Norman times, is situated partly on the downs and partly on the Undercliff, where one will find The Buddle Inn, an old haunt of smugglers, and the Royal Sandrock Hotel, where Queen Victoria stayed when a girl.

St Catherine's lighthouse, built in 1840 on the southernmost point of the island, has the most powerful light in southern England (over 5,000,000 candle-power). It is open to visitors most afternoons.

From here one can walk to **Blackgang**, famous for its Chine, one of the most popular attractions with visitors and the island's answer to Disneyland. The chine is 400ft deep and in the early nineteenth century was regarded as a savage and terrible place, the haunt of smugglers. The worst that can happen to one nowadays is to get lost in the amusements!

On **St Catherine's Down** (an easy walk from the main road viewpoint car-park) is a curious fourteenth-century lighthouse that looks something like a rocket. It stands within the foundations of an oratory that was demolished in the time of Henry VIII, the lighthouse tower being kept as a sea-mark. It was built by Walter de Godeton as a punishment for having stolen from a shipwreck barrels of wine that belonged to a French church. About a mile north stands Hoy's Monument, erected in 1814 to commemorate the visit to the island of Tsar Alexander I. It was erected by Michael Hoy, a local landower, who had spent many years in Russia. Ironically a memorial inscription was added to it 40 years later to honour the British troops who fought in the Crimean War against Russia!

An attractive 2-hour walk can be taken from the viewpoint car-park above Blackgang. Follow the cliff-top path to Niton, then at the second stile beyond the radio station make for Niton church. From there follow Pan Lane and Bury Lane (signposted St Catherine's Down); follow the blue arrows and turn left to the oratory. A short downhill path leads to the car-park. A diversion can be made to Hoy's Monument.

Chale (*Cela* in *Domesday Book*) not only has a strange name but also is an odd place, for though so close to the sea it has no access to it. The village is rather bleak and wind-swept and there is a fine view of the coast from the churchyard.

There is a record of a church being consecrated here in 1114; the present church has been altered and extended over the centuries. The Manor chapel once housed the gun that all parishes were required to have for defence of the island in the sixteenth century. There are gravestones of sailors in the churchyard, many from the *Clarendon*, wrecked near here in 1836. The local hotel was renamed the Clarendon and its modern extension, the Wight Mouse Inn, is well known for its food and drink.

Inland from the south coast the villages are situated in undulating downland. **Whitwell**, north of St Lawrence, is an unassuming place, but its church has a strange history. The medieval church consisted of two chapels side by side, one dedicated to St Radegund and the other to the Virgin Mary; in the sixteenth century the dividing wall was removed.

The White Horse Inn claims to be the oldest on the island. The village has some strange pieces of street furniture — handsome nineteenth-century iron water standards. They were provided by William Spindler, the wealthy owner of Old Park at St Lawrence.

Wroxall, north of Ventnor, is of little interest except for the magnificent shell of Appuldurcombe House, for 300 years the seat of the Worsley family. Rebuilt in classical style in the early eighteenth century with a room, it is said, for every week of the year and a window for every day, it became a school and then lay empty for many years until bombed in 1943. The beautifully-kept grounds were laid out by the famous 'Capability' Brown.

Godshill is the much-visited show village of the island. Not without reason, one might add, for it has a certain charm lacking in some of the popular seaside resorts; the much- photographed group of thatched cottages by the church is particularly attractive. One should come early in the day, before the coaches arrive, to see Godshill at its best.

Lunches at the inns and restaurants, cream teas in attractive gardens, quaint museums and gift shops, a model village (Godshill of course!), antique and curio shops — they are all here for the visitor. But if you want solitude and quiet you must come in the evening or in the winter. It may still be warm enough to sit outside, and you can then appreciate that a quite attractive village lies hidden beneath the commercial façade and that the cottages are really old, not modern 'olde worlde'. Places to visit include The Model Village, the Toy Museum, The Nostalgia Toy Museum, The Old Smithy, the Natural History Centre and The Cottage Herb Garden.

The church is the largest of medieval date on the island and one of the most interesting; like Whitwell church it has two dedications. It is spacious and basically fifteenth century; the present almost Catholic interior is a result of the influence of the Oxford Movement in the 1840s, which attempted to revive High-Church ideals and ritual. Its most remarkable feature is the Lily Cross — a fifteenth- or sixteenth-century wall-painting of the Crucifixion on a flowering

St Catherine's lighthouse

Godshill

lily, the only example in Britain. There are several memorials to members of the Worsley family.

Gatcombe church was built as a private chapel for the manor house. A nave window has the only surviving medieval glass on the island and the east window glass is by William Morris and the Pre-Raphaelites. Rookley Country Park, between Godshill and Newport, has several amenities, such as an adventure playground eminently suitable for children.

The chalk downland ridge forms the backbone of the western half of the island, much of it wooded as at Brighstone Forest. Three of the island's most attractive villages are situated along the foot of these downs.

Shorwell, the easternmost, is perhaps the best of the three, with its old thatched cottages and three mansions dating from Elizabethan and Jacobean times. It is a quiet, unspoilt village, the antithesis of Godshill and Brighstone, for it has no tea-gardens and makes no concessions to tourists, except for the Crown Inn, which is worth a visit. Its church was rebuilt in the mid-fifteenth century and is remarkably interesting. Its stone pulpit, a rarity, is set half-way along the nave and so has caused the central pews to face inwards. The original gun-chamber in the south aisle is said to be the only one in existence. Other interesting features are the large wall-painting of St Christopher and the rare Cranmer Bible of 1541.

Yafford Mill, a mile south-west, is a well-restored nineteenth-century water-mill with an overshot wheel, which used to grind feeding-stuffs for animals. Among many things to see here are waterfowl, seals, rare breeds of cattle and a collection of implements and tools.

Brighstone rivals Godshill as a tourist centre and though not quite as attractive it has its share of photogenic cottages. It was known for a long time as 'Brixton' and is still pronounced as such locally. It is a favourite stop for coaches on their trips round the island and the tea-gardens do a big trade in the summer.

St Mary's church has a Norman north arcade and a thirteenth-century chancel but suffered drastic Victorian restoration. Three of its rectors became bishops — Wilberforce (son of the famous William), Ken and Moberly.

The first lifeboat in the island was stationed at Brighstone (at Grange Chine); it was named the *Rescue* and was donated by the Royal Victoria Yacht Club. A recommended walk through

Brighstone Forest can start at the National Trust car-park on the west side of Brighstone Down. The path follows the Tennyson Trail and returns along forest rides between plantations of beech and Corsican pine. Plants such as clematis are abundant and many different birds may be seen. From the top of the town there are magnificent views on a clear day.

The manor at **Mottistone**, part sixteenth century, part earlier, can be seen from the road; it is one of the most beautiful houses on the island, its mellow grey stone contrasting with the colourful terraces of roses. The porch is dated 1567 but the longer lower wing may be late fifteenth century. It was formerly a farm; the picturesque stone walls in the front gardens are remains of barns and farmyards. The beautiful gardens are open to visitors on certain days. The church opposite was rebuilt in the fifteenth century and restored in the nineteenth. A footpath near the manor leads up to the downs, passing the remains of a neolithic long barrow known as the Long Stone.

The fossilized remains of a pine forest known as the Pine Raft can be seen at low tide on the shore at Hanover Point near Brook Bay. At **Brook** (or Brooke as the local council spells it) one of the two earliest lifeboats in the island (the *Dauntless*) was stationed. At St Mary's church up the hill there are several lifeboat memorials, including one from a Spanish captain in bizarre English. The old roofless lifeboat station still stands near the cliffs. J.B. Priestley once lived at Brook Hill House, visible high above the village. A nature trail can be followed uphill from the village and then along the downs to the west where many typical chalk-loving plants can be seen. Isle of Wight Pearl at Chilton Chine has an extensive display of pearl jewellery, and Chessell Pottery at Shalcombe produces fine porcelain. From Brook the Military Road goes on to Freshwater Bay.

The Military Road from Niton to Freshwater Bay closely follows the cliffs in the south-west of the island and affords magnificent views of the downs further inland and of the cliffs below Tennyson Down. It was constructed in the 1860s to serve the garrisons of troops stationed along this coast during the French invasion scare.

The road was not surfaced until the 1930s; at that time no thought was given to its proximity to the cliffs, and it is now apparent that in some places it will eventually be breached by cliff recession or landslips, as happened between Niton and Blackgang in 1928. Near Brook Bay a coastal mud-slide has encroached to within 80ft of the road and cliff recession at Compton Down has brought the cliff edge to within 40ft of the road.

To enable the road to be used for as long as possible and to give warning of impending landslips, instruments known as tiltmeters have been installed under a section of road at Compton Down. These measure the increase in tilt of the ground and are connected to warning signs on the road. If the amount of tilt exceeds a pre-set limit the warning signs will be illuminated and traffic will be diverted over a more inland route.

The thatched church of St Agnes at Freshwater Bay is not as old as it looks, having been built in 1908. Further west is Farringford, now a hotel, which was rented by Tennyson in 1853 for £2 a week before he bought it 2 years later. He was a familiar figure here for many years in his black cloak, walking in the village or on the downs. In May 1892 he left the island for the last time. His monument on Tennyson Down was placed there as a beacon for sailors.

George Morland the painter was a frequent visitor to Freshwater, and Robert Hooke the scientist and architect was born here in 1635. Julia Cameron, the famous early photographer, lived for a time at a cottage named Dimbola.

All Saints church from the outside looks to be late thirteenth century, but inside a Norman nave is revealed. The expansion of Freshwater in the Victorian period necessitated the enlargement of the church. It is very much associated with the Tennysons; there are memorials to members of the family inside the church and the graves of Lady Tennyson and others of the family in the churchyard. There are fine views from the churchyard; the River Yar is tidal to this point.

The Needles Pleasure Park at Alum Bay (alum was first worked here in 1561) has a chair-lift to the beach where visitors can purchase souvenirs made of the multi-coloured sands in the cliffs, where the strata have been folded vertically so that a large number are encountered in a short distance.

A monument in the car-park commemorates the world's first wireless telegraph station, where Marconi conducted experiments from 1897 to 1900. From here the first radio messages were exchanged with a boat in Alum Bay; scientists came from all over the world to see the station.

From the park a mini-bus service runs to **The Needles Old Battery** at the western end of the downs (no cars allowed), which has been opened to the public by the National Trust. Built in 1861-3 as

Mottistone Manor

Freshwater Bay

Alum Bay and The Needles

Yarmouth

part of the Solent defences against possible attack by the French, it mounted six heavy guns. A hundred years of military history on this bleak headland ended with its recent use as a space-rocket testing-site. From the end of the searchlight tunnel there is a splendid view of the Needles, the most famous landmarks of the island, and their lighthouse of 1858. The Museum of Clocks at Alum Bay has a world-wide collection of clocks and watches, all working.

An exhilarating way to reach the Needles is the 3-mile walk over **Tennyson Down** from Freshwater Bay. Once the path out of the bay has been climbed it is easy walking on level ground with views over the English Channel to the south and across the Solent to the Hampshire coast to the north. On Tennyson Down is the best collection of chalk grassland lichens in Great Britain.

Golden Hill Fort has recently been opened to the public. It was built in 1863-9 as a fortified barracks to protect the five coastal batteries that had been constructed to defend the Needles passage. It held 136 men and had six guns on the roof; from the battlements there are splendid views in all directions. It is being developed as a tourist centre with craft shops in its multitude of little rooms and passages.

Between Totland and Yarmouth is **Fort Victoria Country Park**. Fort Victoria and Fort Albert were built to defend the western entrance to the Solent; Fort Victoria had fifty-two guns.

Yarmouth is an historic little port, compact and attractive, its harbour always full of yachts. By the twelfth century it was the chief port of the island and the first town to have a charter (supposedly about 1135). It became a borough in 1440 and remained one until 1891. Because of its narrow streets visitors are well advised to use the large car-park outside the town.

The castle was completed in 1547 on the 'King's land' outside the borough; its single 'arrow-head' bastion, which gave complete lateral covering fire, is the earliest surviving example in England.

Steamers first came to Yarmouth from Lymington in 1830; until then the crossing was usually by rowing-boat and not always pleasant. The attractive timber pier or landing-stage dates from 1876. The church was rebuilt in 1614-26 and its unattractive tower was added in 1831. In the chapel is a statue of Sir Robert Holmes, governor of the island in the late seventeenth century, said to have the body of Louis XIV and the head of Sir Robert!

The old tide-mill of 1793 which stands at the head of the mill-pond went out of use when the railway embankment was built across the pond. The railway line from Yarmouth to Freshwater is now a footpath and nature trail, following the east bank of the River Yar for part of the way. Cranmore Vineyard, between Yarmouth and Shalfleet, is one of several on the island.

Shalfleet (which means 'shallow creek') is situated where the road to Newport crosses the Caul Bourne; its church has a restored twelfth-century nave and a massive and impregnable tower, which was used as a refuge by the locals at the time of French raids.

From the National Trust car-park near the New Inn one can walk to the old quay situated on one of the creeks of the Newtown River. Once busy with boats unloading coal and loading corn, it is now a quiet haven for yachts and bird-watchers.

Calbourne is a quiet, unspoilt little village with a green, an ancient church and a manor house. Grants Cottage was the birthplace of William Long, author of the *Isle of Wight Dialect Dictionary*.

The village's main attraction is Winkle Street (its more prosaic real name is Barrington Row), a row of pretty thatched and tiled cottages facing a minute stream; it is advisable to come late in the day for a photograph, when the sun is on the cottages and the crowds have gone. The attractive thirteenth-century church has been well restored. Its tower was rebuilt in 1752, as an inscription on it records. Inside there is an interesting brass of a crusader knight.

Calbourne Mill is an early seventeenth-century water-mill in working order. The Museum of Rural Life here has a wonderful collection of curios — old dairy utensils, domestic appliances, war relics, old notices and housekeeping articles of all ages and descriptions.

It is hard to realise that **Newtown** was once a flourishing town, founded by the Bishop of Winchester in 1218 when it was freed from manorial duties, then being called *Francheville*. Its old streets are visible today mostly as grass tracks; the east-west ones were named Gold Street and High Street. All is quiet now, and standing in the former Broad Street is the old Town Hall of 1699, the only remaining monument of the ancient town; it is now a museum containing old borough records. Newtown was a 'rotten borough', returning two Members of Parliament until 1832.

A footpath leads to the old harbour site on the Newtown River, which was very busy even up to the late eighteenth century, though the town had never really recovered from earlier French raids. There

Places of Interest in and Around Yarmouth and the West

Yafford Mill and Farm Park
One mile south-west of Shorwell
Eighteenth-century water-mill in
working order; old agricultural
implements and tools. Waterfowl,
seals and rare breeds of farm
animals. Nature trail and children's
play area.

Brighstone Forest
2 miles north-west of Brighstone
Forestry Commission wood with
three way-marked walks. Trees,
flowers and abundant wildlife to
look for. Nature trail.

Mottistone Manor Garden
Mottistone (National Trust)
Beautiful terraced gardens laid out
in the 1970s in the grounds of
medieval Mottistone Manor.

The Needles Pleasure Park
A chair-lift takes visitors to and
from the beach at Alum Bay,
where the multi-coloured sands
from the vertical strata are sold as
souvenirs. Glass-working can be
seen at the works and studio of
Alum Bay Glass.

The Needles Old Battery
(National Trust)
Built 1861-3 as part of the Solent
defences. There is a superb view
of the Needles rocks from the end
of the searchlight tunnel.

Tennyson Down
(National Trust)
The Tennyson Trail follows the
crest of the east-west chalk ridge.
The Tennyson Monument was
erected as a beacon for sailors.

Golden Hill Fort
Freshwater
Victorian fort in 50 acres of
parkland, with antique, gift and
craft shops, a military museum and
audio-visual theatre.

Museum of Clocks
Alum Bay
A collection of clocks from all over
the world — all working.

Fort Victoria Country Park
Fort Victoria and Fort Albert
formed part of the Solent defences. Marine aquarium.

Yarmouth Castle
(English Heritage)
Completed in 1547 soon after the
death of Henry VIII; its 'arrow-
head' bastion is the earliest
surviving example in England.

Cranmore Vineyard
Solent Road, Yarmouth
Guided tours of the vineyard and
wine-tasting.

Calbourne Water Mill and Museum of Rural Life
Seventeenth-century water-mill in
working order. The museum has a
large collection of old dairy relics,
domestic curios and farm implements.

Newtown Old Town Hall
(National Trust)
A relic of Newtown's former status
as a borough, built in 1699.
Exhibits include borough records.

Clamerkin Farm Park
One mile east of Newtown
A working farm with cows, sheep
and rare breeds of pigs. Woodland
walks.

Chessell Pottery
Shalcombe
Handmade and decorated fine
porcelain, seen in the making in
the studio. Exhibition showroom.

Isle of Wight Pearl
Military Road, Chilton Chine
Extensive display of pearl jewellery
for sale.

was a salt-extracting industry here — the old salt-pans are still visible. Further on is a nature reserve of 300 acres where many species of birds can be seen. Breeding birds are joined in the autumn by migrants such as waders, brent-geese and others; the unimproved grassland surrounding the estuary provides feeding and roosting-grounds for the birds. Since a flood in 1954 part of the estuary has reverted to salt-marsh.

Clamerkin Farm Park, a mile east of Newtown, is a working farm open to visitors.

USEFUL INFORMATION FOR VISITORS

Details are correct at the time of publication but are liable to alteration from year to year. Visitors should note that last admission time at most of these places is half an hour or one hour before official closing time. Almost all of them are closed on Christmas Day, Boxing Day and New Year's Day. At many of them dogs are not admitted.

ARCHAEOLOGICAL SITES AND ANCIENT MONUMENTS

Sites with no fixed opening hours have free access at all times.

Appuldurcombe House
(English Heritage)
Wroxall, Isle of Wight
☎ (0983) 852484
Open: Good Friday to end September, daily 10am-6pm; beginning October to Maundy Thursday, Tuesday-Sunday 10am-4pm.

Basing House
Old Basing
Basingstoke

☎ (0256) 467294
Open: April to September, Wednesday-Sunday and bank holidays, 2-6pm.
Souvenirs, tea-room.

Beacon Hill
Burghclere
Iron Age hill-fort.

Bishop's Waltham Palace
(English Heritage)
Bishop's Waltham
☎ (0489) 2460
Open: Good Friday to end September, daily 10am-1pm, 2-6pm; beginning October to Maundy Thursday, Tuesday-Sunday 10am-1pm, 2-4pm.

Brading Roman Villa
Brading,
Isle of Wight
☎ (0983) 406223
Open: April to September, Monday-Saturday 10am-5.30pm, Sunday 10.30am-5.30pm.
Picnic area.

Butser Hill
Queen Elizabeth Country Park
Iron Age farm
(see under Country Parks).

Danebury Ring
Danebury Hill
Stockbridge
Iron Age hill-fort.

Flowerdown Barrows
(English Heritage)
Littleton
Bronze Age disc barrow and bowl
barrow.

The Grange (English Heritage)
Northington
☎ (096 273) 4720
Open: daily, summer 9.30am-
6.30pm; winter 9.30am-4pm.

**King James's Gate and Landport
Gate** (English Heritage)
Portsmouth
Two gateways of the old fortifica-
tions.

Ladle Hill
Footpath from Watership Down or
Burghclere
Iron Age hill-fort.

Martin Down
West of Martin village
Bokerley Ditch, Grim's Ditch.

Netley Abbey (English Heritage)
Netley
Southampton
☎ (0703) 453076
Open: Good Friday to end
September, daily 10am-1pm,
2-6pm; beginning October to
Maundy Thursday, Saturday,
Sunday 10am-4pm.

Newport Roman Villa
Cypress Road
Newport
☎ (0983) 529720
Open: Easter to September,
Sunday-Friday 10am-4.30pm.

Old Winchester Hill
South of West Meon
Iron Age hill-fort.

Rockbourne Roman Villa
Rockbourne

☎ (072 53) 541
Open: April to June and Septem-
ber, Monday-Friday 2-6pm,
Saturday, Sunday 10.30am-6pm;
July, August, daily 10.30am-6pm.

Royal Garrison Church
(English Heritage)
Portsmouth
Open: April to September,
Monday-Thursday 9.30am-6.30pm,
Friday, Saturday 9.30am-1pm, 2-
6.30pm, Sunday 2-6.30pm.

St Catherine's Hill
Winchester
Iron Age hill-fort, Mizmaze.

St Catherine's Oratory
(English Heritage)
St Catherine's Hill
Isle of Wight
Medieval lighthouse on the site of
a medieval oratory.

Silchester Roman Town Wall
(English Heritage)
Silchester
(see also Calleva Museum).

Titchfield Abbey
(English Heritage)
Titchfield
☎ (0329) 43016
Open: daily, Good Friday to end
September 10am-1pm, 2-6pm.

Wolvesey Castle
(English Heritage)
Winchester
☎ (0962) 54766
Open: daily, Good Friday to end
September 10am-1pm, 2-6pm.

ART GALLERIES

The Allen Gallery
Church Street
Alton
☎ (0420) 82802
Open: Tuesday-Saturday 10am-
5pm.

Guildhall Gallery
The Broadway
Winchester
☎ (0962) 840820
Open: beginning April to end
September, Monday-Saturday
10am-5pm, Sunday 2-5pm;
beginning October to end March,
Tuesday-Saturday 10am-5pm,
Sunday 2-4pm.

John Hansard Gallery
The University
Southampton
☎ (0703) 592158
Open: Monday-Saturday 10am-
6pm during exhibitions. Closed
between exhibitions.

Quay Arts Centre
Sea Street
Newport,
Isle of Wight
☎ (0983) 528825
Open: Tuesday-Friday 11am-5pm,
Saturday 11am-4pm, Sunday
2-5pm.
Café.

Southampton City Art Gallery
Civic Centre
Southampton
☎ (0703) 832769
Open: Tuesday-Friday 10am-5pm,
Saturday 10am-4pm, Sunday
2-5pm (sometimes open Thursday
until 8pm).
Gift shop.

The Winchester Gallery
Winchester School of Art
Park Avenue
Winchester
☎ (0962) 842500
Open: Monday-Friday 10am-5pm,
Saturday 9am-12noon.

BEACH GUIDE

Barton on Sea,
pebble and shingle, bathing safe
when sea is calm.

Milford on Sea,
pebble, bathing dangerous when
rough.

Lepe,
sand and shingle, good for bathing
except at Stone Point.

Netley,
shingle and mud.

Lee-on-the-Solent,
shingle, bathing safe.

Stokes Bay,
sand and shingle, good for
bathing.

Southsea,
shingle, bathing safe except at
harbour mouth and at east end.

Hayling Bay,
sand, good for bathing.

Ryde and Seaview,
sand, bathing safe.

Whitecliff Bay,
sand at low tide.

Sandown and Shanklin,
sand, bathing safe.

Ventnor,
sand, bathing safe but beach
restricted at high tide.

St Catherine's Point,
bathing dangerous.

Brighstone Bay,
sand and shingle.

Freshwater Bay,
pebbles and shingle, bathing safe
when calm.

Alum Bay,
pebbles and sand, swimming
dangerous too far out.

Colwell Bay and Totland,
sand and shingle, bathing safe.

Gurnard Bay,
shingle, bathing safe.

BUILDINGS OPEN TO THE PUBLIC

Alresford House
Old Alresford
☎ (0962) 732843
Open: August, Wednesday-
Sunday 2-6pm.
Pick your own fruit and vegetables
(mid-June to August 10am-6pm),
tea-garden.

Arreton Manor
Arreton, Isle of Wight
☎ (0983) 528134
Open: one week before Easter to
October, Monday-Friday 10am-
6pm, Sunday 12noon-6pm.
Gift shop, restaurant, picnic area.

Avington Park
Avington, Winchester
☎ (0962) 78202
Open: May to September, Saturday, Sunday and bank holidays
2.30-5.30pm.
Tea-bar (Sunday and bank
holidays).

**Beaulieu Palace House
and Abbey**
Beaulieu
☎ (0590) 612345
Open: daily, mid-March to mid-
April 10am-6pm; mid-April to
May 10am-5.30pm; June to early
July 10am-6pm; early July to early
September 10am-6.30pm; early
September to October 10am-6pm;
November to mid-March, Mon-
day-Saturday 10am-4.30pm,
Sunday 10am-5pm.
Gift shop, restaurant.

Breamore House
Breamore, Fordingbridge
☎ (0725) 22468
Open: Easter to April, Tuesday,
Wednesday, Sunday; May, June,
July, September, Tuesday,

Wednesday, Thursday, Saturday,
Sunday, bank holidays; August,
daily 2-5.30pm.
Gift shop, tea-room.

Broadlands
Romsey
☎ (0794) 516878
Open: Easter to July, Tuesday-
Sunday and bank holidays; August
to September, daily 10am-4pm.
Gift shop, restaurant, picnic area.

Haseley Manor
Arreton, Isle of Wight
☎ (0983) 865420
Open: daily 10am-6pm.
Licensed tea-room, picnic area.

Highclere Castle
Highclere
☎ (0635) 253210
Open: July to September, Wednesday-Sunday 2-6pm.
Gift shop, tea-room, garden centre,
picnic area.

Hinton Ampner House
(National Trust)
Hinton Ampner, Bramdean
☎ (096 279) 361
Open: Good Friday to end Septem-
ber; house, Wednesday 1.30-
5.30pm; garden, Wednesday -
Sunday 1.30-5.30pm.
Tea-room.

Jane Austen's House
Chawton, Alton
☎ (0420) 83262
Open: April to October, daily;
November, December, March,
Wednesday-Sunday; January,
February, Saturday, Sunday 11am-
4.30pm.

King John's House
Church Street
Romsey
☎ (0794) 512200
Open: April, May, October,
Saturday 2-4pm; spring bank
holiday Monday to September,
Monday 2-4pm, Tuesday-Saturday
10.30am-12.30pm, 2-4pm.

Medieval Merchant's House
(English Heritage)
58 French Street
Southampton
☎ (0703) 221503
Open: Good Friday to end September, daily 10am-6pm; beginning October to Maundy Thursday, daily except Monday 10am-4pm.
Gift shop.

Morton Manor
Brading, Isle of Wight
☎ (0983) 406168
Open: daily except Saturday, Easter to end October 10am-5.30pm.
Gift shop, tea-room, licensed bar, plants for sale.

Mottisfont Abbey (National Trust)
Mottisfont, Romsey
☎ (0794) 40757
Open: April to September; grounds Sunday-Thursday 2-6pm; house Wednesday 2-6pm; rose garden also open early June to mid-July, Tuesday, Wednesday, Thursday, Sunday 7-9pm.
Gift shop.

Newtown Old Town Hall
(National Trust)
Newtown, Isle of Wight
Open: Easter to June and September, Monday, Wednesday, Sunday; July to August, Sunday-Thursday 2-5pm.

Nunwell House and Gardens
Brading, Isle of Wight
☎ (0983) 407240
Open: May bank holidays and early July to end September, Sunday-Thursday 10am-5pm; June, garden only 1.30-5pm.
Gift shop, tea-room, picnic area.

Osborne House (English Heritage)
East Cowes, Isle of Wight
☎ (0983) 200022
Open: daily, Good Friday to end September 10am-6pm; October 10am-5pm.
Gift shop, café.

The Pilgrims' Hall
The Close
Winchester
Open: daily all year.

Prince Consort's Army Library
Knollys' Road
Aldershot
☎ (0252) 24431
Open: Monday-Thursday 9am-5pm, Friday 9am-4.30pm.

Rotherfield Park
East Tisted
Alton
☎ (042 058) 204
Open: Sunday, Monday at spring and summer bank holidays; Sunday-Thursday in August 2-5pm.

Sandham Memorial Chapel
(National Trust)
Burghclere
☎ (063 527) 394/292
Open: daily 11am-6pm or dusk.

St Catherine's Lighthouse
Niton, Isle of Wight
☎ (0983) 730284
Open: Monday-Saturday 1pm-dusk.

St Cross Hospital
St Cross, Winchester
☎ (0962) 51375
Open: Monday-Saturday, April to October 9.30am-12.30pm, 2-5pm; November to March 10.30am-12.30pm, 2-3.30pm.

Stratfield Saye House
Stratfield Saye
☎ (0256) 882882
Open: beginning May to last Sunday in September, daily except Friday 11.30am-5pm.
Licensed restaurant, tea-room, picnic area, gift shop.

The Vyne (National Trust)
Sherborne St John, Basingstoke
☎ (0256) 881337
Open: Good Friday to mid-October, daily except Monday and

Friday (open Good Friday and bank holiday Mondays) 1.30-5.30pm (tea-room and garden 12.30-5.30pm); bank holiday Mondays 11am-5.30pm; closed on Tuesday after bank holiday Mondays.
Gift shop, tea-room, plant sales.

West Green House
(National Trust)
Hartley Wintney
Open: house, by written appointment only, Wednesday 2-6pm; garden — see under Gardens.

Winchester College
College Street
Winchester
☎ (0962) 64242/841021
Open: chapel, cloister and chantry, summer, Monday-Saturday 10am-5pm, Sunday 2-5pm; winter, Monday-Saturday 10am-4pm, Sunday 2-4pm; college, guided tours April to September at 11am, 2pm, 3.15pm and 4.30pm.

CANALS AND STEAM RAILWAYS

Basingstoke Canal Trips
Colt Hill Bridge
Odiham
☎ (0252) 549037
Open: trips May to early October, Sunday 2.30pm; August, Wednesday 2.30pm; bank holidays 11am and 2.30pm.
Bar, refreshments, gifts on board.

Isle of Wight Steam Railway
Havenstreet, Isle of Wight
☎ (0983) 882204
Open: trains run Easter and April, Sunday, Thursday; May, Sunday, Wednesday, Thursday; June to August, Sunday, Tuesday, Wednesday, Thursday; September, Sunday, Thursday; week before August bank holiday, daily 10.45am-4.15pm; station open daily May to August.

Gift shop, café, museum, picnic area, playground.

Mid-Hants Railway
Alresford
☎ (0962) 734200/733810
Open: trains run mid-March to May, Saturday, Sunday; June to mid-July, Saturday, Sunday, Tuesday, Wednesday, Thursday; mid-July to August, daily; September and October, Saturday, Sunday 10.30am-6pm.
Gift shop at Ropley station.

CASTLES AND FORTS

Calshot Castle (English Heritage)
Calshot
☎ (0703) 892023
Open: daily, Good Friday to end September 10am-6pm.

Carisbrooke Castle
(English Heritage)
Carisbrooke, Isle of Wight
☎ (0983) 522107
Open: daily, Good Friday to end September, daily 10am-6pm; beginning October to Maundy Thursday, Tuesday-Sunday 10am-4pm.
Tea-room (April to September), Isle of Wight Museum.

Fort Brockhurst
(English Heritage)
Gunners' Way, Elson, Gosport
☎ (0705) 581059
Open: Good Friday to end September, daily 10am-6pm; beginning October to Maundy Thursday, Tuesday-Sunday 10am-4pm.

Fort Nelson and the National Museum of Arms and Armour
Down End Road
Fareham
☎ (0329) 233734
Open: Easter to October, Saturday, Sunday, bank holidays 12noon-4.30pm.

Golden Hill Fort
Freshwater, Isle of Wight
☎ (0983) 753380
Open: daily 10am-5.30pm.
Antique, craft and gift shops, café,
public house, Military Museum.

Great Hall, Winchester Castle
Winchester
☎ (0962) 846476
Open: March to October, daily
10am-5pm; November to February,
Monday-Friday 10am-5pm,
Saturday, Sunday 10am-4pm.

Hurst Castle (English Heritage)
Milford on Sea
☎ (0590) 2344
Open: Good Friday to end
September, daily 10am-6pm;
beginning October to Maundy
Thursday, Saturday, Sunday
10am-4pm. Ferry from Keyhaven
May to October every 30 minutes
until 5.30pm, November to April
limited service.

The Needles Old Battery (National Trust)
West Highdown
Totland Bay, Isle of Wight
☎ (0983) 754772
Open: Good Friday to early
November, Sunday-Thursday
(open Good Friday and Easter
Saturday); July, August, daily
10.30am-5pm.
Minibus service from Alum Bay.

Odiham Castle
North Warnborough
Open: unlimited access.

Portchester Castle
(English Heritage)
Portchester
☎ (0705) 378291
Open: Good Friday to end
September, daily 10am-6pm;
beginning October to Maundy
Thursday, Tuesday-Sunday 10am-
4pm.

Round Tower and Point Battery
Broad Street

Portsmouth
Open: unlimited access.

Southsea Castle
see under Museums.

Spit Bank Fort
15 Hill Head Road
Fareham
☎ (0329) 664286
Open: daily, Easter to end of
September. Ferries from Gosport
Pontoon, Clarence Pier (Southsea),
Sandown Pier and Cowes Espla-
nade (weather permitting).
Licensed café.

Yarmouth Castle
(English Heritage)
Yarmouth, Isle of Wight
☎ (0983) 760678
Open: Good Friday to end
September, daily 10am-6pm.

CATHEDRALS AND CHURCHES

Only those with restricted opening
hours are listed.

Portsmouth cathedral
Monday-Friday 8.30am-6pm,
Saturday 9am-5pm.

Beaulieu
until 12noon.

St Michael's Abbey church
Farnborough
Conducted tours Wednesday
3.30pm (mid-July to mid-September), Saturday 3.30pm, Sunday
4pm.

Romsey Abbey
8.30am-5.30pm.

St Michael
Southampton
April to September 11am-1pm,
2-4pm.
Usually open at above times —
included on city guided walks.

Whippingham
Monday-Friday 10am-5.30pm.

COUNTRY PARKS AND OPEN SPACES

Sites with no fixed opening hours have free access at all times.

Farley Mount Country Park
3 miles west of Winchester
Nature trails, picnic tables.

Fort Victoria Country Park
Yarmouth, Isle of Wight
☎ (0983) 760283
Open: daily 10am-6pm (aquarium Easter to October).
Café, picnic area, guided walks.

Holly Hill Woodland Park
Barnes Lane, Sarisbury
Woodland walks, picnic areas.

Itchen Valley Country Park
Eastleigh
☎ (0703) 614646/643025
Nature trail, nature reserve, picnic areas.

Lakeside
Southampton Road
Eastleigh
☎ (0703) 643025/622211
Angling, sports and recreation.

Lepe Country Park
Exbury
☎ (0703) 899108
Restaurant, picnic areas.

Martin Down
West of Martin village

Parkhurst Forest
Near Newport
Two way-marked walks.

Queen Elizabeth Country Park
Horndean
☎ (0705) 595040
Open: Park Centre, March to October, daily 10am-6pm;

November to February, Sunday 10am-dusk; Ancient Farm, April to September, Sunday-Friday 10am-5.30pm, Saturday 2-5.30pm; park always open.
Gift shop, café, picnic areas, trails.

Rookley Country Park
Rookley, Isle of Wight
☎ (0983) 721606
Open: daily 8am-6pm.
Gift shop, restaurant, picnic area.

Royal Victoria Country Park
Netley
☎ (0703) 455157
Open: Easter to end September, Tuesday-Sunday; beginning October to Maundy Thursday, Sunday 10.30am-5pm.
Café, picnic areas, gift shop, visitor centre.

Sir George Staunton Country Park
Havant
☎ (0705) 453405/451618
Open: daily, 9am-6pm or dusk.
Snacks, play area, Ornamental farm, Leigh Park Gardens.

Upper Hamble Country Park
Pylands Lane
Bursledon
☎ (0489) 787055 or (0703) 455157
Open: unlimited access.
Drinks kiosk, picnic areas (see also Hampshire Farm Museum).

Wellington Country Park
Stratfield Saye
☎ (0734) 326444
Open: beginning March to end October, daily; beginning November to end February, Saturday, Sunday 10am-5.30pm.
Gift shop, café, picnic areas, nature trails, National Dairy Museum.

Yateley Common Country Park
Yateley
☎ (0252) 874346
Picnic areas, nature trail, fishing by permit.

CRAFT CENTRES AND WORKSHOPS

Alum Bay Glass
The Needles Pleasure Park
Alum Bay, Isle of Wight
☎ (0983) 753473
Open: glass-works, Good Friday to October, Sunday-Friday 9.30am-5.30pm; November to Maundy Thursday, Monday-Friday 10am-5pm. Shop, daily all year (both closed 2 weeks at Christmas).

Arreton Country Craft Village
Arreton, Isle of Wight
☎ (0983) 528353
Open: Easter to end of September, Monday-Friday 9.30am-5pm, Sunday 12noon-5pm, also Saturday and Sunday at bank holiday weekends 9.30am-5pm. Licensed restaurant, shops.

Branksome China
Shaftesbury Street
Fordingbridge
☎ (0425) 52010
Open: Monday-Thursday 9am-4.30pm, Friday, Saturday 10am-4.30pm. Not bank holidays.

Chessell Pottery
Chessell, Isle of Wight
☎ (0983) 78248
Open: studios, Monday-Friday 9am-4pm; showroom Monday-Saturday 9am-5.30pm (May to September, Saturday, Sunday 10am-5pm).

Denmead Pottery
Forest Road
Denmead
☎ (0705) 261942
Open: daily 9am-5pm, guided tours of factory Monday-Friday. Woodland walk, play area, lake, aviary.

Haseley Manor Pottery
Arreton, Isle of Wight
☎ (0983) 865420
Open: daily 10am-6pm.

Isle of Wight Glass
Old Park
St Lawrence, Isle of Wight
☎ (0983) 853526
Open: glass-works Monday-Friday 9am-4pm; showroom Monday-Friday 9am-5pm (also Saturday and Sunday in summer 10am-5pm).

New Forest Brass-Rubbing Centre
St Mark's Church
Ramley Road
Pennington
Lymington
☎ (0590) 77507/78474
Open: Easter to October during school holidays and half-term holidays, Monday-Saturday 10am-12noon.

The Old Granary Art and Craft Centre
Bank Street
Bishop's Waltham
Open: Tuesday-Saturday 10am-5pm.

Viables Craft Centre
Harrow Way
Basingstoke
☎ (0256) 473634
Open: Tuesday-Friday 1-4pm, Saturday, Sunday 2-5pm (closed 2 weeks after Christmas). Tea-room (Saturday, Sunday), wine-bar, restaurant.

GARDENS

Barton Manor Vineyard and Gardens
Whippingham, Isle of Wight
☎ (0983) 292835
Open: weekends in April, Easter holiday, beginning May to second Sunday in October, daily 10.30am-5.30pm.
Gift shop, wine-bar, café.

Bohunt Manor
Petersfield Road

Liphook
☎ (0428) 722208
Open: daily 10am-6pm.

Exbury Gardens
Exbury
☎ (0703) 891203
Open: mid-March to mid-July,
mid-September to mid-October,
daily 10am-5.30pm.
Tea-room, gift shop, plant sales.

Fountain World
see Medina World.

Furzey Gardens
Minstead
☎ (0703) 812464
Open: daily 10.30am-5pm or dusk.

Greatham Mill
Greatham, Liss
☎ (042 07) 219
Open: mid-April to mid-September, Sunday, bank holidays 2-7pm.

Hollington Herb Garden
Woolton Hill
☎ (0635) 253908
Open: mid-March to September,
Monday-Saturday 10am-5.30pm,
Sunday and bank holidays 11am-5pm; October to mid-March,
Monday-Friday 10am-5pm.
Tea-room, shop.

**The Hillier Gardens
and Arboretum**
Jermyns Lane
Ampfield, Romsey
☎ (0794) 68787
Open: Monday-Friday all year
10am-5pm, Saturday, Sunday,
bank holidays, March to mid-November 1-6pm.
Tea-room, picnic area.

Houghton Lodge
Houghton, Stockbridge
☎ (0264) 810502
Open: Easter Sunday and Monday,
bank holidays in May, March to
August, Wednesday, Thursday 2-5pm.
Plant sales.

Jenkyn Place
Bentley, Alton
☎ (0420) 23118
Open: mid-April to mid-September, Thursday-Sunday, bank
holiday Mondays 2-6pm.
Plant sales.

Leigh Park Gardens
see Sir George Staunton Country
Park.

Macpenny's
Bransgore, Christchurch
☎ (0425) 72348
Open: Monday-Saturday 9am-5pm, Sunday 2-5pm.
Plant sales.

Mottisfont Abbey Rose Garden
see Mottisfont Abbey

Mottistone Manor Garden
(National Trust)
Mottistone, Isle of Wight
Open: Easter to end September,
Wednesday and bank holiday
Mondays 2-5.30pm.

Sea Front Gardens
Southsea
☎ (0705) 834148
Open: daily, dawn-dusk.

Spinners
Boldre, Lymington
☎ (0590) 73347
Open: daily, end of April to
beginning September 10am-6pm.
Plant sales.

Swan Garden Centre
see under Zoos, Wildlife Parks etc.

Ventnor Botanic Garden
Ventnor, Isle of Wight
☎ (0983) 855397
Open: garden — unlimited access;
Temperate House — Monday-Sunday 10am-5pm.
Licensed bar, restaurant, crafts
centre, picnic area.

West Green House
(National Trust)
Hartley Wintney
Open: Easter to end September,
Wednesday, Thursday, Sunday
2-6pm.

LOCAL EVENTS AND SHOWS

These are the more important
events of the year; details of many
more can be obtained from local
papers and Tourist Centres.

Tichborne Dole: 25 March
New Forest Fair, Brockenhurst: 4th
week in May
Aldershot Army Display: last
weekend in June
Hampshire County Fair, Queen
Elizabeth Country Park: 2nd week
in July
Southampton Show, Southampton
Common: 2nd week in July
New Forest Agricultural Show,
New Park, Brockenhurst: 4th week
in July
Cowes Week: 2nd week in August
Navy Days, Portsmouth Dockyard:
4th week in August
Farnborough Air Show: September
every 2 years

LONG-DISTANCE WALKS

The Solent Way
53 miles from Milford on Sea to
Emsworth.

The Wayfarer's Walk
70 miles from Emsworth to the
Berkshire border and Inkpen
Beacon.

The Test Way
45 miles from Southampton to the
Berkshire border and Inkpen
Beacon.

The Clarendon Way
Salisbury to Winchester.

Holidays are available, based on
Winchester, covering these four
walks, also a holiday exploring a
different part of Hampshire on
each of six days. Information from
Hampshire County Council
Recreation Department, Andover
Road, Winchester (☎ 0962 64221).

Isle of Wight Long-Distance Trails
Bembridge trail
Shide, Newport to Bembridge
Point: 8 miles.

Hamstead trail
Brook Bay to Hamstead Ledge: 8
miles.

Nunwell House trail
St John's station, Ryde to Sandown
station: 10 miles.

Shepherds trail
Whitcombe Cross, Carisbrooke to
Shepherds Chine, Atherfield: 10
miles.

Stenbury trail
Blackwater, Newport to Week
Down, Ventnor: 10 miles.

Tennyson trail
Nodgham Lane, Carisbrooke to
Alum Bay: 15 miles.

The Freshwater Way
Yarmouth bridge to Compton with
spur from Freshwater causeway to
Freshwater Bay: 6 miles.

Worsley trail
Shanklin old village to Brighstone
Forest: 15 miles.

Isle of Wight Coastal Path
65 miles. Leaflets for this walk and
the long-distance trails are
available from the Isle of Wight
Tourist Board or the County
Surveyor, County Hall, Newport.

MILLS

Bembridge Windmill
(National Trust)
Bembridge, Isle of Wight
☎ (0983) 873945
Open: Easter to September,
Sunday-Friday; July, August, daily
10am-5pm.

Calbourne Water Mill and Rural Museum
Calbourne, Isle of Wight
☎ (0983) 78227
Open: daily, Easter to end October
10am-6pm.
Gift shop, café.

Eling Tide Mill
Eling, Southampton
☎ (0703) 869575
Open: Wednesday-Sunday 10am-4pm.
Museum, books, crafts and flour
for sale.

Whitchurch Silk Mill
Whitchurch
☎ (0256) 893882
Open: Tuesday-Sunday 10.30am-5pm.
Gift shop, tea-room.

Winchester City Mill (National Trust)
1 Water Lane
Winchester
☎ (0962) 53723
Open: Easter to mid-October,
Saturday, Sunday, Tuesday-Thursday (open Good Friday and
bank holidays) 1.45-4.45pm; mid-October to Easter by appointment,
Wednesday, Thursday, Friday
10am-4.45pm.

Yafford Mill and Farm Park
Shorwell, Isle of Wight
☎ (0983) 740610
Open: daily, Easter to October
10am-6pm.
Licensed bar, café, gift shop, picnic
area.

MUSEUMS

Airborne Forces Museum
Browning Barracks
Alison's Road
Aldershot
☎ (0252) 24431 ext 4619
Open: Tuesday-Sunday 10am-4.30pm.
Gift shop.

Aldershot Military Museum
Queen's Avenue
Aldershot
☎ (0252) 314598/24431 ext 2701
Open: daily, March to October
10am-5pm; November to February
10am-4.30pm.
Gift shop.

Andover Museum
Church Close
Andover
☎ (0264) 66283
Open: Tuesday-Saturday 10am-5pm.

Animal World
Brading,
Isle of Wight
☎ (0983) 407498
Open: daily, May to September
10am-10pm; October to April
10am-5pm.

Army Physical Training Corps Museum
Queen's Avenue
Aldershot
☎ (0252) 24431 ext 2131
Open: Monday-Friday 10am-12noon, 2-4.30pm (not bank
holidays).

Bear Museum
Dragon Street
Petersfield
☎ (0730) 65108/66962
Open: Monday, Tuesday, Thursday, Friday 10am-1pm, 2-5pm,
Wednesday, Saturday 10am-1pm.

Bishop's Waltham Museum
Brook Street
Bishop's Waltham
☎ (048 93) 4970/2365/5500
Open: April to October, Sunday,
bank holidays 2.30-5pm.

Blackgang Sawmill Museum
Blackgang, Isle of Wight
☎ (0983) 730330
Open: daily, Easter to June,
September, October 10am-5pm,
July, August 10am-9pm.

Breamore Carriage Museum
see Breamore House.

Breamore Countryside Museum
see Breamore House.

Calleva Museum
Rectory Grounds
Silchester Common
☎ (0734) 700362
Open: daily, daylight hours.

**Charles Dickens Birthplace
Museum**
393 Old Commercial Road
Portsmouth
☎ (0705) 827261
Open: daily, March to October
10.30am-5.30pm.

City Museum
The Square
Winchester
☎ (0962) 63064
Open: beginning April to end
September, Monday-Saturday
10am-5pm, Sunday 2-5pm;
beginning October to end March,
Tuesday-Saturday 10am-5pm,
Sunday 2-4pm.

City Museum and Art Gallery
Museum Road
Portsmouth
☎ (0705) 827261
Open: daily 10.30am-5.30pm.
Gift shop, café.

Cothey Bottom Heritage Centre
Brading Road
Ryde, Isle of Wight

☎ (0983) 68431
Open: daily 10am-6pm.

Cowes Toy and Model Museum
95 High Street
Cowes, Isle of Wight
☎ (0983) 292272
Open: Monday-Saturday 10am-
5pm (August 10am-9pm), Sundays
in July and August 11am-5pm
(closed Wednesday, October to
March).

**Cumberland House Natural
Science Museum and Aquarium**
Eastern Parade
Portsmouth
☎ (0705) 827261
Open: daily 10.30am-5.30pm.

The Curtis Museum
High Street
Alton
☎ (0420) 82802
Open: Tuesday-Saturday 10am-
5pm.

D-Day Museum
Clarence Esplanade
Southsea
☎ (0705) 827261
Open: daily, 10.30am-5.30pm.

Doll Museum
16A Chapel Street
Petersfield
☎ (0730) 63438
Open: Monday-Saturday 9am-
5.30pm.

Eastleigh Museum
25 High Street
Eastleigh
☎ (0703) 643026
Open: Tuesday-Friday 10am-5pm,
Saturday 10am-4pm.

Eastney Pumping Station
Henderson Road
Eastney, Portsmouth
☎ (0705) 827261
Open: April to September, daily;
October to March, first Sunday in
each month, 1.30-5.30pm.

Emsworth Museum
Fire Station
North Street, Emsworth
☎ (0243) 373780
Open: Easter to end October,
Saturday, bank holidays 10.30am-
4.30pm, Sunday 2.30-4.30pm.

Fareham Museum
Westbury Manor
West Street, Fareham
☎ (0329) 823786
Open: Monday-Saturday 10am-
5pm, occasional Sunday opening.

Museum of Isle of Wight Geology
High Street
Sandown, Isle of Wight
☎ (0983) 404344
Open: Monday-Friday 9.30am-
5.30pm, Saturday 9.30am-4.30pm.

**Gilbert White Museum and The
Oates Memorial Library and
Museum**
The Wakes
Selborne
☎ (042 050) 275
Open: mid-March to end October,
Wednesday-Sunday and bank
holidays 11am-5pm.

Godshill Toy Museum
Godshill, Isle of Wight
☎ (0983) 840790
Open: daily, Easter to October
10am-6pm.

**God's House Tower Museum of
Archaeology**
Winkle Street
Southampton
☎ (0703) 220007
Open: Tuesday-Friday 10am-
12noon, 1-5pm, Saturday 10am-
12noon, 1-4pm, Sunday 2-5pm.

Gosport Museum
Walpole Road
Gosport
☎ (0705) 588035
Open: Tuesday-Saturday 9.30am-
5.30pm all year, Sunday 1-5pm
May to September.

Gurkha Museum
Peninsula Barracks
Winchester
☎ (0962) 61781
Open: Monday-Saturday 9am-
4.30pm.

Hampshire Farm Museum
Manor Farm
Upper Hamble Country Park
☎ (0489) 787055
Open: Easter to end October, daily
10am-5.30pm; beginning Novem-
ber to Easter, Sunday 10am-dusk.
Gift shop, café.

Havant Museum and Art Gallery
East Street
Havant
☎ (0705) 451155
Open: Tuesday-Saturday 10am-
5pm.
Gift shop, café.

Historic Resources Centre
75 Hyde Street
Winchester
☎ (0962) 848269
Open: Monday-Friday 9am-5pm.

HMS Victory
Her Majesty's Naval Base
Portsmouth
☎ (0705) 839766/750521
Open: Monday-Saturday 10.30am-
5.30pm (10.30am-5pm November
to February), Sunday 1-5pm.

HMS Warrior 1860
Her Majesty's Naval Base
Portsmouth
☎ (0705) 291379
Open: daily, March to October
10.30am-5.30pm; November to
February 10.30am-5pm.

Isle of Wight Museum
see Carisbrooke Castle.

Light Infantry Museum
Peninsula Barracks
Winchester
☎ (0962) 61781
Open: Monday-Saturday 10am-
5pm, Sunday 12noon-4pm.

The Lilliput Antique Doll and Toy Museum
Brading, Isle of Wight
☎ (0983) 407231
Open: daily, mid-March to end April 10am-5pm; beginning May to Whitsun 10am-6pm; Whitsun to end August 9.30am-10pm; beginning September to end September 10am-6pm; beginning October to Christmas Eve 10am-5pm.

The Longshoreman's Museum
Esplanade
Ventnor, Isle of Wight
☎ (0983) 852176/853176
Open: Easter to December 10am-5pm (closes later July, August).

The Mallinson Collection of Rural Relics
The Selborne Cottage Shop
Selborne
☎ (042 050) 307
Open: March to October, Monday-Thursday, Saturday 10.30am-1pm, 2-5.30pm, Sunday 2-5.30pm.

Maritime Heritage Centre (Maritime Museum)
Ocean Village
Southampton
☎ (0703) 224216
Open from December 1990: Tuesday-Friday 10am-5pm, Saturday 10am-4pm, Sunday 2-5pm.

Maritime Museum
Bembridge, Isle of Wight
☎ (0983) 872223/873125
Open: daily, Easter to October 10am-5.30pm.
Gift shop.

Maritime Museum
Bucklers Hard
☎ (059 063) 203
Open: daily, Easter to spring bank holiday 10am-6pm; spring bank holiday to September 10am-9pm; October to Easter 10am-4.30pm.
Gift shop, licensed restaurant.

Maritime Museum
Cowes Public Library
Beckford Road
Cowes, Isle of Wight
☎ (0983) 293341
Open: Monday-Friday 9.30am-6pm, Saturday 9.30am-4.30pm.

Mary Rose Exhibition and Ship Hall
Her Majesty's Naval Base
Portsmouth
☎ (0705) 839766/750521
Open: daily, March to October 10am-5.30pm; November to February 10.30am-5pm.
Gift shop.

Military Museum
see Golden Hill Fort.

Museum of Army Flying
Middle Wallop
☎ (0264) 62121 ext 421/428
Open: daily 10am-4.30pm.
Gift shop, café.

Museum of Clocks
Alum Bay, Isle of Wight
☎ (0983) 754193
Open: Good Friday, Easter Sunday to Friday; April to spring bank holiday, Sunday only; spring bank holiday to end October, Sunday-Wednesday 11am-5pm.

Museum of the Dockyard Apprentice
Unicorn Training Centre
Market Way, Portsmouth
☎ (0705) 822571
Open: April to September, Monday-Friday 10am-1pm, 2-5pm.

Museum of the Iron Age
Church Close
Andover
☎ (0264) 66283
Open: Tuesday-Saturday 10am-5pm, Sunday (April to October) 2-5pm.

Museum of Smuggling History
Ventnor Botanic Garden
Ventnor, Isle of Wight

☎ (0983) 853677
Open: daily, Good Friday to end
September 10am-5.30pm.

National Dairy Museum
see Wellington Country Park.

National Motor Museum
Beaulieu
☎ (0590) 612345
Open: daily, mid-March to mid-
April 10am-6.30pm; mid-April to
May 10am-6pm; June to early July
10am-6.30pm; early July to early
September 10am-7pm; early
September to October 10am-
6.30pm; November to mid-March,
Monday-Saturday 10am-5pm,
Sunday 10am-5.30pm.
Gift shop, restaurant.

**National Museum of Arms and
Armour**
see Fort Nelson.

National Wireless Museum
see Arreton Manor.

**New Forest Museum and Visitor
Centre**
Lyndhurst
☎ (042 128) 3914
Open: daily, from 10am
(closing time varies).
Gift shop, audio-visual theatre.

Nostalgia Toy Museum
Godshill, Isle of Wight
☎ (0983) 840181
Open: daily, end of May to
October 10am-5pm.

Odiham Pest-House
South side of churchyard, Odiham
Open: no set times.

Old Town Hall
Brading, Isle of Wight
Open: daily, Whitsun to September
10am-5pm.

**Portsmouth Royal Dockyard
Historical Society**
Her Majesty's Naval Base
Portsmouth

☎ (0705) 664659
Open: daily, May to October 10am-
5pm.

**Queen Alexandra's Royal Army
Nursing Corps Museum**
Royal Pavilion
Farnborough Road
Aldershot
☎ (0252) 24431 ext 4301
Open: Monday and Friday by ap-
pointment, Tuesday, Wednesday
9am-12.30pm, 2-4.30pm, Thursday
9am-12.30pm.

**Regimental Museum of the Royal
Corps of Transport**
Buller Barracks
Alison's Road
Aldershot
☎ (0252) 24431 ext 3834
Open: Monday-Friday 9am-
12noon, 2-4pm (not bank holi-
days).

Romany Folklore Museum
Selborne
☎ (042 050) 486
Open: daily, Easter to September
10.30am-5.30pm.
Gift shop.

**Royal Army Dental Corps
Museum**
Evelyn Woods Road
Aldershot
☎ (0252) 24431 ext 2782
Open: Monday-Friday 10am-
12noon, 2-4.30pm (not bank
holidays).

Royal Army Pay Corps Museum
Worthy Down, Winchester
☎ (0962) 880880
Open: Monday-Friday (except
bank holidays) 10am-12noon,
2-4pm.
Advance notice required (in
military camp).

Royal Green Jackets Museum
Peninsula Barracks, Winchester
☎ (0962) 61781
Open: Monday-Saturday 10am-
5pm, Sunday 12noon-4pm.

Royal Hampshire Regiment Museum
Southgate Street
Winchester
☎ (0962) 63658
Open: Monday-Friday 10am-12.30pm, 2-4pm, Saturday, Sunday, bank holidays in summer 12noon-4pm.

Royal Hussars Museum
Peninsula Barracks
Winchester
☎ (0962) 63751
Open: Tuesday-Friday 10am-4pm, Saturday, Sunday 12noon-4pm.

Royal Marines Museum
Eastney Barracks
Portsmouth
☎ (0705) 819385
Open: daily, 10am-4.30pm.

Royal Naval Museum
Her Majesty's Naval Base
Portsmouth
☎ (0705) 733060
Open: daily 10.30am-5pm.
Gift shop, café.

Royal Navy Submarine Museum
Haslar, Gosport
☎ (0705) 529217
Open: daily, April to October 10am-4.30pm; November to March 10am-3.30pm.
Licensed cafeteria.

Sammy Miller Museum
Gore Road
New Milton
☎ (0425) 619696
Open: April to October, daily; November to March, Saturday, Sunday 10.30am-4.30pm.

Second World War Aircraft Preservation Society Museum
Lasham Airfield
Alton
Open: Sunday, no fixed times.
Gift shop.

Sherings Fordingbridge Museum
53 Church Street

Fordingbridge
☎ (0425) 52276
Open: April to September, Wednesday 2-5pm.

Sir Max Aitken Museum
The Prospect
Cowes, Isle of Wight
☎ (0983) 295144
Open: by appointment.

Southampton Hall of Aviation
Albert Road South
Southampton
☎ (0703) 635830
Open: Tuesday-Saturday 10am-5pm, Sunday 12noon-5pm.
Gifts, café.

Southampton Maritime Museum
The Wool House
Southampton
☎ (0703) 223941
Open: Tuesday-Friday 10am-1pm, 2-5pm, Saturday 10am-1pm, 2-4pm, Sunday 2-5pm.

Southsea Castle Museum
Clarence Esplanade
Southsea
☎ (0705) 827261
Open: daily, 10.30am-5.30pm.
Gift shop.

Tudor House Museum
Bugle Street
Southampton
☎ (0703) 332513
Open: Tuesday-Friday 10am-5pm, Saturday 10am-4pm, Sunday 2-5pm.

Ventnor Heritage Centre and Local History Museum
Spring Hill
Ventnor, Isle of Wight
Open: Easter to October, Monday-Saturday 10am-12noon, 2-4pm (June to September, Tuesday, Thursday also 7-9pm).

Wax Museum
Brading, Isle of Wight
☎ (0983) 407286
Open: daily, May to September

10am-10pm; October to April
10am-5pm.

Westgate Museum
High Street
Winchester
☎ (0962) 69864
Open: beginning April to end September, Monday-Saturday 10am-5pm, Sunday 2-5pm; beginning October to end March, Tuesday-Saturday 10am-5pm, Sunday 2-4pm.

The Willis Museum and Art Gallery
Old Town Hall
Market Place
Basingstoke
☎ (0256) 465902
Open: Tuesday-Friday 10am-5pm, Saturday 10am-4pm.

Winchester Cathedral Treasury
☎ (0962) 53137
Open: Monday-Saturday 10.30am-12.30pm, 2.30-4.30pm, Sunday 2.30-4.30pm.

Winchester Cathedral Triforium and Library
☎ (0962) 53137
Open: Easter to end September, Monday 2-4.30pm, Tuesday-Saturday 10.30am-1pm, 2-4.30pm.

OTHER PLACES OF INTEREST

Alice Holt Forest Visitor Centre
Bucks Horn Oak
Farnham, Surrey
☎ (0420) 23666
Open: daily, beginning April to end September 10am-5pm.
Gifts, refreshments.

Bembridge Lifeboat Station
Bembridge, Isle of Wight
☎ (0983) 872201
Open: early May to end September, Wednesday, Thursday, Sunday, bank holidays 2-4pm.

Blackgang Chine
Niton, Isle of Wight
☎ (0983) 730330
Open: daily, Easter to May and October, 10am-5pm; June to September 10am-10pm.
Gift shop, licensed bar, café.

The Crusades Experience
St John's House
The Broadway
Winchester
☎ (0962) 56706/841598
Open: daily 10am-5.30pm.
Gift shop.

The Model Village
Godshill, Isle of Wight
☎ (0983) 840270
Open: daily, April to June and September, 10am-5.30pm; July, August 10am-dusk (Friday, Saturday 10am-5.30pm); October 10.30am-4.30pm.

Natural History Centre
Godshill, Isle of Wight
☎ (0983) 840333
Open: daily, March to May, October, November 10am-6pm; June to September 10am-10pm.
Gift and craft shop.

The Needles Pleasure Park
Alum Bay, Isle of Wight
☎ (0983) 752401
Open: daily, Easter to October 10am-5pm (open later in summer).
Gift and craft shops, restaurant, bar.

Ocean Village
Dock Gate 2, Eastern Docks
Southampton
☎ (0703) 228353
Open: daily, 10.30am-8pm, unlimited access to marina.
Shops, restaurants, bars, cinemas, Heritage Theatre, museum.

Paultons Park
Ower
Romsey
☎ (0703) 814442
Open: early March to early

November, daily 10am-6.30pm,
earlier closing in spring and
autumn.
Restaurant, tea-room, gift shops,
picnic areas, playground.

Pirates Ship
Newport Quay
Newport, Isle of Wight
☎ (0983) 529789
Open: daily, Easter to end October
10am-5pm.

Puckpool Park
Ryde, Isle of Wight
Open: unlimited access.
Café, games, barbecue site.

The Pyramids Resort Centre
Clarence Esplanade
Southsea
☎ (0705) 294444
Open: summer, daily from 10am;
winter, Wednesday-Sunday from
11am.

Shanklin Chine
Shanklin, Isle of Wight
☎ (0983) 866432
Open: daily, Easter to late May
9.30am-5.30pm; late May to late
September 9.30am-10pm; late
September to mid-October 9.30am-
4pm.
Gift shop, tea-room, inn.

SS Shieldhall
Ocean Village
Southampton
Open: Easter to September,
Saturday, Sunday 11am-5pm.

**Southampton Common Studies
Centre**
Cemetery Road
Southampton
☎ (0703) 636094
Open: Monday-Friday 10am-5pm;
Saturday, Sunday, summer 2-5pm,
winter 1.30-4.30pm.

Southsea Model Village
Southsea
☎ (0705) 294706
Open: March to October, daily;

November to February, Saturday,
Sunday 10am-dusk.

Winchester Heritage Centre
Upper Brook Street, Winchester
☎ (0962) 51664
Open: Tuesday-Saturday 10.30am-
12.30pm, 2-4pm, Sunday 2-4pm.

TOURIST INFORMATION CENTRES

** Open in summer only

Aldershot
Military Museum
Queen's Avenue
☎ (0252) 20968

Andover
Town Mill car-park
Bridge Street
☎ (0264) 24320

Beaulieu
National Motor Museum
☎ (0590) 612345

Cowes **
4 Marina Walk
High Street
☎ (0983) 291914

Eastleigh
Town Hall
Leigh Road
☎ (0703) 641261

Fareham
Westbury Manor
West Street
☎ (0329) 221342

Farnborough
The Library
Pinehurst Avenue
☎ (0252) 513838

Fleet
Gurkha Square
Fleet Road
☎ (0252) 811151

Gosport **
Falkland Gardens
☎ (0705) 522944

Havant
1 Park Road South
☎ (0705) 480024

Hayling Island
Sea Front
South Hayling
☎ (0705) 467111

Lymington **
St Thomas Street car-park
☎ (0590) 672522

Lyndhurst
New Forest Museum
☎ (042 128) 2269

Newport **
Church Litten car-park
☎ (0983) 525450

Petersfield
27 The Square
☎ (0730) 68829

Portsmouth
The Hard
☎ (0705) 826722

Continental Ferry Terminal **
☎ (0705) 698111

Clarence Esplanade **
Southsea
☎ (0705) 832464

Ringwood **
Furlong Lane car-park
☎ (0425) 470896

Romsey **
Bus station car-park
☎ (0794) 512987

Rownhams
M27 service area (westbound)
☎ (0703) 730345

Ryde **
Western Esplanade
☎ (0983) 62905

Sandown
Esplanade
☎ (0983) 403886

Shanklin
67 High Street
☎ (0983) 862942

Southampton
Above Bar
☎ (0703) 221106

Ventnor **
34 High Street
☎ (0983) 853625

Winchester
The Guildhall, The Broadway
☎ (0962) 67871

Yarmouth **
The Quay
☎ (0983) 760015

USEFUL ADDRESSES

British Airways
Reservations and advance travel
information
☎ (0703) 639744
☎ (0430) 66031

British Rail
Enquiry bureaux
☎ (0256) 464966 Monday-Saturday
7.30am-9pm, Sunday 8.15am-
8.45pm.

☎ (0705) 825771 Monday-Saturday
7am-9.30pm, Sunday 8am-9.50pm.

☎ (0703) 229393 Monday-Saturday
7am-9pm, Sunday 8.15am-8.45pm.

☎ (071) 928 5100 24-hour service.

British Telecom
70 High Street, Southampton
☎ (0703) 229966

British Tourist Authority
Information Centre
64 St James's Street, London SW1
☎ (071) 499 9325

Overseas Offices
94 Cumberland Street, Suite 600
Toronto
Ontario M5R3N3
☎ 416 925 6326

875 N. Michigan Avenue
Chicago, Illinois 60611
☎ 312 787 0490

Cedar Maple Plaza, Suite 210
2305 Cedar Springs Road
Dallas, Texas 75201
☎ 214 720 4040

Room 450, 350 South Figueroa
Street
Los Angeles, California 90071
☎ 213 6283525

40 West 57th Street
New York 10019-4001
☎ 212 581 4700

Caravan Club
East Grinstead House
East Grinstead, East Sussex
☎ (0342) 26944

English Heritage
Osborne House, Isle of Wight
☎ (0983) 200022

Forestry Commission
Conservancy Office
Queen's House, Lyndhurst
☎ (042 128) 3141

Camping Enquiries
Southampton Road, Lyndhurst
☎ (042 128) 3771

Hampshire Bus
Travel and ticket enquiries
☎ Andover (0264) 52339

☎ Basingstoke (0256) 464501

☎ Southampton (0703) 225805

☎ Winchester (0962) 52352

Head Office
☎ Eastleigh (0703) 641186

**Hampshire and Isle of Wight
Naturalists' Trust**
71 The Hundred, Romsey
☎ (0794) 513786

**Hampshire County Museum
Service**
Chilcomb House
Chilcomb Lane
Winchester
☎ (0962) 846304

Hovertravel
Quay Road, Ryde, Isle of Wight
☎ (0983) 65241

Hurst Castle Ferry and Cruises
19 Everton Road
Hordle, Lymington
☎ (0425) 610784

Isle of Wight Tourist Office
Town Quay
Newport, Isle of Wight
☎ (0983) 524343

National Express Coach Services
Travel Information
☎ (0329) 230023

National Trust
36 Queen Anne's Gate
London SW1
☎ (071) 222 9251

35a St James' Street
Newport, Isle of Wight
☎ (0983) 526445

New Forest Wagons
Balmer Lawn Road, Brockenhurst
☎ (0590) 23633

Red Funnel Steamers
12 Bugle Street, Southampton
Weekdays — vehicle reservations
and passenger enquiries
☎ (0703) 330333

Weekends — vehicle reservations
☎ (0703) 330342

Weekends — passenger enquiries
and hydrofoil reservations
☎ (0703) 227599

Sealink Ferries
Isle of Wight Reservations
☎ Lymington (0590) 73301
☎ Portsmouth (0705) 827744

Southampton City Museums
125 High Street
Southampton
☎ (0703) 224216

Southern Tourist Board
40 Chamberlayne Road
Eastleigh
☎ (0703) 616027

Winchester City Museums
75 Hyde Street
Winchester
☎ (0962) 848269

VINEYARDS

Adgestone
Brading, Isle of Wight
☎ (0983) 402503
Open: Monday-Friday 9am-5pm,
Saturday 10am-1pm.

Barton Manor
Whippingham, Isle of Wight
☎ (0983) 292835
Open: Good Friday to Easter
Monday and April, Saturday; May
to second Sunday in October, daily
10.30am-5.30pm.
Gift shop, wine-bar, café.

Cranmore
Solent Road
Yarmouth, Isle of Wight
☎ (0983) 761414
Open: daily.

Lymington
Wainsford Road
Pennington
Lymington
☎ (0590) 672112
Open: beginning May to end
September, Sunday-Friday
10.30am-4.30pm.

Morton Manor
Brading, Isle of Wight
☎ (0983) 406168
Open: first Sunday in April to end
October, Sunday-Friday 10am-
5.30pm.
Tea-room, wine-bar, shop.

Wellow
Merryhill Farm
Tanners Lane
East Wellow
☎ (0794) 522860/522431
Open: daily, tours and tastings by
appointment.
Wine bar, snack-bar, gift shop,
train rides, picnic area.

YOUTH HOSTELS

Burley
Cottesmore House, Cott Lane
☎ (042 53) 3233

Overton
Red Lion Lane
☎ (0256) 770516

Portsmouth
Wymering Manor, Cosham
☎ (0705) 375661

Sandown
The Firs, Fitzroy Street
☎ (0983) 402651

Southampton
461 Winchester Road, Bassett
☎ (0703) 790895

Totland Bay
Hurst Hill, Summers Lane
☎ (0983) 752165

Whitwell
Whitwell, Ventnor
☎ (0983) 730473

Winchester
City Mill, 1 Water Lane
☎ (0962) 53723

ZOOS, WILDLIFE PARKS, FARMS, ETC

Birdworld and Underwater World
Holt Pound
Farnham, Surrey
☎ (0420) 22140
Open: Birdworld: daily 9.30am-one hour before dusk.
Underwater World: daily 9.30am-6pm.
Gift shop, café, picnic place, play area.

Brickfields Horsecountry
Newnham Road
Binstead, Isle of Wight
☎ (0983) 66801
Open: daily 10am-5pm.
Gift shop, licensed café, restaurant, bar, play area.

Butterfly World
see Medina World.

Clamerkin Farm Park
Newtown, Isle of Wight
☎ (0983) 78396
Open: daily, Easter to October 10.30am-6pm.
Tea-room, picnic area, play area.

Deer Sanctuary
Bolderwood, New Forest
Open: unlimited access.

Finkley Down Farm Park
Andover
☎ (0264) 52195
Open: daily, beginning April (Easter if earlier) to beginning October 10.30am-6pm.
Gift shop, café, picnic area.

Flamingo Park
Springvale
Seaview, Isle of Wight
☎ (0983) 612153
Open: daily, Easter, April 2-5.30pm; May to September 10am-5.30pm; October 2-5pm.
Gift shop, café, picnic area.

The Hawk Conservancy
Weyhill
Andover
☎ (0264) 772252
Open: daily, beginning March to last Sunday in October 10.30am-4pm (10.30am-5pm in summer).
Café.

Isle of Wight Zoological Gardens
Sandown, Isle of Wight
☎ (0983) 403883/405562
Open: Easter to end October, daily; November to Easter, Sunday only 10am-6pm.
Gift shop, bar, café.

Little Amazon
Swan Garden Centre
Gaters Hill, Southampton
☎ (0703) 474089
Open: daily 10am-5pm (garden centre 9am-6pm).
Gift shop, café, picnic area.

Longdown Dairy Farm
Deerleap Lane
Longdown, Ashurst
☎ (042 129) 3326
Open: daily, Easter to end October 11am-5pm.
Gift shop, picnic area.

Marwell Zoological Park
Colden Common
Winchester
☎ (096 274) 406
Open: daily, summer 10am-6pm; winter 10am-one hour before dusk.
Licensed bar, restaurant, gift shops, picnic areas, play area.

Medina World
(Butterfly World, Fountain World and Medina Garden Centre)
Staplers Road
Wootton, Isle of Wight
☎ (0983) 883430
Open: daily, Good Friday to end October 10am-5.30pm (garden centre open all year).
Restaurant, shop.

New Forest Butterfly Farm
Longdown, Ashurst
☎ (042 129) 2166/3367
Open: daily, Easter-end October
10am-5pm.
Restaurant, gift shops, picnic area,
playground.

Ornamental Farm
see Sir George Staunton Country
Park.

Reptiliary
Holidays Hill
Lyndhurst
Open: daily, beginning May to end
September, daylight hours.

Robin Hill Adventure Park
Downend, Isle of Wight
☎ (0983) 527352/528029
Open: daily, March to November
10am-dusk.
Gift shop, cafeteria, licensed bar,
picnic gardens.

Sea Life Centre
Clarence Esplanade
Southsea
☎ (0705) 734461
Open: daily 10am-6pm.
Restaurant, play area.

Stubbs Farm Trail
Kingsley
☎ (042 03) 4906
Open: beginning May to end
September, Saturday, Sunday,
bank holidays 1-5.30pm.
Tea-room, picnic area.

Tropical Bird Park
Old Park
St Lawrence, Isle of Wight
☎ (0983) 852583
Open: daily, spring and summer
10am-5pm; autumn and winter
12noon-4pm.
Gift shop, café.

Underwater World
see Birdworld.

INDEX